AS GOOD AS MY WORD

Praise for *As Good as My Word*

'*As Good As My Word* is a richly detailed memoir, recounting K.M. Chandrasekhar's long and distinguished career as a civil servant and diplomat. From his very first posting in Kerala to his tenure as Cabinet Secretary via senior positions in Europe, Chandrasekhar tells us of the challenges and satisfactions of a life on India's public-service frontlines. An insightful read.'
—Shashi Tharoor, author and Member of Parliament

'K.M. Chandrasekhar's memoir takes us on a fascinating journey with one of India's most accomplished civil servants as he navigated some of the momentous challenges in India's recent history. This is a rare and penetrating look at governance in India in all its complexity.'
—Shyam Saran, former Foreign Secretary, India

'K.M. Chandrasekhar's unmatched problem-solving approach and the openness to collaborate with multiple stakeholders, as narrated in this book, is bound to inspire the administrative discourse. This autobiography captures what it takes for an administrator to navigate through complex roles and relationships to render one's duties effectively, while keeping the greater interests of the people and the nation at heart. A must-read!'
—Dr S. Ramadorai, former CEO & MD, Tata Consultancy Services

'A dispassionate, masterly and informative account of the concatenated role of bureaucracy and politics in governance from an insider's perspective.'
—Prabhu Chawla, Editorial Director, *The New Indian Express*

'The author provides his candid comments on the eventful, indeed turbulent, years when he was at the helm of the civil service, and equally candid comments on some recent trends in India that are clearly a matter of concern to him. What the reader gets, therefore, are rich insights into the working of an administrator's mind, from his early career to his post-retirement engagements. Some telling asides and anecdotes provide added flavour.'
—Shri T.N. Ninan, former Chairman & Director,
Business Standard Private Limited

AS GOOD AS MY WORD

a memoir

K.M. Chandrasekhar

HarperCollins *Publishers* India

First published in India by HarperCollins *Publishers* 2022
4th Floor, Tower A, Building No 10, DLF Cyber City,
DLF Phase II, Gurugram, Haryana – 122002
www.harpercollins.co.in

2 4 6 8 10 9 7 5 3 1

P-ISBN: 978-93-5489-500-5
E-ISBN: 978-93-5489-487-9

Typeset in 11/115 Adobe Garamond Pro at
Manipal Technologies Limited, Manipal

Printed and bound at
Thomson Press (India) Ltd

To
Sri Sai Baba of Shirdi, who has been with me since I was seven

Contents

Prologue

'I am growing up … I am losing my illusions, perhaps to acquire new ones.'

—*Virginia Woolf*

When writing about a long career like mine, it is difficult to decide what to include and what not to. During my service, I accomplished many things—some good and some not so good. I made many mistakes, too. But all of it has been a learning experience and I hope to cover some parts of it in this book. The reader must, however, be conscious of the fact that the writer invariably views happenings in his or her own perspective. One of my favourite books is *Living Zen: The Diary of an American Priest* by Harvey Daiho Hilbert Roshi. He says, 'There is a precept that we Zen Buddhists take. "I vow not to elevate myself by slandering others." This precept addresses our fairly common mechanism to make ourselves feel good by making others look bad.' I sincerely hope that I am not guilty of this error in any part of this text. I have also tried consciously not to embellish any part of the story or to exercise my writer's privilege to depart from facts. Yet, there may be many who disagree with the facts or my opinions. I have only tried to tell my story from my viewpoint.

I have often wondered why I became an Indian Administrative Service (IAS) officer. As a child, I wanted to grow up to become an engine driver on railway trains. With my father working for the Indian Railways, there was nothing more majestic that I could visualize than being at the helm of a railway engine, gliding it smoothly away from the platform, gathering speed, racing across the countryside, leaving mountains and rivers and houses and roads behind, steaming furiously into railway stations teeming with thousands of people waiting expectantly for friends and loved ones, or preparing for their own onward journeys. Some of that excitement still remains with me. A railway station still evokes greater emotion than an airport, even though I rarely travel by train these days and have travelled by plane scores of times, both while living in our own country and abroad.

Yet, I chose to join the civil services. Why? Largely because it was my father's burning ambition to see his only child in the corridors of power. It is also a fact that in the 1960s and '70s, opportunities were limited and government service seemed like the best option. I had already been living in Delhi for fifteen years, from 1956 to 1970, and Delhi is the place where the big Babus have been living since the days of the Mughals. To live in a big Lutyens' bungalow with its sprawling lawns was a dream that came true in the last four years of my extended service in the IAS, which spanned a full forty-one years.

Have I regretted this choice? Was I railroaded into this career? I cannot say that I have never thought about the opportunities that I may have missed. I used to write English superbly in my teens. I started reading when I was very young—when I was just seven or eight. By eleven, I had read all of P.G. Wodehouse. With no other distractions, I continued to read—classics, plays, thrillers, the works. The length of a book never fazed me. I could read three books in a day, lying on the upper berth of a train, merrily chugging along, all the way from Delhi to Madras. In the process, my vocabulary grew no end. As writing lengthy essays was part of schooling in those early days, my language developed. Often, I have wondered whether journalism would have suited me more. Perhaps it would have. Perhaps I would have become a journalist or a writer; written a few books and maybe won one or two awards. But choosing such a career back then was difficult for the son of a middle-class government servant with no means of his own. Journalism, in those days, was a limited profession—a low salaried one, insecure to boot. Could I have made a name for myself then as an academic? Perhaps, because I have always had a capacity to get into the details and absorb them, and use my analytical skills. Perhaps not, because I am shy and reclusive and teaching would have been a challenge.

But after all these years, I am happy with the choice I made, even though it entailed sacrifice—choosing ideals over practical and monetary considerations. I live in a small flat because I cannot maintain a large house. Also, at the end of the day, who needs a great deal of space? I had a larger house, built by the inimitable Laurie Baker, an Englishman who chose to live in Trivandrum and sparked off a veritable revolution in tastefully designed, low-cost housing, not just in Kerala but all over India and the so-called 'third world'. I knew I did not have the means to keep it shipshape and chose, instead, to sell it off and buy a little flat. I recall P. Chidambaram telling me once that an honest civil servant can easily be identified after retirement because he would have no more than a small flat and a small car, which he would drive himself, and that his main occupation would be occasional trading in the stock market. I did not accept this then because it was difficult to visualize the end when one was so close to the zenith of power.

Yet, the service has innumerable compensations. It exposed me to a variety of jobs and many different worlds which I would never have known had I been confined to a narrow field. Quick transitions from one area to another is an essential component of a civil services career. This means that when I entered any new sector, be it agriculture or fisheries or industry, I would be completely ignorant at the start. To hold my own in areas that required technical expertise, I had to learn fast. To each new job I took up, I carried my learnings from previous assignments. This gave me the ability to see connections and opportunities to do new things, which specialists would have lacked. In a huge, diverse and fast-changing field like public administration, functioning in a democracy with its shifting priorities, it is a special skill that the IAS officer possesses which makes him still relevant in a system that is rapidly becoming compartmentalized. I also developed an entirely different set of skills after dealing with different kinds of people—the fisherman for whom his world is the sea; the policeman, arrogant in his uniform; the farmer who develops incredible skills on his little piece of land; the politician who subsists on his profession; the 'suited-booted' corporate honchos; and the suave, courteous and exceedingly shrewd diplomat. Yes, I am happy at the end of my career to have met several great people, made friends in India and abroad, and honed my skills and pitted them against the best in the world.

The railway mindset, however, never died in me. It continued as an unwavering affinity for trains and journeys. The Indian Railways is surely the lifeline of India. It carries millions of passengers every day, thousands of tonnes of various goods, raw materials and fuel for industries everywhere. It connects the length and breadth of the country like no other institution, except the ubiquitous post office, provides and facilitates hundreds of thousands of jobs, acts as the face of modernization, and provides connectivity to countless towns and villages. It is one of the key building blocks of our history, an institution that creates a sense of belonging in a diverse society which is divided in every possible way otherwise.

The railway culture runs in my veins, regardless of the fact that throughout my working career, I have not had much to do with it. As I have said earlier, my father was a railwayman, and my mother was an inveterate temple-goer. A good part of my childhood was therefore spent in trains, railway retiring rooms, guest houses, the homes of other railwaymen—friends of my father's—and in temples. My father was not very high up in the railway hierarchy in those days and was, therefore, entitled only to what was called a four-wheeled railway saloon, much smaller than six- or eight-wheeled saloons, but still equipped with a kitchen and an attached toilet. The four-wheeled saloon was too small to be attached to express or mail trains and, therefore, we chugged along slowly as the last carriage attached to passenger and goods trains. These were simple carriages, made of wood, not steel, with pull-down windows and shutters. The first-class compartments in those times, with their attached toilets, were reasonably well-provided by Indian middle-class standards, directly opening on to the platforms. When wood yielded to steel in the making of railway bogies, the first-class compartment became part of a line of compartments sharing an adjoining corridor. Today, non-air-conditioned first class compartments are rarely to be seen. Air conditioned two- and three-tier carriages predominate.

Each train journey was an adventure in itself. The changing landscape, the different languages and modes of dressing, and the mannerisms and preferred foods of our co-passengers taught us valuable lessons in the diversity of India and how bonding can easily develop between simple, ordinary folk, who are separated otherwise by language, religion, culture and caste. Earlier, passengers had direct access to the hawkers selling sweets, snacks, bangles and what have you on railway platforms. As the trains meandered slowly across the countryside, pulled by steam engines which had often to stop and refresh themselves with fresh infusions of coal and steam, nature floated by in its myriad colours and forms.

Today, the railway's trains and culture have undergone a great transformation, symbolic of India's own metamorphosis from a poor, 'third-world' country living in abysmal poverty to one that is on its way to becoming an economic superpower. Some changes are almost unbelievable. I left Kerala for Central Service in 1996 and came back only in 2011. In the pre-1996 days, tea, coffee and snacks were served in chair cars by Malayali attendants. Today, we see no Malayali attendants but only people from the northern states and Bengal, even from our neighbouring countries—standing testimony to the growing prosperity of Kerala and the willingness of people to travel across the country and even from their own homelands to earn a living. This clearly underscores the essential unity among the people of India—indeed, the entire subcontinent—and their infinite capacity to imbibe the cultures of one another. These people are the 'migrant labourers'—euphemistically now called 'guest workers', who shed their invisibility after the recent dramatic lockdown of the country in response to the Covid-19 pandemic.

The stately steam engine is gone, replaced by the more powerful diesel and electric engines—but they pale in comparison to the stately, bullet-shaped WB engine as it rolled majestically on to the platform, spewing and spitting steam angrily like a mythical dragon. Gone are the huge, old-style retiring rooms with their four-poster beds and capacious bathrooms with copper vessels and giant bathtubs. Gone are the railway refreshment rooms of yore which matched the best hotels in town with their own specialities. Gone are most of the metre gauge and narrow gauge tracks.

From Groundwork to Launch

'Starting a new job can be nerve-racking, but it's also exciting. You are embarking on a new future, positioning yourself to write a fresh story on a clean slate.'

—*Arianna Huffington*

After six months of training at the National Academy of Administration in Mussoorie, it was the Grand Trunk Express headed for Madras that took four of us IAS probationers to Trivandrum, the capital of Kerala, the state to which we had been allotted. The Grand Trunk Express has a history of its own. A connection between the north of India and the south was considered a difficult proposition until 1921, when a military train carried the families of a regiment from Cannanore (now Kannur) to Peshawar. The train had its genesis in the form of just two carriages attached to multiple trains serviced by different railway companies. Later, it became a full-fledged train from Mettupalayam to Delhi. This train played a big role in my life as it carried us on our trips to Kerala during my school summer vacations, year after year, and I saw it metamorphose from a wooden train hauled by steam engines to its present dieselized and partly electrified form.

We had heavy trunks to carry this time around as we were not going to be returning for a whole year. Railway inspectors took one look at our luggage and promptly fined us for not having weighed our trunks at Delhi and paid the excess fare. I tried to speak of my father's position in the railways—it was of no avail and we had to pay the penalty. At that time, travel, whether by air or by rail or by road, invariably meant that the traveller was at the mercy of the lower bureaucracy. This situation changed only with the advent of competition in airlines and digital ticketing in the railways. Yet, at opportune times, particularly in times of crisis or shortage, the bureaucracy continues to assert its ugly power over others. Not that the inspector who charged us for extra luggage was wrong. It was I who was wrong because I believed—as it was commonly believed then—that one can could evade the law by quoting proximity to authority.

Kerala was very different from the archetype inculcated in us at the academy in Mussoorie. We had been instructed to be prim and proper when we went to the Secretariat for the first time. So we went wearing suits and solemn looks on our faces to the Chief Secretary's office, only to find him wearing a simple shirt and trousers, and chappals on his feet. We were probably the only people in all of Trivandrum wearing suits on that day. It was the then Special Secretary, Bhaskaran Nair, who told us not to be ridiculous and to stop coming to the Secretariat wearing suits. At that time, we had Secretaries and Special Secretaries, the latter being senior to the former. Later, in conformity with practices prevailing in other states, these seniority levels were reversed and the Secretary became senior to the Special Secretary. Later still, when one Secretary arrogated for himself the title of 'Principal Secretary', all Secretaries became Principal Secretaries and the 'Special' Secretary became Secretary.

Looking back on the training in Mussoorie and my career in the civil services, there was, indeed, a considerable mismatch between the training and real life. In Mussoorie, one of the first cyclostyled notes we received was on how to use forks and knives, and how to behave at the dining table. While some of my batchmates with sophisticated backgrounds were openly contemptuous, I must confess that I was ignorant of dining table etiquette and learnt the basics from that note. The Mussoorie academy also had a 'dry day', when only 'dry' food was served—sandwiches, cutlets and the like. The logic was that, during the course of our service, we would be touring places where 'normal' food, to which we as Indians are accustomed, would not be readily available. We had to learn horse riding also, in the unlikely event of our having to travel to places which could not be accessed by motorized vehicles. Obviously, the National Academy of Administration, as it was then called, was running as it had been in the British era, when district officials had to travel to remote places on horseback and camp in tents with a retinue of cooks and attendants waiting on them. By the time we had joined the academy, in 1970, horses were difficult to find and when we had to travel to places not accessible by road, we walked.

To its credit, the academy brought the batch together—an association that remained alive throughout our careers and even later. Today, as we are joined together by a WhatsApp group to celebrate the silver jubilee of our batch, I find that the camaraderie has not ceased and the gossip continues, even though we are older and, hopefully, wiser. The silver jubilee event in Mussoorie, however, fell prey to the pandemic and never took place, but may take place sometime this year.

When I visited Mussoorie again, many years later, the landscape had changed. The old building, including the room in which I had stayed, atop the Central Hall, had burnt down and been replaced by a set of stone constructions. As an old-timer, it was difficult for me to digest the changes, but conditions of living are definitely better, even though the old-world charm of the quaint Charleville Hotel, which had been made into the academy, is no more to be seen. As Cabinet Secretary many years into the future, I recall one occasion on which the then Director Padamvir Singh told me that the academy was struggling to get government sanction for starting a bar, a facility which was available in the National Police Academy and the Administrative Staff College of India in Hyderabad. I thought there was justification for a bar. Controlled and time-restricted drinking within the academy was better than forcing probationers to go all the way to Landour Bazaar for a drink. So, I told the director to give me a note on file, even while I was in Mussoorie. I sanctioned it on the spot, not really knowing whether I had the power to do so but, in the process, cut short the protracted correspondence between the academy and the Department of Personnel and Training. The department, fortunately, accepted without demur the decision of the Cabinet Secretary and, hey presto, the academy had a new bar in no time. Alas, this was a short-lived joy as the bar was scrapped mercilessly when Prime Minister Narendra Modi visited Mussoorie a few years later.

Going to the allotted district for training as an Assistant Collector was an entirely new experience. I had cleared the IAS straight after college. The college atmosphere persisted in Mussoorie, too, which was more like an extension of university life for most of us. I gather that it is not the same any more. Probationers are much older, several of them married, with children, too—the outcome of repeated increases in the age of entry for the services. The character of the service has also changed. Most of us came from academic backgrounds in the humanities, while today, most probationers have completed professional courses. Yet my own assessment, having met scores of them in different parts of the country, is that, by and large, there is no diminution in their enthusiasm and zeal while joining the service. I have realized that generational change is inevitable, even though the conflict between generations continues with each considering the other not sufficiently energetic. A senior officer carries with him the wealth of his experience and skills, acquired through field work in various capacities. A new entrant brings boundless energy and a great deal of technical knowledge, essential in a world which undergoes rapid transformation. Where both these streams can work together in harmony, there is significant achievement. As in all aspects of human endeavour, there are some who succeed and some who don't. Success and failure are as much products of circumstance and opportunity as of ability. Sometimes, a reversal turns out to be a breakthrough that carries one forward. At other times, a big opportunity can turn out to be a major flop show. To take life as it comes, without rancour towards anyone, is one of the primary lessons to be learnt by a civil servant.

The district taught me pragmatism in decision-making. It taught me that what seems to be the most fair and transparent solution need not necessarily be the best; that there are many interests—political, commercial and financial—that are often intertwined. I was lucky to be posted in the northern district of Calicut (now Kozhikode) for my training. The district had inherited many of the administrative practices and value systems of the British Raj, as Calicut used to be the seat of authority of the Collector of Malabar. There were several British Collectors who had left their imprint on the district and on administration. *Malabar Manual* of 1887, the work of a past Collector, the Scotsman William Logan, was a meticulous journal on almost all aspects of life and administration in Malabar as it had been in the late nineteenth century. The Connolly Canal, constructed between 1848 and 1850, owes its existence to the then Collector H.V. Connolly. The Tottenham system of office procedure—the work of Sir Richard Tottenham, Collector of North Arcot, written in the first half of the twentieth century—brought order and rigour into public administration. It held sway over the entire Madras Presidency for many decades until it gradually crumbled and faded away, yielding to the onslaught of democracy and the multiplicity of needs that it had generated. Yet, during the early part of my career in Kerala, it was this Tottenham system that held the administration together, prevented files from getting lost and ensured continuity, even as officers changed.

I was an admirer and scrupulous follower of the Tottenham system as I found it gave me control over my job, even as I was shifted from place to place and job to job. Now, of course, the system is irrelevant, having been swept away by the digital revolution.

There is a big difference between Collectors then and those of today. Back then, Collectors stayed in the district for years on end. In many cases, they contributed heavily to the uncovering of the region's history and understanding its geography and culture, even more minutely than old residents of the area. Today, postings are much shorter. In fact, during my tenure of one year in Calicut, there were three Collectors, from all of whom I learnt different and valuable lessons. In the first two years of my official career post-training, I held four different jobs in four different places, traversing the length and breadth of the state of Kerala.

The First Brush with Power

*'If we all did the things we are capable of, we would literally astound
ourselves.'*

—Thomas Edison

My first official posting was as Subcollector of Devicolam (now
Devikulam) in the then newly created Idukki district. When I
got the posting orders whilst still at Mussoorie for the second leg of our
training, I was very excited. Devicolam was up in the hills, nestled in
the lap of nature; the subdivision was a relatively large one (by Kerala
standards), densely forested in places, home to tea and cardamom
plantations, rich with spices and teeming with wildlife. An idyllic spot,
I thought. On my way up from Kottayam, as I ascended the slopes
of the Western Ghats in a ramshackle jeep, the euphoria gradually
turned into dark foreboding as a growing desolation gnawed at my
vitals. When I reached Munnar, now a bouncing tourist town, it felt
lonely, cold and dismal and I felt more and more isolated. I lunched

at the Munnar guest house, then took a short nap. As I awoke, I got out of my bed and stepped on to my spectacles, smashing them to smithereens. There was no way of getting another pair, as the nearest point of civilization was Kottayam, a good four hours away by roads which were in a woeful state of disrepair. There was nothing to do but to manage without my spectacles until my next trip to meet the Collector, a month hence.

The high ranges of Kerala have a long history. There was a megalithic civilization in these areas with many dolmens (stone tombs) and caves in the Marayur area, apparently dug out by sages of yore. The Western Ghats, stretching all the way from Kerala to Maharashtra, have a long history of enlightened masters and spiritual evolution. Inevitably, there are legends of the Pandavas of Mahabharata fame, hiding in the forests of Marayur. Years after I left the subdivision, rock paintings made of kaolin (a type of clay), red ochre and ashes, and ancient Tamil inscriptions, were found in rich abundance in these areas. The area had Buddhist traditions too, and an unmistakable Buddha image can be found in a temple near Marayur. The temple of Ayyappan at Sabarimala was then located in this subdivision—now it falls within a new district, Pathanamthitta. Occasionally, looking at the idol in the temple, I have wondered at its similarity to idols of Jain Tirthankaras I have seen elsewhere in our country.

The Duke of Wellington had visited these hills in 1790. A great trigonometric survey of the land was made in the mid-nineteenth century. Towards the end of the nineteenth century, enterprising British adventurers took a lease of over 200 square miles of land from the Rajas of Poonjar, cut down the dense forests and started cultivation of many crops, predominantly tea. The British established a new company, the Kanan Devan Hill Produce Company, which dominated the economy of the area for decades thereafter.

Therefore, when I reached Devicolam, I may have been the Subcollector and the Head of the Revenue Division, but the man who really mattered was the British General Manager of the Kanan Devan Company. I reached there shortly before the Independence Day of 1972 and found that my predecessor had already requested the British general manager to hoist the national flag in the revenue divisional office. Today, such a thing would have roused a huge furore and heads would have rolled, including mine, rather prematurely. In those days of poor communication and greater tolerance, this act of sacrilege passed unnoticed.

The Subcollector's official residence was an ancient one, quaintly furnished with large, commodious chairs, four-poster beds and chess tables. Around the house was a dry moat, intended to keep out marauding wild elephants. There was an old jeep, lying disconsolately in the garage, because it had met with an accident months ago and the government had not yet sanctioned money to repair it. During the few months that I stayed in the subdivision, I had to beg and borrow vehicles from better-provided departmental officers for all my tours. On most days, I used to go to office using transport buses. In fact, using public transport was quite common in those days, unlike today, when the entire governmental system is flooded with cars of all kinds.

Immediately after I took charge, I suddenly found that I was in a state of paralysis when I dealt with files. I could not think straight or write a word. I could only affix my initials and return files. For days, I agonized over whether my career would end then and there in ignominy. Then, one day, there was a burst of energy, the sun shone through the clouds, and I started writing elaborate notes, agreeing or disagreeing with proposals and opinions as they came from below. In the past half a century, I must have written millions of words. I enjoyed writing longhand on files, even though I was conscious that my vocabulary was declining as bureaucratese of the Kerala kind had crept into my language.

I didn't last long in Devicolam. After I got married in October 1972, I was promptly transferred to Fort Cochin, where my wife and I lived in an old Dutch fort at the mouth of the harbour. The story goes that in olden times, ships going into the harbour and those going out had to dip their flags as they passed the fort in which the Dutch factor lived. There were many who saw ghosts in that house, but we did not. It was, however, amusing to frighten my new wife with stories of dead white women haunting the mansion. Stories embellished by our old Muslim driver, Koya, who used to see many phantoms in that ancient palace. We had to contend with leaky roofs and howling winds, and the odd smuggler bringing bottles of Scotch whisky into Cochin, as smuggling was the trade of choice in those days when customs duties were unconscionably high. It looks like smuggling has re-entered the Kerala economic system in recent times, but in different ways and at different levels.

A singular feature of the subdivision was that Subcollectors traditionally settled civil disputes. They were not within his judicial powers, but lawyers and clients chose to bring petty civil cases to the Subcollector's court, where disposal would be quick and the decisions largely fair. I was very young then, in my early twenties, and I have no doubt that many people would have taken advantage of my naiveté. This again is something every young officer has to overcome. No one can be right all the time. On many occasions, the speed of decision-making solves more problems than hair-splitting accuracy.

From Cochin, I was transferred to Quilon (now Kollam), where I stayed for fifty-two days. The next stop was Cannanore in the northern extremity of Kerala, which has since been split into two and a half districts. If in my first two jobs I was exercising magisterial and revenue powers, the next two—as Project Officer of the Small Farmers Development Agency and the Marginal Farmers Development Agency in Quilon and Cannanore districts—were exactly the reverse. Here, the assignment was to help small and marginal farmers improve their living standards through a mix of schemes—wells and pump sets to improve productivity, soil conservation; and subsidiary occupations such as cattle rearing, poultry, piggery and the like. Subsidies were given but these were linked to loans from banks and cooperative institutions, so the job involved tramping all over the place, not only to the farms but to bank branches and primary cooperative credit societies. I must say I enjoyed this job a great deal more than exercising magisterial power, as it was possible to be creative and innovative. I have never been particularly enamoured of power, a mindset that remained with me until the end of my career.

A Novice in the Marketplace

'We need to accept that we won't always make the right decisions, that we'll screw up royally sometimes—understanding that failure is not the opposite of success, it's part of success.'
                                                    —Arianna Huffington

In 1975, I joined as Managing Director (MD) of the State Cooperative Marketing Federation in Calicut. It was here that I was able to express myself fully at work and gain a reputation as an officer of some capacity. This was virtually a defunct organization with barely twenty-three employees, an accumulated loss that equalled its annual revenue, and headed thus far by an Assistant Registrar of Cooperative Societies. Its main business then was to export a little pepper and, that too, only to the Soviet Union and Eastern European countries, which had a rupee payment arrangement with India, whereby they would export goods to India on rupee payment and use the money to buy goods, also in rupee. For a nation starved of foreign exchange, this was an ideal arrangement. The Soviet Union and other countries in Eastern Europe bought their pepper through agents, who were paid some half a percent commission on the value of purchases. With this half a percent, the agent had to take care of himself and his family, the trade representatives of the country purchasing pepper, and also provide money to run some publicity campaigns within India. In those days, there were Prabhat Book Houses all over India, funded by means of rupee reserves accumulated in the country through such trade. From my point of view, these bookstores were invaluable—as they sold good books, largely leaning to the left—at throwaway prices.

The Kerala state policy was markedly left of centre. As Subcollector of Cochin, one of the first instructions I received from the state government was that in disputes between labour and management, I must always take a position that would favour labour, regardless of the rights and wrongs of the case. A starry-eyed Subcollector, straight from the mint, would accept such instructions as the words of God. Such early catechism in the ways of Kerala created an indelible impression on me. So much so that I was one of those who were disturbed by the 1991 reforms in the country because it was impossible for my mind, conditioned by leftist thinking, to readily embrace the freedom now being given to industry. It took me a long time to adapt to the change.

Selling pepper was no easy task. It required tremendous physical stamina. The agent informed me, one evening, that the Soviet trade representatives were waiting in Trivandrum in a sea-facing hotel at the beach resort at Kovalam, south of Trivandrum, then owned by the India Tourism Development Corporation. They wanted to have breakfast with me. There was no option but to have my driver drive me through the night to get to Trivandrum. I reached the resort dead tired and bleary-eyed, only to find my interlocutors equally bleary-eyed and guzzling Scotch whisky early in the morning. The drinking continued afresh with a new burst of energy now that I had entered the scene. Breakfast came, but it didn't look much like breakfast, with lobster and crab, even as the bacchanalia continued. After breakfast, drinking started again in full flow in preparation for lunch, after which the next round started in celebration of dinner. As a good host, I had to keep pace. I think my drinking proclivity convinced them that doing business with me would be good. I don't remember whether we discussed business on that day as we were all in a kind of daze, but what I do remember is getting several orders from the Soviet Union that year.

In the same year, there came a stroke of luck. D.K. Panicker, a promoted IAS officer, had acquired a huge reputation for creating a new beedi cooperative that could compete with the best in the land. He was then MD of the Kerala Cashew Development Corporation. His main problem was that he could not get enough raw cashew to run his factories, even partially. Most of the raw cashew was leaking out to neighbouring states, where labour costs were lower and processing, consequently, less expensive. Between Panicker and Gopal Krishna Pillai, the then Cashew Special Officer, they conjured up a scheme for the monopoly procurement of raw cashew. This struck a chord with the Communist Party of India (CPI) ministers who were successively in charge of industry, M.N. Govindan Nair and P.K. Vasudevan Nair, who felt that farmers growing raw cashew were getting very low prices for their produce and needed to be supported. Of course, private cashew processors were up in arms and even the government was not entirely confident. Gopal and I traversed parallel paths several times thereafter; when I finally retired as Cabinet Secretary, he was Home Secretary at the Centre.

Gopal and Panicker looked around for an organization that could take up monopoly procurement and, luckily, hit upon the State Cooperative Marketing Federation that I was heading. I have always been the kind of officer who would jump at a challenge, even if I did not have the necessary equipment or resources. So, I took it up. I had no money, no staff and no facilities to procure and dry raw cashew. The Cashew Development Corporation came to my assistance, offering their factories as collection and drying centres, and their staff to manage quality and drying. Gopal rescued me with money by issuing orders to cashew processors to take delivery of non-existent stocks from our yards. I was, therefore, able to procure cashew using the money given in advance by processors and roll it over. It was only later that I managed to secure a working capital loan from the United Commercial Bank.

Initially, raw cashew was trickling in very slowly. We suspected smuggling of cashew across the state borders, and Gopal and I—more particularly Gopal—would spend sleepless nights scouring border areas. At that time, Gopal took leave and went to Delhi on vacation. Suddenly and unexpectedly, raw cashew began flowing into our yards in abundance. I was then still depending on advance payment from processors to pay for the raw cashew. As the Cashew Special Officer was not in situ, there was no one to issue release orders. I was badly strapped for money. I remember sending a frantic telegram to him in Delhi asking him to come back. I recall his wife, Sudha, herself a distinguished and capable officer, joking about my telegram later. Gopal did not return immediately, but the problem sorted itself out, as all problems do, eventually.

At the end of the season, we were left with stocks which no processor would pick up because of poor quality. There was no recourse left other than to auction what remained. Ultimately, after doing that, we were able to clear our loan and also make a profit of a couple of crores. Thus, when I left the Marketing Federation shortly thereafter to take over as District Collector of Idukki, its annual turnover had increased from Rs 15 million to Rs 400 million, and the accumulated loss had completely been wiped out.

The Marketing Federation taught me many things. It taught me that if there is sincerity in purpose and solid teamwork, it is possible to accomplish even that which seems unattainable in public service. It also taught me how to work closely with elected representatives of the people. My Chairman, Meloth Narayanan Nambiar, was a Congressman of Gandhian vintage, a close associate of A.K. Antony, who later became the Chief Minister when he was just thirty-three, and with whom I was closely associated when he was Defence Minister at the Centre. Another Director of the Federation was P.J. Kurian, who became Minister at the Centre, and more recently, served as Deputy Chairman of the Rajya Sabha for several years. Aryadan Mohammed was another Director who went on to become Minister several times in the state. I also worked closely with the State Cooperative Bank and its President, Chandrasekharan Nair, who was initially horrified at the thought that the IAS was extending its reach into the cooperative sector but later played a big role in my growth as an officer who could achieve results.

Ups and Downs

'Believe me, my journey has not been a simple journey of progress. There have been many ups and downs, and it is the choices that I have made at each of those times that have helped shape what I have achieved.'

—Satya Nadella

I see myself as having been a nondescript Collector in Idukki. There are phases in one's career when results do not come easy. Yet, it was when I was Collector at Idukki that there happened a postscript event to the Marketing federation story. This was when I received the Annual Report of the federation. My successor in the federation had pushed up its turnover by another Rs 100 million or so, largely due to increased cashew procurement and larger exports of pepper. Yet, the cover page of the Annual Report showed a graph depicting a small increase in 1976–77, when I was there, and a massive upswing in 1977–78, when my successor was in charge. I had a hard time believing it because I knew that the annual turnover had gone up from Rs 15 million to Rs 400 million in 1976–77, and from Rs 400 million to a little more than Rs 500 million in 1977–78. It was then that I found the graph had been manipulated at the y-axis (the vertical axis). The intervals on the y-axis were equidistant and showed 20, 40, 45, 50, 55 from the bottom up. It made my blood boil for some time but then I let it go. I am not confrontational by nature and I am aware that people have exploited this weakness of mine many a time. Willingness to fight is a necessary quality in civil servants today, which I must confess I never possessed. This episode also showed how easy it was to manipulate facts and manoeuvre positions to one's own advantage in the government.

After my district tenure, I spent a year as MD of Travancore Titanium Products, which, in my view, was the worst stretch of my career. I was completely at sea against aggressive trade unions and I came to understand the problem Kerala faced in attracting new investment and industry. In Kerala, the struggle against the unions does not end with a wage or bonus negotiation. The unions, particularly their leaders, believe in keeping the management constantly on edge, raising issues virtually every day. For a novice like me, running the company was too much of a task, and my stress levels must have been the highest at this job, out of all those I have held. It showed in the results, too. For the first time ever in the history of the company, it showed a loss in the year in which I was MD, owing to a protracted strike on the quantum of bonus. By a strange coincidence, the next strike in the company also took place when I was Chairman of the company in my capacity as Industries Secretary, many years later.

I lasted barely a year in the company and then left for Ernakulam to take charge of the Civil Supplies Corporation. This role was one of the high points of my career. During this period, I worked directly with a minister who was a visionary, a political leader of standing and a pillar of support for civil servants willing to take risks to achieve results. Not only was it a pleasure to work with the gentle and unassuming E. Chandrasekharan Nair, but he also taught me many a lesson in administration. With the support of all of us who worked with him, it was he who transformed the face of non-formal public distribution in Kerala.

I knew him from my earlier tenure in the Marketing Federation. He was the then Chairman of the State Cooperative Bank, which, too, he built up in his own inimitable way. The decision to appoint me as MD of the Marketing Federation was taken at a meeting of their board held in the conference room of the State Cooperative Bank. I was later told that Chandrasekharan Nair had asked the President of the federation whether it was necessary to commit the sin of appointing an IAS officer to a state-level cooperative institution in his conference room! Clearly, IAS officers were not too popular in Kerala at that time.

It was, therefore, of particular pleasure to me that he himself asked for my appointment as Chief Executive of the Civil Supplies Corporation. I was happy to leave Trivandrum and go to the less rigid, less bureaucratized, more happy-go-lucky city of Ernakulam, despite the enormous work pressure the minister went on to put on me.

Chandrasekharan Nair was firmly resolved to restrain the rise in prices of vegetables and groceries during Onam in the year 1981. Onam is the harvest festival of Kerala, a period of continued feasts and festivity, celebrated by all, regardless of caste or religion. Traders made merry during Onam, raising prices of vegetables and groceries to dizzying heights at the expense of hapless consumers.

The minister's solution lay in opening a chain of temporary outlets through which the Civil Supplies Corporation would sell vegetables to consumers at lower prices. 'A mad, hare-brained scheme,' many called it. But I was as mad as he was, willing to take that risk, with the help of the officers of the Department of Civil Supplies. This meant organizing supplies, planning locations where temporary outlets would be set up with the help of local bodies and district administrations, determining how many officers and staff we would have to take on deputation, arranging materials, looking at the nuts and bolts of organizing such a massive venture far beyond the known capacity of the corporation—a mammoth task, the likes of which had never been done before. It meant trusting officers, giving them a free hand, standing behind them.

The first Onam fair was a tremendous success. We were desperately nervous before it started, but when we rose on the morning of the day it kicked off in multiple locations, we were greeted with the sight of huge queues of people waiting patiently before our outlets. It was also fascinating to see the enthusiasm and excitement of our officers and staff as they strove to make the mission a total success. Shortages did arise in some outlets and I issued a general order authorizing officers to purchase from local markets and sell below market price.

The media, which had been sceptical, was astounded at the manner in which the markets had been flawlessly organized, and wrote column after column in open praise. Prices in the open market remained steady as well, as poorer people patronized the corporation's outlets and private vegetable shops had few customers. We had gone much beyond expectations. Of course, we made a loss on that operation, but the gain for the people of the state far outweighed the losses of the corporation. While the minister was undoubtedly the man of the hour, I too established a kind of reputation in the Kerala bureaucracy as a worker of miracles of sorts. Of course, as a civil servant, I endeavoured also to cover my backside by quickly estimating the losses we might have made and getting ratification directly from the minister, bypassing traditional channels, including the most feared Finance Department. Those were days when officers could expect to get support from ministers and senior officials, even if we made mistakes while striving to achieve results. It is an unfortunate fact that some of us who were among the most daring field officers later emasculated the system ourselves when we held senior positions endowed with Constitutional or statutory authority.

The minister had categorically told me that the corporation must not expect resources from a cash-strapped government. We had to incur losses doing things for the benefit of the people, which would be ratified, but we would have to make up for these losses ourselves by making profits elsewhere. We were already selling cement, as agents of the government, which gave us some profit. When I first took charge, I found that we had a few tonnes of palmolein oil, imported from Malaysia by the State Trading Corporation, which was lying unsold because no one wanted it. I decided to mount a large publicity campaign, extolling the virtues of palmolein as a cardiac-friendly cooking oil and emphasizing particularly its low prices. Again, it worked. The few decrepit retail outlets I had inherited saw long lines of people before them, all with tins and bottles and containers. I made good profit on palmolein.

We were also selling dust tea, which was bought in bulk from a tea company in the high ranges. Suddenly, the company decided to raise their prices. I thought this was unjustified because this increase was not reflected in the tea auction prices in Cochin. So, I decided that the corporation would venture into this unknown field by itself. We found dealers and exporters of tea on Willingdon Island in Cochin with some experience in blending tea. They agreed to buy for us from the auctions and produce a blend similar to the one we had been marketing earlier. We started marketing it, supporting our sales with another strong publicity campaign. We did well, and in due course, hired our own tea taster. The corporation became the third biggest buyer in the Cochin auctions after Brooke Bond and Lipton. My officers and I were invited frequently to meetings of planters' associations, principally the United Planters' Association of Southern India (UPASI) and our work was known and appreciated by the Tea Board, located in distant Calcutta (now Kolkata).

We also started the practice of buying rice in bulk from rice-producing states. I visited Bhopal, Bhubaneswar and Hyderabad to interact with state agencies involved in the procurement of rice. My confidence in support from the government was so great that I could negotiate and buy whole trainloads on my own. Buying was easier than getting the rice into Kerala. It was an impossible task to get railway rakes to move the rice. We had no option but to appoint 'expeditor agents', to whom we paid a commission to help us procure rakes. We indulged in other experiments too, in our compulsive urge to make profits to cover our losses. I remember we bought some rice bran oil, which we never managed to sell.

At one point, we suddenly found that we had accumulated more rice than we could sell. We had given up our retail outlets by then and were selling only through cooperative fair price shops. One day, General Manager Gopalakrishnan Nair came to me and said that we needed to think of opening a few retail outlets again. I rated Gopalakrishnan Nair very highly and I trusted his judgement. I sought the approval of my minister, who gave me permission to open outlets in a restrained manner, as the earlier attempt at retail marketing by the corporation had been an unmitigated disaster. Since I had learnt the essence of marketing by then, we decided to give a fresh brand image to our venture with a new name, a well-designed facade and colour scheme. Out of the names we suggested, the minister chose the name 'Maveli' and he also selected the colour scheme. Thus the corporation's retail marketing started again and fourteen shops were opened on the first day.

The minister got a letter shortly thereafter from former Chief Minister C. Achutha Menon, himself a great visionary who had envisioned Kerala as the future embodiment of learning, culture and education. Both Achutha Menon and Chandrasekharan Nair belonged to the same political party, the CPI. Indeed, in the earlier years of the state, when the culture of politics was different, the CPI produced a plethora of great ministers and chief ministers—men and women of unimpeachable integrity, daring dynamism and absolute commitment to the state and its people.

In his letter, Achutha Menon beseeched the minister to ensure that Maveli stores not be allowed to proliferate, lest the Civil Supplies Corporation turn into another money guzzler like the Kerala State Road Transport Corporation. Indeed, this is exactly what happened in later years, when the concept of profits to offset losses was given up totally in the medley of competitive politics. When I came back to Kerala as Vice Chairman of the State Planning Board after my retirement, I found that the corporation was subsisting on huge dollops of taxpayers' money.

Towards the end of my tenure in the corporation, I found another avenue for making some profit. I had known, over the years, that there was a great deal of profit being made by distributors and sellers of Indian Made Foreign Liquor (IMFL). P.J. Joseph, who had been the MLA in Idukki district when I was Collector, had just become Excise Minister. I went to him and asked whether we could be given some IMFL retail outlets. He obliged, and we entered the new field of retail marketing of whisky, brandy and the like. We ran into an immediate barrier, when sellers of big brands, sensing disruption in not-too-savoury distribution systems, refused to directly give us top brands. As our shops languished in the absence of big brands, I had a brainwave. I asked my office to put up notices in our outlets saying that consumers may not find some brands because we only buy liquor directly from manufacturers to ensure quality, and hence where manufacturers were unwilling to supply directly, their brands were not being sold. Again, it worked. Crowds of buyers started forming outside our shops. The work we had started became the precursor of the highly profitable State Beverages Corporation of today.

My tenure in the Civil Supplies Corporation, in retrospect, was an unqualified success. There was a huge element of luck there. Many of the things I did could have failed miserably. Solid support from the minister gave me confidence and the will to enter untested waters. Ministers come and go, and governments change every five years in Kerala. Chandrasekharan Nair was followed by a Muslim League minister, U.A. Beeran, who also trusted me. The risks I took in the Civil Supplies Corporation are unimaginable today. At that time, we did not have TV and news channels competing with each other to attract viewers by denigrating government programmes and projects. Many of the things I did in the corporation would have provided big stories for these channels because they were far outside normal bureaucratic process and it would not have been difficult for a media person to depict them as acts of high corruption. The investigative agencies, the Constitutional authorities and the courts would have together made mincemeat of me and there would have been no one above me who would take the responsibility and support me. As I see good officers languishing in jail or facing huge investigations, I am reminded of what my friend and colleague Jawhar Sircar of the West Bengal cadre, now a Rajya Sabha Member of Parliament, once told me. 'More officers', he said, 'have suffered in service out of overenthusiasm, not malpractice.' Indeed, my officers and I were unduly enthusiastic in the Civil Supplies Corporation. Today, we might all have been crushed under the combined weight of unrelenting media, unforgiving regulatory and investigative institutions and a helpless political and bureaucratic structure at the top.

After an amazing send-off, the likes of which I had never had before or since, I went to Leeds, UK, under a Colombo Plan programme. I was going abroad for the first time, after twelve years in the civil services, rather unusual amongst a set of colleagues who considered foreign trips as a status symbol. Going abroad was never a high priority for me, but the forces of the Universe conspired to make me stay abroad for six years later in my career. England itself was a revelation. It was as though I was in familiar land—Trafalgar Square, Oxford Street, the moors of Yorkshire and the lush countryside made the classics that I had read and P.G. Wodehouse come alive. The river Thames was a big surprise. It loomed large in all the books I had read, but when I saw it for the first time, it seemed puny in comparison to the Ganga, the Brahmaputra, the Godavari and the Cauvery.

A Piscean World

'I love to watch the movement of light on water and I love to play in rivers and lakes, swimming or canoeing. I am fascinated by people who work with water—fishermen, boatmen—and by a way of life that is dominated by water.'

—*Bierlie Doherty*

A few months later, in the middle of 1982, I was back in Kerala. I could have taken some months off to write a thesis on the tea industry in Kerala, the subject I had chosen, for which I had already done quite some research at the Leeds University library. I had been in Leeds for a postgraduate degree in management studies. In those days, with computers still a distant dream in India, it was easier to collect material from a library linked to many others, and most of my material was gathered at Leeds. The thesis on the tea industry brought me in close contact with the Tea Board and its chairman, Jagdish Khattar, who found my work interesting. He had heard from industry sources about the work I had done in the Civil Supplies Corporation for the marketing of tea. He thought I would be useful in the Tea Board and persuaded V.C. Pande, then Additional Secretary in the Commerce Ministry, to post me in the newly created position of Deputy Chairman of the Tea Board at Coimbatore. This was turned down by my Chief Secretary, R. Gopalaswami, because I had only just assumed charge of the post of Director of Fisheries. My name, however, remained within the purview of the Commerce Ministry, and when the position of Chairman, Cardamom Board, fell vacant in 1985, I was chosen. The thesis on tea, too, was a success, and I was awarded an MA degree with distinction, which was rare for Leeds University.

I took up my position as Director of Fisheries immediately after I came back from Leeds in 1983. Once more, I was the first IAS officer ever to take up what was essentially a technical position. I recall that some of my colleagues sympathized with me for having been handed a dud job, which nobody else wanted, and that too so soon after I had distinguished myself in the Civil Supplies Corporation. Some were secretly happy that I had been brought down a peg. I, too, felt sorry for myself. However, once I took it on, I found the job fascinating and realized that I would be able to do some new things at it.

Perhaps it helped that being a Piscean, I had a natural affinity for water and fish. Besides, it brought me in contact with the Congress Chief Minister K. Karunakaran, who had picked the Fisheries portfolio in a Cabinet reshuffle. He was one of the greatest ministers I have worked with; a powerful politician with an inherent administrative sense, and a minister who believed in evaluating his officers initially, then trusting them completely and backing them up when necessary. I worked closely on many occasions with the 'Leader', as he was called, and his faith in me gave me the same kind of freedom that I enjoyed under Chandrasekharan Nair.

One of my seniors, S. Krishnakumar, who later entered politics and became a Union Deputy Minister, had served as Fisheries Secretary for some time. He was a creative officer while in the service and had a penchant for thinking differently and doing new things. He had been my Collector when I was Subcollector, Fort Cochin, and I had learnt from him how public service offered one the unique opportunity to strike out on different paths and explore new avenues, never mind the occasional inevitable mistake. Krishnakumar had conceived of forming 'fishermen villages' under a separate act of the Legislature with elected management committees. A hundred of them were formed with impressive objectives but no resources, and not the faintest notion of what to do with them. My first task was, therefore, to find a role and the money for them; the state government had no money. I tried to find out whether the National Cooperative Development Corporation (NCDC) would help. I had dealt with this institution in the past when I was in the cooperative sector. The NCDC said they could not finance the village societies because they were not formed under the Cooperative Societies Act. I asked them whether they would be prepared to finance a federation of these villages formed under the Cooperative Societies Act. They said they would, and thus was formed the Kerala Fishermen's Welfare Cooperative Federation, which we named Matsyafed for short, and is now a familiar presence in all parts of Kerala.

I was MD of the federation, in my capacity as Director of Fisheries, and Government Secretary R.C. Choudhury was the Chairman of the first board nominated by the government. I was looking for a young officer who would invigorate the organization and came to know of Amitabh Kant, who had built a reputation as an enterprising Subcollector in the northern subdivision of Tellicherry, now Thalassery. Incidentally, PM Modi has much to thank Thalassery for. Amitabh is now the Chief Executive Officer of NITI Aayog, while Ajit Doval, now National Security Advisor, used to be Assistant Superintendent of Police, Thalassery, in his early days.

Since the minister in charge of Fisheries was the Chief Minister himself, I had no difficulty in getting Amitabh posted to what was virtually a non-job. I do not know whether or not he was disappointed because there were many others who wanted to offer him more glamorous postings. We had to build an organization from scratch. Amitabh had unorthodox ways. One objective we had set for ourselves was to merge three loss-making public sector undertakings—the Kerala Fisheries Corporation, the Kerala Fishermen's Welfare Corporation and the Kerala Inland Fisheries Development Corporation—into Matsyafed. Normally, this procedure would have taken months, even years. But one afternoon, Amitabh came and told me, 'I went to the three corporations and took all their documents and papers.' By fiat and this act of grand larceny, the three corporations became part of Matsyafed. The Kerala Fishermen's Welfare Corporation used to distribute outboard engines to traditional fishermen at a subsidized cost. The engines they distributed were exclusively of Yamaha make. Mitsubishi never got a look in. One day, Amitabh told me, 'I have bought 200 Mitsubishi engines.' Since Yamaha was firmly established and had many backers, I expected trouble in the meeting of the Board of Directors of the federation. So I told the board that I myself had taken the decision to buy the Mitsubishi engines, that their quality was good and that we needed competition in the market to get better prices. As I had acquired some repute and had the confidence of the Chief Minister, no one raised any objection.

Between us, Amitabh and I fashioned an organization out of thin air, which continues to flourish even today. I think both of us learnt lessons there that have lasted a lifetime. One lesson is that the less glamorous jobs which nobody wants provide the best opportunities for creativity. That teamwork based on mutual trust pays. That the support and confidence of a senior political leader like Karunakaran makes all the difference in trying to achieve results. Both Doval and Amitabh were favourites of Karunakaran. When Doval was in Kerala, Karunakaran was Home Minister and used to openly say, 'If I have five officers like Doval, I can transform Kerala Police.' Amitabh worked with me later, too, and he bought into my pet theory that in order to be an effective officer, one has to think ten years ahead and visualize how the nation and society will change.

In the Central Government for the First Time

'Failure is instructive. The person who really thinks learns quite as much from his failures as from his successes.'

—*John Dewey*

My tenure in the Fisheries Department ended in 1985 with my deputation to the central government as Chairman of the Cardamom Board. This lasted a full five years, my longest-ever tenure in any government posting. Full of enthusiasm and a youthful, know-all spirit, bolstered by my successes in certain aspects of my career, I blundered right away. The global market for small cardamom was dominated by purchasers in the Middle East and Saudi Arabia, who frequently drink a concoction called 'kahwa', prepared out of equal quantities of coffee and cardamom—this is not the same as the Kashmiri kahwa, which contains other spices, saffron, almonds, rose petals and honey. On the supply side, India dominated for years and years until it was found that cardamom can grow in parts of Latin America, too. Guatemala entered the fray, and relying on the economies of scale and the productivity of virgin forest soil, severely undercut Indian producers and swept the market. The Arab buyers still preferred the taste of Indian cardamom, but when the price differential was too high, they turned to Guatemala.

Small cardamom was sold through auctions. The main growing area was Idukki district in Kerala, although some quantities were also grown in Coorg, Karnataka. Flushed with my previous successes in marketing agricultural commodities, I got the notion that I could control prices by laying minimum and maximum caps for the quantities offered in auctions. At the very first auction, prices went plunging down and never recovered thereafter. The growers were up in arms against the Cardamom Board and me, in particular. Large demonstrations were organized in front of my office. My relationship with growers of small cardamom was uneasy thereafter, right until the end of my tenure.

We retrieved the position for small cardamom later by marketing it heavily in Indian markets, promoting two health schemes. Boil water before drinking, we said, because microbes are destroyed in the process of boiling. To add a bit of flavour to the water, add a pod of small cardamom. The second theme was to chew a pod of cardamom when one felt the urge to smoke. These were not my ideas—they came from the experienced Secretary of the board, K.G. Nayar. The campaign yielded results and the vast Indian market began to open up for small cardamom. Over the years, long after I had left the board for greener pastures, an industry which had seemed on the verge of extinction had survived and was flourishing in the Indian market. This was not what I was required to do by the Commerce Ministry. Their focus was on exports, at a time when keeping domestic markets closed and starved was the leitmotif in Indian economic policy. New Delhi, with its many priorities and problems, hardly noticed this act of lèse-majesté.

A decision had been taken by the Government of India to bring other spices under the purview of the board and to convert it into a Spices Board. The procedures took quite some time, but ultimately an Act was passed in Parliament and we became the Spices Board. P. Shivshankar, a lawyer from Andhra, was the Commerce Minister then. The Government Joint Secretary at the time, D.P. Bagchi, told me that the minister wanted to appoint a politician as Chairman of the board and make me its Executive Director. The idea of working in a secondary position in an organization I had chaired did not appeal to me. I told him I would rather go back to my state government. Somehow, the minister's idea did not materialize and I took over as Founder–Chairman of the Spices Board.

Before the Spices Board came into being, there used to be two organizations, the Cardamom Board—which I was heading—and the Spices Export Promotion Council, managed by an elected body of spice exporters. I had two immediate problems—to integrate the employees of the council into the new board, and to win over the spice exporters who were not comfortable with the bureaucratic takeover of an organization they had hitherto managed. The former task was accomplished with the help of the O&M (Organization and Methods) Wing of the Commerce Ministry, which was persuaded to create so many new posts that virtually everyone in both organizations got promotions—even some double promotions—in the new board. In the process, the staff union in the board vanished as their leaders became officers, while the officers of the council were treated with respect and understanding, and they merged seamlessly into the new board. The second task, I knew, would be a slow and laborious process.

In 1987, the US Food and Drug Administration (USFDA) hit the pepper exporters hard with an injunction of automatic detention of black pepper in US markets. This meant that our pepper would not enter the US markets without clearance from a laboratory approved by the FDA in the US. This meant more costs for the exporters and put them at a disadvantage vis-a-vis exporters from Brazil, Malaysia and

Indonesia, who were India's competitors. The main problem was the rodent droppings found in some consignments in excess of the limits prescribed by the FDA.

Solving this problem, therefore, became my priority. A delegation went to the US to meet their officials and importers. Led by the government's Joint Secretary M.R. Sivaraman, it comprised several leading exporters and included me, as the Chairman of the board. Sivaraman had the reputation of being difficult, a tough taskmaster. When I met him for the first time in his chambers in Udyog Bhavan in Delhi, he cross-examined me very closely. Since I have always had the habit of going deep into all details relating to my job, I obviously met his expectations. We worked well thereafter, not only at that job but many others. In the civil services, it often happens that some officers loom large in one's life and career due to more than one official relationship. Sivaraman was one such person in my career.

Some of the American importers were, frankly, rude. That was a time when India was treated as a poor and inconsequential third world country. When Sivaraman naively asked one group of importers if there were no rats in the US, one replied, 'No rats here, except the ones to whom we have given green cards.' Many Americans live under the delusion that being rude is the same as being outspoken. It takes time to understand their cultural mores. I came to realize later that they respect strength and deal more carefully with those who can benefit them commercially or politically.

The American culture shock also gave us an opportunity to set our own house in order. We mounted a massive campaign to improve processing of pepper for exports. Not only at the level of processors and exporters, but even in farmyards. We trained farmers on how to dry pepper carefully and safely, while protecting it from rodents, birds and animals. Everyone cooperated and the quality of Indian pepper exports were soon rivalling those of Malaysia, which was considered the gold standard back then.

A few months after that, T.K.A. Nair, then Chairman of the Marine Products Export Development Authority (MPEDA), invited a senior functionary of the USFDA to India. The MPEDA had been struggling with automatic detention for years for their frozen marine products. These products could not enter US markets without undergoing further checks in an approved laboratory in the US. Nair was kind enough to let me borrow the official for two or three days. We took him up and down the hills, made sure he wined and dined well, and were very hospitable hosts. We took him around some of our modernized and cleaned up processing units, and took him to farms to see how well the farmers had begun to clean and dry their pepper. Soon after his return, pepper was removed from the stipulation of automatic detention, much to the relief and joy of our exporters. Marine products, however, continued to remain blocked. On a future occasion, I overheard the rather crude and brash Vice Chairman of MPEDA upbraiding the soft-spoken T.K.A. Nair for having let the Spices Board hijack the US official.

For me, the removal of automatic detention was a singular triumph. Not only was the problem behind us, we gained the respect and friendship of Indian exporters who suddenly realized that the Spices Board was working towards their prosperity. We built a close relationship, strengthened by successive chairpersons, which remained intact for many years until it broke recently. Together with the exporters, we organized an international meet of exporters and importers of spices, which, over the years, became a permanent fixture in the spice calendar for spice traders around the world. Today, I believe the Spices Board is no longer a part of the organization of this event. It is run entirely by the traders.

As Chairman of the Spices Board, I realized quickly that I could no longer remain bound to Kerala. Kerala has no doubt been recognized for centuries as the home of spices—Vasco da Gama sailed across the seas and landed in Calicut, looking for spices, more specifically, black pepper. He was followed in succeeding epochs by the Portuguese, the Dutch, and finally, the English; the seeds of the British Raj were sown in Kerala. But as Chairman of the Spices Board, I knew that Kerala was only the third biggest producer of spices after Andhra, which grew chillies, and Rajasthan, which grew seed spices like coriander, cumin and fennel. I endeavoured, therefore, to establish links with all these states, as also others, like Gujarat.

A visit to Gujarat stands out in my memory. I made my first—and only—Hindi speech in Gujarat in a village in its interiors. Rajiv Gandhi rode high in those days and his speeches were festooned with the expression, 'hamein sochna hai…' in Hindi, meaning 'we must think…' I was deeply impressed by him and hence liberally used these words, with the result that a young Kerala exporter who had travelled with me said in a tongue-in-cheek fashion that my speech sounded like that of Rajiv Gandhi. I remember also that we were given pooris and aloo for lunch in the village. They came covered in layers of houseflies, which put off some who had come with me, but I ate with gusto. I have been a foodie all my life and the pooris were delicious.

Before I leave my story of the Spices Board—and eating—behind, let me recount another lunch episode, this time in the heartland of Saudi Arabia. I was travelling with a bunch of cardamom exporters and also my trade officer, headquartered at Bahrain, Sumit Dutt Majumdar, who retired many years later as Chairman of the Central Board of Excise and Customs, and is now considered a national authority on the Goods and Services Tax (GST). Sumit had told me in advance about a certain cultural practice prevalent in the depths of Saudi Arabia, so I cannot say I was not forewarned.

An Arab sheikh had invited us for lunch. Some of us were vegetarian, a concept he failed to understand. He advised my vegetarian friends to remove the meat from the rice and eat it. Eventually, when my friends insisted on food without any trace of meat or fish, it got through to him that they were strange creatures who needed to be treated differently. Finally, some fruits were produced before them. I was, of course a full-blooded Malayali, willing to experiment with any meat, fish or fowl. As the chief guest on the occasion, I was seated next to the sheikh on the carpeted floor. He bit into a rich and luscious piece of meat, found it delicious and passed it on to me to eat the rest. Since Sumit had already cautioned me, I chomped on it contentedly, making the appropriate noises of appreciation.

Besides eating different kinds of food, I also learnt more about marketing during my days in the Spices Board. I learnt the hard way that government agencies and officials must not poke their noses into commercial and economic matters about which they know little. I realized once again the value of teamwork, of keeping my ears open to all ideas and suggestions, of finding ways to get along with all kinds of people. Once more, I understood that life is never a straight line, that there are ups and downs, hits and misses, and that one's own high opinion of oneself is not necessarily shared by others and that they may not be wrong in judging one by one's shortcomings.

Back to the State

'You're always you, and that don't change, and you're always changing, and there's nothing you can do about it.'

                                                              —Neil Gaiman

From the Spices Board, it was back to the Secretariat, this time as Secretary in charge of Animal Husbandry, Dairy Development and Fisheries in 1990. I had some knowledge of fisheries, having been Director of that department, and also for a short period of six months Chairman of MPEDA, when T.K.A. Nair went back to his state, Punjab, and the Commerce Ministry was taking time to post his successor. I was able to refresh and expand my knowledge of animal husbandry and dairy which I had acquired many years ago in the Small Farmers Development Agency. I didn't remain there for long. Karunakaran came back to power after a year, and he thought that I should be in charge of a more glamorous department. His Chief Secretary, S. Padmakumar, thought likewise and I was posted as Industries Secretary. Padmakumar himself was a colourful personality. We did not get along too well when I was MD, Travancore Titanium Products, but during my tenure as Industries Secretary and for long thereafter, we worked well together and remained good friends. Padmakumar was also the most powerful and influential Chief Secretary the state had ever seen—I doubt whether in succeeding years, too, there ever was a Chief Secretary as influential as him. From him, I learnt the important lesson of managing top jobs in an essentially political environment.

While I was new to Industries, my minister, P.K. Kunhalikutty of the Indian Union Muslim League, was new both to the department and to governance itself, as he had become minister for the first time. For both of us, therefore, it was a learning process rendered easier by the fact that there were some outstanding officers in the department, like the incorruptible V. Somasundaran in the State Industrial Development Corporation, and the incomparable G. Vijayaraghavan, setting up the first-ever Technopark in the country. Together, we organized an event in Delhi involving top corporate honchos at the behest of the Chief Secretary, essentially to market Kerala as an ideal investment destination. Confronted as I was, for the first time, with the big names of the corporate world, I was understandably in a state of utter panic, which was not made easier by the fact that after his initial welcome speech, the Chief Secretary left it to me to front the whole event. We came through reasonably successfully, as far as the event was concerned, but of course, no investment followed. Throughout my career, I have come across many such events organized by many states at much grander scales, with money flowing like water as investors were lavishly entertained. Many Memoranda of Understanding (MoUs) are signed and grandiose announcements are made regarding the manna that will fall upon the state, but ultimately, hardly anything happens.

Investors are clever people. They might be pleasant to political leaders and senior officials, but they will put their money where they can get the best returns and the best terms from state governments. This is all there is to 'ease of doing business', which is much talked-about lately. The fate of the investor is written by his shareholders and his creditors.

This was followed by an exercise of scripting a new industrial policy for Kerala. Somasundaran and I burnt the midnight oil, trying to be as clever as possible. One day, Padmakumar walked into my room and told me, 'Chandran, somehow I don't feel comfortable with what has been written. It doesn't seem striking and impactful.' Since the Minister wanted the policy announced early, we did not have enough time to make it more analytical and abstruse. Instead, we just took out the main policy initiatives and strung them together to produce a short document without any embellishments. Strangely, this proved to be a big hit and gained much applause, despite my initial trepidation. I went abroad sometime thereafter to Jamaica on a short assignment of the Commonwealth Secretariat, but the reports from Kerala were encouraging.

In retrospect, Technopark was the singular achievement of that period. What started as a glimmer of an idea turned out to be a venture that transformed Trivandrum, and Kerala at large. When it was being built, there were many who scoffed at it as another white elephant created at taxpayers' expense by the state government. Who, they asked, would come to backward, provincial Trivandrum? Not that their concerns were completely misplaced. When we first came to Trivandrum as IAS probationers, there were barely two or three cinema theatres and, in these, the audience had to sit on folding chairs. Other than the state-owned Hotel Mascot, there was not a single restaurant or hotel of note in the city. There was no social activity after seven in the evening. The nearby seaside hamlet of Kovalam was beautiful but deserted. In place of the rocks and cliffs we used to climb back then, there is now a seven-star hotel and the entire seaside is crowded with resorts and eateries.

Yet, we laboured on in the fond expectation that if the infrastructure is provided, industry will come—if not today, then tomorrow or in good time. Vijayaraghavan, who can rightfully be called as the founding father of Technopark, was a dedicated young man of unimpeachable integrity. Work proceeds much faster and far more effectively when there is mutual trust among those in the team. I trusted Vijayaraghavan so much that when he brought his bills to me for approval, I signed them without even looking at them. This is a habit that has stayed with me. When I trust someone, I trust him or her completely, and let the work go on without putting spokes in the wheel. Even when I became Finance Secretary of the state a couple of years later, when I trusted a colleague and felt that he would apply the same standards in the examination of issues as I would, I signed blindly without allowing the file to get lost in the labyrinth that was the Finance Department. At the same time, when I smelled a rat, there was no way I was going to be coerced into any action, however mighty the personage involved might be.

Today, Technopark has changed the face of Trivandrum. All the big names are here. The likes of Tata Consultancy Services (TCS) and Infosys have set up large establishments and there are many foreign companies jostling for space. Technopark has itself had to expand considerably, and despite its growth, there is still a waiting list of firms that want to set up shop there. Start-ups have proliferated, new technologies have mushroomed and some 50,000 people have found jobs. High-rise buildings dot the landscape, and hotels and restaurants of many kinds and descriptions have come up aplenty. The biggest and most satisfying change that I have seen is that Trivandrum is no longer a prim and proper Malayali bureaucratic town. There are people from all across the country living in the city, and one hears the sound of many different languages. Technopark has brought India into Kerala.

Technopark has also created a new model of industrial development in the state; industrial development that is led by infrastructure creation and by technology. Having broken the belief that adverse labour conditions will prevent industry from settling comfortably in Kerala, medium and small industries have sprouted all over and are spreading their wings not merely in the state, but in other states and even abroad. My friend, C. Balagopal, who worked capably with me as General Manager of the Civil Supplies Corporation, is writing a book on this and I cannot wait to read it. Between Technopark and the seaside resort of Kovalam, Trivandrum has turned into a commercial city. This transformation will reach fruition with the establishment of the Vizhinjam International transhipment port, being built by the Adani group, and I am gratified that I had a role to play in that too, many years later, as Vice Chairman of the State Planning Board. The icing on the cake would be a spanking new airport. Since the Government of India has decided to privatize it and the Adani Group has now taken over the management of the airport, we can soon expect to see phenomenal changes.

There was another change of Chief Secretary in 1994, and Ramachandran Nair took over. He felt that I would do well as Finance Secretary. Kerala was under great stress financially, so much so that during 1993–94, the state treasury had to be closed half a dozen times because we could not clear our overdraft with the Reserve Bank of India (RBI) on time. Expenditure control is the normal and traditional method adopted by governments when they are in financial distress, but the Chief Secretary and I decided to turn this practice on its head. Instead of expenditure, we shifted focus to resources. We had an Expenditure Department under Finance at the time, as all the focus at all times was on expenditure. I brought my trusted officer, Somasundaran, to Expenditure and we managed as before—like a house on fire. To the horror of my officers in the Finance Department, I made a presentation to other Secretaries on the state of our finances and how we were going to go bust by Onam that year unless all of them cooperated by limiting their expenditure and enhancing revenue by collecting more fees for the various services rendered by governmental departments. This was unusual because the finances of the state are supposed to be kept very secret, but it nevertheless yielded great results as my colleagues began to work with me, rather than in opposition to me.

On the resources side, we looked at taxes and how we could make up our backlog. We also set up a new centre for taxation studies, which today has become the Gulati Institute of Finance and Taxation, with a sprawling building in the heart of Trivandrum. When we started the centre, however, we had to make do with a makeshift basement, which previously housed a failed small-scale industry owned by a film actor. We found big opportunities for stepping up collection of national savings. The focus on revenue paid off, and in the year 1994–95 we never went into overdraft with the RBI nor ever had to take an advance from them. On the other hand, we parked funds in the RBI and earned interest on it. This had never happened before in the history of the state.

As Finance Secretary, I met Union Finance Minister Manmohan Singh for the first time in 1994. We were going to be in serious trouble by Onam that year; we may not even have been able to pay salaries on time. Traditionally, Onam is a difficult month because government servants were not just paid their salaries but an additional month's salary as bonus. I received Manmohan Singh at the airport in Thiruvananthapuram, shaking off airport security and meeting him on the tarmac. On the next day, the state Finance Minister Padmarajan and I met Manmohan Singh at Raj Bhavan. The Union Finance Minister was defensive and non-committal, and I thought he cast a baleful eye at both of us. However, he did give us a Plan advance and we sailed through Onam without too much trouble. He remembered us again next year, and told his Expenditure Secretary, N.K. Singh, to check whether we needed any money before Onam. By a strange coincidence, I had sought an appointment with N.K. Singh as a courtesy call. He asked me whether I needed money, and I told him, 'No sir, I am okay.' He was astonished. He told me to write a report on how we had turned around the state's finances so that he could put it up to his Minister. Somehow, I never got around to writing the report.

By 1996, I had decided that it was time for me to go to the centre. My name still had some currency in the Commerce Ministry, and I was offered a deputation to the centre as there was a vacancy in the Trade Policy Division, which looked after matters relating to the World Trade

Organization (WTO). P. Chidambaram was the Minister of State at the time. The Commerce Secretary then was Tejendra Khanna, who examined the panel presented by the Department of Personnel and Training, and thought I might fit the bill. Chidambaram was, however, a meticulous man. He looked through all my confidential reports and made enquiries of many people I had worked with. Having satisfied himself, he put my name on the panel for selection by the Civil Services Board. The Cabinet Secretary at the time was Surendra Singh, who was the Additional Secretary in the Commerce Ministry when I was in the Spices Board. He had no difficulty in agreeing to my posting, and it went through the process. Unfortunately, after that, a small drama unfolded. Chidambaram went out of Commerce and his place was taken by a minister from Bihar. The rule was that if a minister changes, any appointment file would go back to the new minister for review—in this case, D.P. Yadav. Yadav was in Commerce for less than a month and he approved my appointment on his last day in office, but the file had to go back to yet another new minister, Bolla Bulli Ramaiah, from Andhra Pradesh. Ramaiah kept the file to himself, trying to see whether my name could be replaced by an officer of his choosing, preferably from Andhra Pradesh. He was told by the Secretary that the process was too far advanced to make a change at that point, and finally, he approved. Thus, a process that should normally have taken a few days took months to be completed. My appointment was approved not by one minister, but by three ministers in quick succession!

I had to leave for Delhi in a hurry because my Secretary wanted me to attend a meeting of officials from developing countries on trade and investment, an ongoing and controversial issue at the WTO. I handed over charge quickly and left for Delhi without the benefit of protracted send-off parties given by friends and colleagues. Normally, I would have expected to come back to Kerala in five years upon the conclusion of my tenure. However, as things turned out, I came back only after fifteen years, and that too, after my retirement from the civil services.

Return to Delhi

'Delhi is a soldier's town, a politician's town, journalists' and diplomats' town. It is Asia's Washington, though not so picturesque, and lives by ambition, rivalry and opportunism.'

—*Jan Morris*

Delhi is where I spent a good part of my childhood and teenage years. Now, I was back in the city which held memories of both my school and college days. I had joined Delhi Public School (DPS), Mathura Road, in 1956 and, coming from Madras, I experienced an immediate culture shock at school. The lack of knowledge of Hindi at once made me the laughing stock of my new class. The children of Delhi were loud, at times nasty, rarely friendly. In a way, this was an expression of a cultural trait of Delhi that I have noticed throughout my life. Delhi has great admiration for the rich and powerful, and not much concern for others. Not only are power and wealth important, they need to be garishly flaunted to hold value. This is not to be seen in Kerala, where you can never distinguish between the very rich and the middle class. At the same time, Delhi retains its magnificence and its deep roots in history and its acceptance of multiple cultures. The common people in the city continue to be hospitable, open and hearty.

We stayed initially in Karol Bagh, in a first-floor flat overlooking a cremation ground. I was eight years old at the time and my mother thought it better not to tell me that the fires burning in the place across the road were bodies being cremated. Not that it would have made much of a difference, because for a boy of that age, death is just another event and one could only feel mildly curious about bodies being burnt. At any rate, I was used to seeing dead bodies being carried across the road in front of our house in Madras, with the mourners riotously celebrating, dancing, singing and playing musical instruments. Among some sections of Tamilian society, death is a liberation into an eternally joyous state from a world riddled with pain and suffering.

We did not live for long in Karol Bagh, moving to Lajpat Nagar, then a backwoods area, where jackals could be heard in the night. This was when I used to spend all my time playing cricket in an open ground adjoining our house or scouring the area for puppies, which were many. I knew all the stray dogs in the area personally, and was miserable when corporation employees came and shot one of them and threw its body in the garbage bin. That was the barbarous mode of removal of these mute and friendly creatures at that time. Animal lovers, not least of them the indomitable Maneka Gandhi, deserve to be felicitated many times over for introducing the nation to more humane ways of dealing with these devoted friends of mankind.

I plodded along in school, not much interested in anything, least of all science and mathematics. However, I read voraciously, devouring books of all kinds. Late every evening, I would see a tall Sikh boy wending his way on a bicycle to his house in E Block. As far as I knew, he never joined other young people for any games or sports and was hardly seen outside his house. He also studied in DPS with me. He was three years my senior and known to be brilliant in studies, outshining all others. In later years, we had a great deal to do with each other. His name was Montek Singh Ahluwalia.

I failed ignominiously in the ninth class (then known as seventh standard) and my father chose to put me in the Bharatiya Vidya Bhavan Public School on Curzon Road. Around that time, we also shifted houses, moving closer to the heart of the city, somewhere between Connaught Place and Turkman Gate. We lived in that area in different houses until I appeared for the IAS, got selected and went off to Mussoorie for training. In this phase of my life, I became increasingly lonely, reclusive and painfully shy. Books became my sole refuge. My grades improved, and I managed to secure a first division in my final school examination, which, after an interview, secured me admission in the Economics Honours course at the famed St. Stephen's College, at that time considered by far the country's best institution for higher education. Economics was regarded as the prime course in the college and I therefore became part of the creme de la creme. My shyness acted as a barrier and I did not make many friends, going straight back home from college. Moreover, I belonged to a lesser category—the 'day scholar' in contradistinction to the residents of the college hostels. A day scholar in a humanities honours course was just one step above the lowly science students in the social ladder of the college.

From Economics Honours, I moved to History for my MA. Throughout my life, I have had a good grasp over the fundamentals of economics but I never managed to secure better than modest marks. I enjoyed history, particularly in my second year, when I specialized in ancient Indian history and encountered one of the great historians and social activists of our time, Romila Thapar, who left a deep and lasting impression on me, even though we never had an occasion to interact after my college days.

My love for history would take me on long walks to Feroz Shah Kotla, not far from my house. I used to enjoy walking anyway, particularly in the salubrious winters and springs, and it was exhilarating to sit in the inner quadrangle of Feroz Shah Kotla, facing Emperor Asoka's pillar edict, surrounded on all sides by dark cubicles, where I could visualize vibrant life, people flitting about in heavy clothes and armour, chatter and merriment, from a time long ago in the past.

While I was still studying, during the second year of my MA course, my father persuaded me to appear for the Indian Police Service (IPS) examination. In those days, one could appear for the IPS examination at the age of twenty but had to wait until twenty-one to appear for the IAS. I qualified in the written examination and for the interview, I recall going to the Union Public Service Commission (UPSC), desperately nervous, wishing the earth would open up and swallow me. However, as I was sitting in the outside hall, waiting to be called in for the interview, a sudden transformation took place—I cannot say why and how. From a state of utter hopelessness, a wave of confidence swept over me and the interview that followed went off like a breeze. On this occasion, and many later, I have observed that one's mind can undergo magical changes in a jiffy. From a state of despair, the mind can rise in exuberance just as one can plunge to the depths of depression from the heights of exultation. Today, when I read about young men and women committing suicide when they perceive setbacks in what others would consider scintillating careers, I understand even more deeply how a fickle and unsteady mind imagining rather than experiencing situations can defeat a human being.

My father had told me that the IPS examination was a precursor for the main one, which was the IAS. If I finished in the first half of the list, I would not be part of the IPS, but rather would sit and work for the IAS. Most unexpectedly, I was at the top of the list, at the fourth position, having scored exceedingly well in the interview, which had hitherto been considered my weak point and for which I was supposed to have to make up in the written examination. Life takes unexpected twists and turns. Thus, the preparation for IAS started, and like other aspirants, I joined Rau's IAS Study Circle above the Palace Heights restaurant in Connaught Place. Unlike now, when virtually every city and town sports multiple civil service coaching institutions, at that time, we had only the one. Literally only one Rau, the man operated as a lone ranger with no one to support him. He could have his pick of students because he was producing impressive results year after year with at least five or six people in the top ten.

Hence, admission was granted only after an interview. When I appeared for the interview, having been introduced by one of his previous students, Ajay Prasad, who had been my classmate in MA, I entered a small room and saw a diminutive, ill-dressed man, hunched over a typewriter. 'Ha,' I said to myself, 'the secretary.' It was no secretary as he did not have one, it was Rau himself. Somehow, I seemed to have impressed him, because he told Ajay that he thought I had it in me to be one of the toppers, something I never thought of myself then or ever before or ever after. Mind you, this interview was conducted before my IPS results had come out; even before I had secured a first division in my MA examination.

Rau's words came true, and in the IAS examination, as in the IPS exam, I secured the fourth position. I left for Mussoorie, leaving home for the first time in my life; my father saw me off at the Delhi railway station. I owe a deep debt of gratitude to my father. Himself a gold medallist, having secured the top position in all of Madras Presidency as a student of Madras Christian College, he somehow failed to make it as big as he should have. But he devoted himself wholly to helping me become what he could never be. I have no hesitation in saying that intellectually and in the sheer breadth of his learning, I was no match for him.

For twenty-six years after I had joined the IAS, I was away from Delhi. When I returned to take up residence once more in the year 1996, it was a completely different city, no longer safe and staid, as it used to be in my time.

At Sea in the Commerce Ministry

'*The leading rule for the lawyer, as for the man of every other calling, is diligence.*'

—*Abraham Lincoln*

The new post in the Commerce Ministry that I occupied foxed me completely for quite some time. I was used to learning fast as I had held many different positions. At the time, I did not even know what Most Favoured Nation meant or what National Treatment in WTO trade policy was, which were basics for anyone given the task of dealing with trade law. The Trade Policy Division in the Commerce Ministry seemed like a whole new world of arcane trade laws, developed in a disorderly manner to accommodate the diverse negotiating interests of multiple countries, developed and developing. I had some brilliant young officers working with me, including the likes of Vandana Aggarwal from the Indian Economic Service and Jayashree Watal, Arun Goyal and Raghav Chandra from the IAS. Chandra was not dealing with the WTO but helped me in developing trade with Latin America, another responsibility added to the post of Joint Secretary, Trade Policy Division.

I had a distinguished predecessor, Anvarul Huda, who had spent many years in the division. He dropped into my chambers one day and told me that the best way of understanding the subject was to go deep into each file that came up, study the law pertaining to the issue contained in the file and go into the jurisprudence. While I adopted this method to study individual files, the whole structure was not coming together in my mind. This changed when I was called to the Lal Bahadur Shastri National Academy of Administration at Mussoorie to deliver a lecture. In the library there, I found some simple books which explained how the entire set of agreements, laid out in a document called the 'Legal Texts', were strung together after the Uruguay Round negotiations in the mid-nineties and how they evolved from basic principles laid down in the earlier 'General Agreement on Tariffs and Trade'. Thereafter, I was able to relate the parts to the whole, and my understanding was further bolstered by the hectoring ways of the very learned, aggressive and well-meaning Ambassador to the WTO at the time, S. Narayanan.

Narayanan could be so fierce that people like me would quake in his presence. Ashok Lahiri from the Finance Ministry, now an MLA in Bengal, and Krishnan Venugopal, lawyer and the son of the present Attorney General K.K. Venugopal—who I was trying to lure into the field of multilateral trade law as there was no one else in the country who had specialized in this thicket of unintelligible legal jargon—were in awe of him. When Narayanan started with the words, 'Let me be brutally frank …', we would cower because we knew a devastating snub was on its way. Yet, he and his wife, Sunanda, were exquisite hosts and I have seldom seen a more pure-hearted and transparent man than Narayanan. We continue to be friends to this day.

A few months later, we had the First Ministerial Conference of the WTO in Singapore in December 1996. There was great pressure from the US and European communities, particularly the latter, to bring new issues into the ambit of the WTO—investment, competition policy, government procurement and trade facilitation. This was firmly opposed at Geneva by Narayanan and a bunch of other ambassadors representing developing countries. The meetings were long and arduous, stretching into the night. Finally, some language was found which gave some comfort to the US and European Union (EU) without compromising our position too much. It provided only for setting up working groups on investment, competition policy and government procurement, to study these issues and obtain greater clarity. On trade facilitation, a decision was made to help developing countries achieve better understanding of the issues involved, drawing upon the resources available to the United Nations Council on Trade and Development (UNCTAD).

Following the agreement in Singapore, there was uproar in the Indian Parliament leading to a short adjournment. The impression that people strove to create was that our interests had been totally compromised. The negotiations at Singapore had been led by Secretary Tejendra Khanna, together with Ambassador Narayanan. Minister Bolla Bulli Ramiah was virtually a bystander, a lone and ineffectual figure, shepherded helplessly from room to room as the negotiations progressed. This was a far cry from the next negotiation that I attended at Doha, where Murasoli Maran was the roaring lion who held the entire meeting in thrall.

When we came back to India, Prime Minister Deve Gowda called us for a meeting the very next evening. Deve Gowda had a reputation of not being very attentive when serious discussions took place. In this meeting, Tejendra Khanna launched forth on all that had transpired. Deve Gowda closed his eyes. Khanna spoke on and on for nearly an hour. Deve Gowda's eyes remained firmly closed, but he did not snore, nor did his head droop. When Khanna's peroration was over, the PM opened his eyes. And then, to my utter surprise, he asked a series of incisive questions, which revealed beyond doubt that he had heard and understood every word. At the end of the session, the PM said, 'That means my delegation acquitted itself well. All this criticism is meaningless.' It was then that all of us breathed a sigh of relief. On our way back, I told Khanna, 'All these rumours about Deve Gowda going to sleep seem false. He was fully alert.' Khanna smiled and said, 'Our Prime Minister has a native, homespun intelligence which has taken him so far. He is not to be underestimated.'

This was followed by a special discussion in the Parliament on the issue. Knowing the serious limitations of our minister, my team and I had worked on enlisting every single point that we thought could be raised in the Parliament. I gave him a detailed note in question-and-answer form, almost like a guidebook for students appearing for examinations. The Commerce Secretary was all praise for it. Fortunately, we managed to anticipate every single question asked and every single point raised, and the minister sailed through with flying colours by just reading from my text.

Tragedy and a Brush with the Occult

'There is a saying in Tibetan, "Tragedy should be utilized as a source of strength". No matter what sort of difficulties, how painful experience is, if we lose our hope, that's our real disaster.'
                            —*His Holiness the Fourteenth Dalai Lama*

My tenure in Delhi as Joint Secretary was also a period of personal turmoil. On 7 October 1997, I reached my office as usual. I was due to leave for Ernakulam that evening to attend a function held by my old organization, the Spices Board. Around 9.30 in the morning, as I was sitting at my desk, I received a call from Coomi Kapoor of *The Indian Express*.

My elder daughter, Priya, who had studied at the Asian College of Journalism, had begun to work for *The Indian Express*, Ernakulam, and later, Trivandrum. When I moved to Delhi, I sought to get her transferred to the Delhi edition, and the then editor, Shekhar Gupta, had been kind enough to agree.

She came with me to Delhi, where we stayed initially in Kerala House, until I was allotted a government flat on the ground floor in the multistorey government residential complexes at R.K. Puram. She used to travel by the rickety old blue-line buses of the day—now extinct—to her office located far away, beyond Tilak Bridge near ITO. Occasionally, on Sundays and holidays, I would drop her to her office in my Maruti 800. It was easy to make her laugh, so these long journeys across Delhi were rollicking trips. Often, I would get down with her near her office and we would have a large glass of spiced sugarcane juice each from a little stall nearby. She had to work in her office until the wee hours of the morning and would be dropped back home in a car arranged by the paper. Around 1996, *The Indian Express*, under pressure to publish from Jammu and Kashmir, started a new edition headquartered at Jammu. As they started the edition in a hurry, they managed it by sending groups of editorial staff on deputation from Delhi for a fortnight at a time. When her turn came, I dropped her at the airport. Always, in my life, I have been unduly apprehensive about my loved ones and what might happen to them. As she waved goodbye from inside the airport, suddenly a thought struck me, 'Will I see her again?' I do not consider this to have been a premonition because I was, by nature, a nervy person and such thoughts had crossed my mind on earlier occasions, too.

She was due to return on 7 October. I was due to fly to Ernakulam on the same day. On the previous night, she phoned her sister in high spirits, saying she and her gang had planned to visit Patni Point, about 100 km from Jammu. As the official driver was missing, one of those in the group drove the van himself. Like the rest of our family, Priya, too, was exceedingly fond of pets, particularly dogs. We had two at home. I heard later that there was a dog at the place where she stayed in Jammu, and the dog kept trying to pull her back when she set out for Patni Point with her friends.

Coomi Kapoor said to me that morning, 'There has been an accident in Jammu. We are all going to your house. You also come.' I said, 'What accident? Is Priya all right?' She spoke with greater urgency, 'Please come home at once.' I returned the air ticket to the representative of the Spices Board, who was in my room and immediately suffered a momentary blackout. I told the Commerce Secretary, P.P. Prabhu, about the situation, and rushed home. My wife had gone to her sister's house in Noida to greet her on her birthday. I remembered to tell her to come home immediately as Priya had had an accident. Priya's colleagues in *The Indian Express* and Coomi Kapoor were waiting at home with drawn, solemn faces, almost on the verge of tears.

On its return from Patni Point, the van, while making way for an ascending truck, fell off the side of the road into a ravine 200 metres deep. Only Priya died. All others in the van were able to jump off and sustained some injuries. Instead of my live and bubbly daughter, her body came back, draped in a white cloth by a special aircraft arranged by *The Indian Express* for the injured and for my daughter's body. My immediate priority, of course, was to take care of my younger daughter, Preeti. The two of them were close, like peas in a pod, and they leaned heavily on one another. To keep Preeti strong has indeed been the mission of my life. Both of us faced more than one setback in our lives and I am happy that, despite her troubled past, she has emerged strong and confident, capable of taking care of herself and her family while performing competently at her job, too.

I have always had an interest in the occult and the spiritual side of life, perhaps because my mother had fed me tales of headless apparitions and the like in my childhood. My father, too, believed in ghosts, and believed that he had seen dark shadows in our house in Madras. I went through an episode of constant shivering one night in my maternal grandfather's house at Alangad in Palghat (now Palakkad) district, a huge three-storey mansion amidst paddy fields, without electricity and accessible only by foot. I have never seen a ghost or observed any unusual phenomenon myself. Once, in a guest house in Sakleshpur in Karnataka, I did see a bright, writhing sliver of light climbing up the wall inside my room despite all the windows being tightly shut and the curtains drawn. I thought it might be a ghost, so I covered my face and head, and slept off.

Priya had a friend called Hena, who stayed with us in Delhi until she found other accommodation. It was she who told us that she had often seen an old lady looking at Priya in the middle of the night in their bedroom in my house in R.K. Puram. In those days, Hena had a pager, a handheld device on which messages could be sent and received. On the day after Priya's death, Hena received a message on the pager, saying: 'I am still at H.' There was no indication where it was from and who had sent it. She panicked and rang up the base station from which messages were routed, where she got the information that no message had been transmitted to her. Priya was cremated in the electric crematorium and hundreds of people attended, including my colleagues and those who had worked with Priya. After the funeral, further rituals were observed at Haridwar. In the middle of the rituals, the priest who was conducting it had the temerity to tell me that the larger the amount I pay him, the easier would be Priya's journey into the other world. He also said, 'Now you won't have to spend money on her wedding, so you can spend more here.'

When we returned, the house felt gloomy and sorrowful, even frightening. We went to a nearby 'institute of psychic research'. The man there first made me go and fetch Rs 750. No cheque, he said; he did not want to pay income tax. He heard us thereafter, and said after some reflection that the rituals performed at Haridwar were inadequate. He told us to gather all the things Priya liked—vegetables, fruits, eatables and so on—along with a bottle of water in a bag and leave it at a spiritually potent temple. The South Indian Malai Mandir, dedicated to the hill deity Murugan, was, according to him, spiritually potent. We got together all the things and left it at the temple, evading the bemused looks of suspicious priests.

In a bid to help us move on, my friends worked to get me another house. We shifted soon to Moti Bagh in a ground-floor flat just in front of Basrurkar market and endeavoured to put together the pieces of our lives again. A week after I lost my daughter, I was back at work in Udyog Bhavan. Complete immersion in work served to conceal the pain, even though it would come flooding back during the interludes of rest. Over time, I acquired mastery over my subject. I was then the senior-most Joint Secretary in the Commerce Ministry and was well-regarded. Hence, when there was a vacancy for the Deputy Chief of Mission at our embassy in Brussels, I was appointed initially as Minister (Economic) and later as Deputy Chief of Mission.

Sojourn in Brussels

'The construction of Europe is an art. It is the art of the possible.'
—*Jacques Chirac*

The culture shock started at the very outset. There were no direct flights from Delhi to Brussels at that time. We had to alight at Paris and take a connecting flight to Brussels. Our dog, Sandy, had travelled with us to Paris, but they failed to put him on the flight to Brussels. It took two days for him to reach Brussels, and he came psychologically wrecked. Every now and then, he would stand still as though he was in a state of paralysis following shock. We had to take him to an expensive veterinarian, who gave us some pills to be administered every morning. If he did not recover, the vet said, he would have to be taken to a veterinary psychiatrist. Fortunately, he recovered with the pills, and from that point onwards, flourished and blossomed in the temperate climes of Europe.

On the face of it, India and Belgium are like chalk and cheese. India is large, populous, diverse—not only in the languages spoken, but in ethnicities, religions, castes, geographical features, traditions, cultures, wealth and history. Belgium is a small country. I worked for three years in Brussels at the Indian Embassy. The joke then was that if we drove forty minutes out of Brussels in any direction, we would be out of the country—an exaggeration, of course, but not far from the truth.

Belgium is a beautiful country; a country with many singular features. I have stayed for some years subsequently in Switzerland on a different posting. Switzerland is considered to be the apogee of scenic splendour in all the world. When we talk of the scenic beauty of our own Kashmir valley, we refer to it as the 'Switzerland of India'. The beauty of Switzerland arises from its alpine terrain, which resembles in large measure the stark, awe-inspiring, sometimes terrifying Himalayan landscapes stretching majestically across our northern borders from Kashmir to Sikkim and to the Northeast.

Belgium sits in the plains, but I have seldom seen a more beautiful stretch of country. We lived in a town house close to the Bois de la Cambre, a public park surrounding a small lake at the edge of the Sonian forest, with tall trees, mainly beech and oak. In the middle of the lake was a small island, with a signboard showing the name Chalet Robinson. The original chalet was destroyed by a fire in 1991. I believe it was rebuilt in 2006. The walkway around the lake was my favourite—cool, calm, suffused in the peace of nature, reflecting nature's infinite colours and moods as the seasons changed. The Bois, as it was popularly known, is the direction-finder in Brussels. If you lose your way in any part of Brussels, you can always quickly find a signpost indicating the way to the Bois, and thus climb out of the maze. Brussels is an old city that has grown over centuries, and is not built in rectangles and squares like the more modern cities.

In the heart of Brussels is the Grand Place, a square surrounded largely by hoary buildings constructed over the centuries, largely by workers' guilds. In the approach to Grand Place and around the square

are many eateries serving food from all parts of the world—including India—chocolate shops and souvenir shops. Not too far from the square is Manneken Pis, a small black statue of a boy urinating, which, for some obscure reason, sends tourists into raptures. Within half an hour from Brussels is Lac de Genval, another pretty lake surrounded by woods, an old castle now converted into a hotel and quaint eateries. At about the same distance is Waterloo, now a memorial for the battle that Napoleon lost. Venturing a bit further into the French-speaking region of Wallonia, the tourist is regaled with the sights of Namur and Dinant. I lost my way once driving towards Namur, and drove through vast, empty farmland, broken occasionally by little eateries advertising roasted wild fowl. And then, of course, there is Belgian beer, a thousand different brands of them, of different colours and tastes and potencies. Going towards the Dutch-speaking Flanders, there is the famous little tourist town of Bruges, studded with canals and bridges, such that it is called the 'Venice of the North'. It even boasts of a South Indian restaurant.

The Belgian people love their beer and enjoy their festivals wholeheartedly. There are many of them—the Flower Carpet at Grand Place in August; the Brussels International Fantastic Film Festival dedicated to horror films; the historical Ommegang Festival, celebrated since 1549; the Festival of Europe; the Christmas Market and many others. They enjoy good films from all over the world. I heard once that a cinema hall in Brussels was organizing a film festival featuring the famed Malayalam film director Adoor Gopalakrishnan. Generally, I have not found much of an audience at movie theatres in Brussels. But I was astonished to see the theatre jam-packed for the Adoor Gopalakrishnan festival. Stranger still, my wife and I were the only Indians attending. The rest of the audience was Belgian.

We drove around a lot, particularly in Wallonia. I lost my way often but Wallonia is a beautiful stretch of country and it is rather nice to lose one's way. Once, while going with a friend to Dinant, I was on a narrow road and a bus full of revellers was coming from the opposite direction.

I tried to make way for them and promptly sank into the mud. The picnickers were delighted, seeing my car stuck with its wheels deep in the mud, and waved joyously to me.

Aside from Belgium being a beautiful place, its political structure resembles India's in that it adheres to the federal system of governance. With the growing feeling in India that our federal structure is under threat from a rampaging central government, there is much that we can learn from the genesis and evolution of federalism in Belgium, and indeed, from other countries like Australia, and even our own economic history.

Belgium is composed of two linguistic groups: the Francophones of Wallonia and the Dutch-speaking people of Flanders. The Belgian federal structure comprises several levels. It is called 'double federalism' because it encompasses both 'regions' and 'communities'. There are the regions of Wallonia and Flanders, besides the capital region of Brussels. There are communities representing the linguistic groups, primarily the French and the Dutch, but also one for the small minority of Germans. Then there are 589 municipalities, formed into five provinces. At the top of this structure is the federal government, which has to perform a balancing act between the regions and the communities. As in India, each region has its own powers of taxation. The extent of dependence on the federal government is, however, a great deal less. The 'us versus them' approach that defines the attitude of the centre towards the states in India is, however, not visible in Belgium.

The division of power is premised on the roles assigned to different federal substructures. The communities look after functions relating to citizens—education, parts of public health, social assistance and cultural affairs, including radio and television broadcasting. The regions are responsible for economic policy, zoning, environment, housing, water, agriculture and parts of energy policy, such as energy efficiency, renewable non-nuclear energy, research and development and market regulation.

Regions also supervise provinces and municipalities. They have a great deal of authority and can negotiate directly with foreign governments.

The municipalities have a legal monopoly over the distribution of energy. The role of the federal government is most delicate—it performs all social security functions. This puts it in a difficult position as the years go by. Belgium, with its excellent healthcare facilities, has an increasingly adverse demographic quotient as average life expectancy is steadily rising. This means that the cost of social security will increase year after year, and the burden will have to be borne entirely by the federal government. The federal government has also to ensure balance between the regions, which means that monies generated in the more prosperous Flanders will have to be diverted to poorer Wallonia.

The big difference between Belgian federalism and Indian federalism is that the former is the outcome of a process of evolution through discussion and debate. This evolution has not stopped and the process undergoes modification as circumstances change. The regions were constituted through the First State Reform in 1971. Division of functions between regions and communities took place in 1980 through the Second State Reform. Through the Third State Reform of 1989, regions received expanded responsibilities and full control over resources transferred from the federal government. Division of financial powers was further elaborated in the Fourth State Reform of 1993. The Fifth State Reform of 2001 dealt with some of the requirements of the Brussels community and the French-speaking community.

India started from an entirely different premise. At the time of independence, India was a congeries of princely states and British-administered provinces, with Pakistan having broken away from the country. It was recognized that the formation of a federal system was necessary as India was too large and too diverse to be administered from a single point. Hence, we invented a federal system that divided power and functions, but at the same time, remained strongly unitary. The Australian Oxford academic, K.C. Wheare, considered an authority on federalism, however, is not prepared to accept that the Indian constitution is a federal one at all. According to him, 'The constitution establishes indeed a system of government which is almost quasi-federal, devolutionary in character, a unitary state with subsidiary federal features, rather than a federal state with subsidiary unitary features.'[1]

Since then, India has evolved. The monopoly of the Indian National Congress over political power has been broken, strong regional forces have risen, awareness of regional developmental imbalance has increased, the economy has grown, our global presence has become more significant and different parts of the country have become more aggressive in their demand for a larger share of the pie. In some areas, the yearning for equitable growth has assumed extreme and militant forms, such as in the areas in which left-wing extremists are dominant. With the formation of linguistic states, more people at the bottom of the pyramid have gained access to political power, and consequently, have become more vocal. At the same time, a tug of war has emerged between the centre and the states. The recent abortive attempt to marginalize the role of the states in the management of the pandemic, the failure to recognize the role of the states as being pivotal in the fight against it and the extreme reluctance to empower them—and even further, to trust them—are factors that do not augur well for the future of India's federal democracy. It is time the centre and states sat together and reworked the fundamental tenets of Indian federalism. This is what Prime Minister Modi wanted when he said, 'Federalism is no longer the fault line of Centre–State relations but the definition of a new partnership of Team India. Citizens now have the ease of trust, not the burden of proof and process. Businesses find an environment that is open and easy to work in.'[2]

Luxembourg was another small country attached to the embassy in Brussels. I attended the crowning of the Archduke as India's representative in place of my ambassador, who could not attend the

---

1   K.C. Wheare, *Federal Government* (New York: Oxford University Press, 1964).

2   Narendra Modi, 'Prime Minister Narendra Modi's Address to the British Parliament', PM India (12 November 2015), https://www.pmindia.gov. in/en/news_updates/text-of-pms-address-to-the-british-parliament/

function for some reason. Luxembourg is famous for its fireworks once a year on the eve of their National Day on 23 June. The embassy arranged a room for me in a hotel overlooking the Adolphe Bridge, the point where the fireworks would start. Watching from this vantage point, the festivities were at first impressive, but after many hours, became irksome as we could not sleep amidst the never-ending clamour. Luxembourg was important to the wealthy people of India because it is a major financial centre with favourable tax treaties with many countries and low tax rates. The links between lawyers of Luxembourg and the corporate chieftains of India are, therefore, deep and strong. Political leaders from India, too, came to Luxembourg and returned clandestinely without informing the Mission.

The bulk of my work, however, related to the European Commission, the European Council and the European Parliament. At that time, leadership of the European Council was vested in a head of government from one of the member states and would change every six months. The country which held the presidency of the council influenced the way in which it worked, thus making it an unpredictable body that could abruptly swing from one political extreme to another. The European Parliament, at the time, was a maverick body, more like a giant collection of NGOs, represented by political parties from all member states with wildly different policy perspectives. The European Parliament was wholly unpredictable. Our Mission would often receive a question raised in the European Parliament on an issue of high sensitivity to India, like Kashmir or human rights, late in the evening on Thursday. The answer would have to be given on Monday. We would have to gently nudge them to see the issue our way, and also knock at the doors of members and groups more favourably disposed towards India. Since Friday was the only working day left to do this, there would be a great deal of excitement and tension in the Mission on such occasions. As I dealt more with economic and commercial matters, there was not as much pressure on me as on the ambassador and on the minister dealing with political matters.

The Commission was the backbone of the EU structure. Essentially bureaucratic, its manner of functioning was not unfamiliar to us who knew governments' way of working. Officials ruled the roost and guided the policies of the EU. Our task was primarily to develop close relations with the officials and to gently persuade them. This caused no problems for me because we had to learn diplomatic ways in Kerala, and my experience there stood me in good stead. With multiple political parties, aggressive trade unions and vocal local politicians, negotiation is the only way to do business in Kerala.

When Portugal took over the Presidency of the EU, one of their political objectives was to establish closer links with India, probably because of their colonial legacy and the realization that after the reforms of 1991, India was poised for a sharp acceleration in the economic field. There were many other connections and similarities, like parliamentary democracy, liberal thinking, commitment to equality and to human rights. We prepared the ground for the first-ever summit between the then Indian Prime Minister Atal Bihari Vajpayee, the then Prime Minister of Portugal, Antonio Guterres, President of the European Commission at the time, Romano Prodi, and the then Secretary General of the European Council, Javier Solana, who also dealt with foreign affairs.

For the preparation of the Joint Declaration to follow the summit, there were intensive discussions between the Indian delegation, comprising principally of me on the economic and commercial side, and the Minister (Political) of the Mission on the political side, with support, at times, from New Delhi through the fiery Bhaswati Mukherjee, Joint Secretary (West) in the Ministry of External Affairs, and the learned and persuasive Vivek Katju, who had admirable knowledge of South Asia and adjoining countries, as well as of the dangers and dimensions of growing terrorism. I recall Vivek speaking earnestly of the dangers emanating from Taliban in Afghanistan, and of the continuous encouragement and support given to terrorism by Pakistan. The European delegation was deeply impressed, as my counterpart in the delegation, the suave Laurence Argimon-Pistre, later told me, but they would not agree to any specifics on terrorism. Afghanistan has undergone many political changes since then, but we now seem to be back where we had started.

The Joint Declaration, issued on 28 June 2000, however, stated,

> We share the conviction that terrorism remains a major threat to regional and international peace and security, and constitutes a serious violation of the rights of innocent individuals and the integrity of States. We reaffirm our unreserved condemnation of terrorism in all its forms, wherever it occurs and whatever its motives and origin.[3]

The Joint Declaration covered a wide range of areas, including economic reform and development, human rights, controlling drug trafficking, strengthening social, cultural and people-to-people links, information technology, mutual efforts to arrest environmental degradation, and infrastructure and trade. India and the EU committed to strengthening trade liberalization and the WTO. Above all, the declaration said, 'In recognition of our enhanced relations of a new strategic partnership in the new century, we will hold further regular EU–India Summit meetings in alternative capitals or elsewhere.' Fourteen such summits have been held but it cannot be said that significant progress has been made in deepening the relationship between EU and India. In her definitive and incisive book, *India and EU: An Insider's View*, Bhaswati Mukherjee writes:

> It is ironical that the 'soft' power elements of the partnership, including civil society dialogue under the aegis of the EU–India Round Table, cultural exchanges and think tank interactions,

---

3   From the first India–EU Summit, which took place on 28 June 2000 in Lisbon.

have become marginal or non-existent by 2018. More unfortunate, hard power elements of the relationship, including the India–EU security dialogue, have over time become even more marginalised than the soft power elements. The normative means that the EU established through the First Summit to expand the partnership, including through the Round Table, were not reciprocated by India. Both sides failed to address the question whether the normative elements, insisted on by the EU, were relevant for this strategic partnership.[4]

Indian foreign policy has turned many somersaults since Independence. For the first few years, the young republic, led by an idealistic Prime Minister, Jawaharlal Nehru, exercised influence in the global comity of nations far above its weight in terms of its economic or political power. This was a time when India was a force to reckon with, rapidly being recognized as the most strident voice in the Third World. Unfortunately, it is almost fashionable today to make disparaging remarks about Nehru. People forget fast. We forget that if not for Nehru having guided the fortunes of the country for a decade and a half after Independence, if not for his resolute adherence to constitutional values even in the face of adversity, the Indian democracy would easily have gone the authoritarian way like many other countries emerging out of colonialism. We forget that the base of Indian heavy industry was laid by him at a time when no private corporate entity would have dared to venture into areas like fertilizers and steel or into massive hydroelectric projects, technical education of the highest quality or into space and into atomic energy. We forget also that he strode across the diplomatic world like a colossus, the matchless voice of the underprivileged, an undisputed leader of non-aligned countries.

---

4   Bhaswati Mukherjee, *India and EU: An Insider's View*, (New Delhi: ICWA and Vij Books, 2018).

Today, our approach to foreign policy is that of a business person's. How does a businessman build his empire? By aligning himself to centres of power who could be of benefit to him, hoping that by clinging to the apron strings of the powerful, he himself will be carried forward. Our thinking appears to be the same. Our diplomacy has been centred too much on individuals in power in big countries, organizing big events to make them happy, publicly hugging them, wining and dining them. We make some fundamental mistakes in this process. First, when deep-seated differences arise among the big men we endeavour to befriend, we may find ourselves to be unwitting victims. When Xi Jinping and Donald Trump were at loggerheads, too much proximity to Trump could have upset Jinping. Second, the power system in any country can change. A Joe Biden-led US is not quite the same for India and the excessive and overt friendship with Trump-led US has obviously not paid its expected dividends. Third, while we seek to ingratiate the powerful, those who relied on India to lead them forcefully began to fall away from us. Foreign policy is best conducted on the premise that we are strong, we will become stronger and we will speak up for ourselves and for weaker countries. Recent developments in foreign policy, however, reveal a welcome change with a more confident India, depending no more on this or that power centre, striking its own path in the complex world of diplomacy.

On a Tuesday afternoon in September 2001, I was at home in Brussels when Kishan Singh, a Customs Department representative in the Mission, called me and said, 'Watch the television. Terrible things are happening.' I switched on the TV to see the image of a plane striking one of the World Trade Centre buildings in New York, the building crashing down and terrified Americans running in mad confusion. The story of 9/11 gradually unravelled. The Al-Qaeda and Afghanistan links to the terrorist attack came to light. Hundreds of Belgian people held hands together in front of the World Trade Centre in Brussels. There was an unprecedented meeting of the European Council convened in Brussels on 21 September. This was followed by a series of urgent declarations and special meetings of the Council of the European Union, the European Commission and the European Parliament to pledge total support to the US. I was reminded then of Vivek Katju and his impressive presentation on terrorism in Afghanistan and Pakistan, which failed to make headway in the discussions preceding the finalization of the Joint India–EU Declaration at the first summit. The West had clearly sidelined the terrorism issue as one that afflicted only the Third World. 9/11 changed this perception. But are we going back to the old days once again?

Foray into Trade Diplomacy

While I was still in Brussels, I came to know that I was under consideration for appointment as Ambassador to the WTO in Geneva, an institution with which I was very familiar, having attended umpteen meetings, both in Geneva and other places, while I was Joint Secretary in Delhi. My path to the position of ambassador was, however, not smooth. It was preceded by a huge tussle between the Foreign Ministry and the Commerce Ministry on who should be appointed, an IFS officer or an IAS officer. I was clearly at a disadvantage: a little-known IAS officer from the far reaches of the country with hardly any contacts or support.

The Commerce Minister back then was Murasoli Maran of the Dravida Munnetra Kazhagam (DMK) Party, then part of the National

Democratic Alliance (NDA) headed by the veteran political leader Atal Bihari Vajpayee of the Bharatiya Janata Party (BJP). Maran had recently suffered serious heart problems and was still in convalescence. The first round of selection was won by the IFS officer, but it turned out to be a short-lived victory. The Foreign Ministry had moved the file for his appointment, along with other ambassadors, from the Foreign Minister to the Prime Minister and the President. The posting was approved by the President and orders were issued. The officer, then posted in London, telephoned Ambassador Narayanan in Geneva and conveyed the information. He also wanted to know when Narayanan would be leaving. Narayanan was due to retire a couple of months after the crucial Doha Ministerial Conference of Trade Ministers, involving all member countries of the WTO.

When news of the appointment filtered out, there was consternation in the Commerce Ministry. The Foreign Ministry, in its attempt to post the officer to Geneva, had failed to route the file through the Commerce Minister. Murasoli Maran took it as a personal affront. The position of Ambassador to the WTO has always been considered as the preserve of the Commerce Ministry, since the officer reports directly to that ministry. This was the situation in the past and the same practice has been followed subsequently. Maran was, therefore, livid.

Vajpayee was a seasoned political leader who had seen many ups and downs in his long career in the BJP. He was also essentially a consensus builder who knew how to manage coalitions and leaders of different parties. He knew from long experience how to make compromises in a democratic political system. He had no hesitation in changing his own decision and appointing Maran's choice as the ambassador. At that point of time, I had never met Vajpayee and I hardly knew Maran; I had met him only once in London at a meeting. All my life, I've been known more for the work I've done than for my contacts. I can say with confidence that I never made a special effort at any point in time to achieve anything particular in my career. I have preferred to stay professional and maintain a low profile, but this never prevented me from occupying the highest positions available to any civil servant in the country.

As a precursor to my tenure in Geneva, I was directed to attend the Ministerial Conference of the WTO at Doha. Major policy decisions and strategy initiatives are taken at Ministerial Conferences of Trade Ministers, held every two years. The first of these conferences was held in Singapore, which I attended as Joint Secretary in the Ministry of Commerce. I attended the second one also at Geneva, in the immediate aftermath of the Pokhran nuclear explosion, where India, represented by Ramakrishna Hegde, the Commerce Minister, was treated as a pariah. The third one was held at Seattle and I did not attend it as I was posted in Brussels at the time. The Doha Ministerial Conference was considered to be a crucial one as it was expected to lead to another round of negotiations to further liberalize international trade.

The genesis of the WTO and India's role

First, I must elaborate a little on the history of the WTO. At the Bretton Woods Conference in the aftermath of the Second World War, two international institutions—the International Monetary Fund (IMF) and the International Bank for Reconstruction and Development (popularly known as the World Bank)—were brought into existence. It was then expected that a third organization to manage multilateral trade relations would also come into being. By then the Cold War had begun, notwithstanding the fact that the Western Allies and Russia had come together against Hitler and his allies. The Americans were, therefore, reluctant to create a third organization to lay down rules for international trade.

The formation of the WTO had to wait until the end of the Cold War in the early 1990s. The first attempt at a round of deliberations to put in place strong trade rules was made during the Uruguay Round[5] of negotiations between countries in the '90s, although the toothless General Agreement on Tariffs and Trade (GATT) had been in existence since 1947. Russia was not part of the negotiations of the Uruguay Round, neither was China. India set itself up as the voice of developing countries, and was widely perceived as the 'spoiler' in the negotiations. India almost single-handedly waged a strong battle to limit the scope of the Uruguay Round, initially opposing the inclusion of services within the scope of negotiations, but ultimately playing an important role in the drafting of the Agreement on Services. Almost to the end, India opposed multilateral rules on intellectual property rights, with the result that our negotiators were virtually kept out of the discussions.

Perhaps the Trade Related Aspects of Intellectual Property Rights (TRIPS) would have been less rigorous had India participated wholeheartedly in the negotiation. As a friend mentioned later, India was finally carried to the negotiating table 'kicking and screaming' and made to sign the 'Legal Texts', which encapsulated, in a series of agreements, the entire content of the results of the negotiations that had lasted a full seven years. The Uruguay Round was conducted by savvy and trained Western negotiators, with a bunch of largely unschooled but boisterous negotiators from developing nations, who did not really have the legal acumen and training to read between the lines in the language of the texts. This resulted in acrimonious negotiations ever since the WTO came into existence, as developing nations struggled to win back some lost negotiating space.

---

5   The Uruguay Round brought about the biggest reforms in the world's trading system since GATT. The Uruguay Round was the eighth round of multilateral trade negotiations (MTN) conducted within the framework of the GATT, spanning from 1986 to 1993, and embracing 123 countries as 'contracting parties'. The round led to the creation of the World Trade Organization, with GATT remaining an integral part of the WTO agreements.

India's efforts, right from the commencement of the Uruguay Round, were focused on restricting the role of the WTO. This opposition arose from the fact that, unlike GATT and international bodies, the WTO was armed with punitive powers. Any member country can take perceived violations of any of the agreements to the dispute settlement mechanism set up within the organization. Once a dispute is taken to the WTO, the dispute settlement process is initiated. At the start of the process, the two disputants meet together in Geneva to try and resolve the issues bilaterally. If this fails, a dispute settlement panel is created, usually a three-member panel, chosen by mutual agreement between the disputing members. The panel then hears both parties, deliberates at length with the help of the legal wing of the WTO and gives its verdict, which would be binding. If a violation is found to have taken place, the member country which initiated the dispute becomes entitled to raise retaliatory tariffs on goods and services of interest to the member found to be in violation. There is also an appellate body but it has now been rendered ineffective by the US during Trump's presidency by the simple expedient of not agreeing to fill one of the vacancies that arose. The WTO works on the basis of consensus, which means 100 per cent agreement from all members. Therefore, when the US disagreed, the appeal system came to a dead stop. As a consequence, the entire dispute settlement mechanism became ineffective because no case can reach closure without going through the appeal process. The WTO, therefore, is an ineffectual body today, awaiting resuscitation. At the time of writing, the Biden government is yet to firm up its trade policy and the future of WTO continues to remain uncertain.

India initially wanted the Uruguay Round to be confined to tariffs on goods, as was the case with GATT. India wants the scope of the WTO to be limited because our freedom to evolve and implement our own economic and commercial policies would be curtailed if they could be subjected to dispute settlement. Thus, India opposed the introduction of intellectual property rights within the purview of the WTO, but did not succeed in stopping it. This applied particularly to the pharmaceutical industry where our producers were able to reverse engineer molecules developed at great cost by manufacturers in the West with advanced research and development facilities. Through the simple device of reverse engineering, our manufacturers would be able to sell medicines produced from the same molecules at a fraction of the cost. We opposed the introduction of services, but later changed our stance when we found that we also stood to gain from an agreement on services as it would provide room to our professionals, both skilled and unskilled persons, to migrate to other countries and work there. From that point, we entered the negotiation on services in the early '90s with gusto and were able to get many of our concerns and priorities addressed in the Agreement on Services.

WTO: To grow or not to grow?

The developed countries, particularly the European Communities (EC), wanted the remit of the WTO expanded still further to include policies relating to investment, competition policy, trade facilitation and government procurement. India stoutly resisted these attempts as we wanted flexibility in designing policies in these areas and to not be constrained by international rules, making us open to dispute settlement and retaliatory action. However, during the First Ministerial Conference in Singapore, the developed countries succeeded in bringing these issues into the work programme of the WTO, albeit only in the study mode. These were collectively called 'Singapore issues' in common negotiation parlance. The opposition to this, however, continued unabated. We had a few developing countries backing our position at Geneva, called the 'Like-Minded Group', but it was clear as day that high-pressure tactics being applied by the powerful Western bloc would lead to the total dissolution of this group.

The Ministerial Conference at Doha in 2001 was dominated by one man, Murasoli Maran. The Indian Commerce Minister was in poor health at the time but was in spirit a combative man, willing to take on the world by himself. The coalition that Ambassador Narayanan had painstakingly put together at Geneva to resist the so-called 'Singapore issues' broke apart very quickly on the very first day of the conference, under pressure from the US and the EC. Before I left for Doha, the Director General (DG) (Trade) of the European Commission, Peter Karl, called me and said, 'Please convey to your capital that we are determined to push through the Singapore issues. Your Mission in Geneva thinks there are some other countries supporting you. Please inform your capital that none of them will be there for you, you will be alone.' I did not need to argue with him as I was still only representing my Mission at Brussels. I told him I would convey his message, which I did.

The battle at Doha was hard and arduous. Maran would not yield an inch. Every single trick was tried by the experienced negotiators of the US and EC, but he was immovable. They tried to separate him from his team in the dead of night for a 'Heads of Delegation only' meeting with the big two and a few others, along with the DG of the WTO, Michael Moore of New Zealand. We could hear Maran shouting in the adjoining room, 'You are trying to ambush me!' Yet the effort failed as Maran remained firm. On the final day, all the rest of the members agreed, but India would not agree. An EU spokesman went outside the building and said that consensus was blocked by a lone 'madman' inside the building and that developing countries were being denied a great deal. At long last, Maran agreed to a formulation that Ambassador Narayanan thought we could work with, and the Doha Work Programme was unanimously adopted. We had worked without any sleep for almost forty-eight hours. Many of us were snoring on the table, but the minister was alert and wide awake.

Over to me now, as the new Indian Ambassador and Permanent Representative to the WTO.

Diplomacy in Geneva: The Beginnings

'Diplomacy is listening to what the other guy needs ... You have to develop relationships with other people so when the tough times come, you can work together.'

—*Colin Powell*

Early days

When I reached Geneva two months after the Doha meeting, the immediate briefing I got from my colleagues in the Mission was that India had virtually become an outcast in the diplomatic community. The first task was, therefore, to rebuild confidence and ensure that India regained its position as a premier negotiator. Doha was a watershed moment in the history of the WTO because China had joined the organization for the first time after completing a protracted process of accession, and having been forced to give many more concessions than what other members had had to give in the Uruguay Round. If a country is not there at the start of negotiations of a multilateral or regional agreement, it has to pay a much higher price to join later. The kind of concessions that were wrested from China, and later Russia, were in a way an endorsement of the wisdom our Indian negotiators had displayed in the early '90s while signing agreements, despite the fact that there were many lacunae from our perspective. China and Russia could enter the WTO only after convincing individual member countries of the WTO. The US, EC and other developed countries drove hard bargains.

China never enters a negotiating forum without proper preparation. The Indian Mission was operating with just four or five negotiators on one floor of a rented building. On the other hand, China came in full strength with about fifteen negotiators and built their own protected premises with all facilities, including a first-rate kitchen with cooks flown in from their own country. The expectation among negotiators in Geneva was that the entry of China would result in the dilution of India's negotiating strength. The Chinese had been closely observing Minister Maran's solo performance in Doha and were greatly impressed. The Chinese Ambassador Sun Zhenyu told me that China would follow India's lead in negotiations at the WTO until they developed their own capacity. Indeed, during the first few months, Chinese negotiators were present at all meetings, took copious notes, spoke little and spent time learning the processes and rules of negotiation by working closely with India.

My next objective was to smooth ruffled feathers in the diplomatic community. I met more than forty ambassadors, got on first-name terms with all of them, and became socially active. It was also my belief that an entirely negative stance in negotiation was not in our interest. It was better to indicate our own desire to negotiate and gain maximum possible benefits for the country. I was accepted soon as a congenial colleague by other ambassadors.

India and the European Communities

The first sign of friction between India and the EC developed over a matter which I did not really consider important, but was forced to take a position on, thanks to one of my younger colleagues, who, in a meeting on market access in non-agricultural products, came into direct conflict with an EC representative. While the EC wanted a framework on non-agricultural market access to be developed by April 2002, my officer had insisted on time until June that year. I did not consider this serious because I was aware that time schedules were not so relevant in negotiations and that they would take their own course and their own time.

However, the EC made this an occasion to test India's negotiating strength in the changed circumstances and to reclaim their own influence after the problems created for them in Doha by Maran and his team. In the first few weeks, India was completely isolated and there was a great deal of tension in every negotiating forum. India was once again being seen as an unreasonable negotiator. When my colleague and friend, Ambassador Datuk Supperamaniam Manickam of Malaysia, came forward with a compromise solution, suggesting May 2002 as the date for completion of the work, I was quick to accept it as I really did not see any logical reason for continuing with the dispute. However, the EC had painted themselves into a corner and Peter Karl, DG (Trade) of the commission, and his team in Brussels were adamant about teaching India a lesson.

When Malaysia mooted the compromise solution at a meeting, I expressed my agreement immediately. The EC Ambassador could not withdraw from the position that his 'capital' had already taken. Indian negotiators traditionally have much more negotiating room than those of other countries, particularly the developed ones. Hence, I could quickly seize the initiative.

My friend and colleague from Delhi, S.N. Menon, then Additional Secretary in the Ministry of Commerce, was present at the meeting.

I turned to him and said, 'You saw India was isolated. Now, you see EC isolated. We have turned the tables on them.' Everyone in the room, other than the EC ambassador, was in support of the new May deadline. The dispute dragged on for a few more weeks, with India now in the driver's seat, urging the EC to join the consensus. Finally, an old friend from my Brussels days and a counterpart negotiator when I was Joint Secretary in Delhi, Hervè Jouanjean, came up with a revised formulation. He told me that this was the most that the EC was willing to do on the matter. As I recall, the new formulation gave a 'best endeavour' twist to the time limit prescribed. I magnanimously agreed and the issue was resolved.

That evening, at a dinner organized by one of the ambassadors, I said to the EC ambassador, 'Welcome back to the WTO.' The American Ambassador, Linnet Deily, was seated next to me at the dinner table. I related this incident to her and she was highly amused. She later told me that she had conveyed this story to her colleagues in Washington, and they too found the situation comic. While the US and EC were outwardly negotiating partners in the Geneva negotiations, there was always an undercurrent of tension between them, primarily because their interests differed in many areas, even though they worked together to secure their common interests wherever they could. Peter Karl, however, was not amused with the way his plans to show India its place had not fructified. In a meeting which he attended, he said to me, 'I hear you have been very active.'

Speaking of Jouanjean, there is an amusing incident I can never forget. This was during my tenure as Joint Secretary in New Delhi. Jouanjean and his EU team had come for a negotiation. I was leading the negotiation as a representative of India. The meeting was being held in a ground-floor conference hall at Udyog Bhawan, the seat of the Ministry of Commerce. The European team was seated across the table, facing the windows while we sat with our backs to the windows. We were some way through the meeting when I found Jouanjean—and, indeed, all the Europeans—looking increasingly restless and uneasy.

Finally, Jouanjean burst out, 'There is a monkey at the window!' And there indeed was one, pretty fierce-looking, not happy that he had no access to the eats on the table. One of the members of my delegation decided to shoo him away. He went towards the window and made some aggressive gestures. This enraged the monkey no end and he retaliated by making faces at the officer, who finally returned to his chair, red-faced and defeated. The monkey stayed for as long as it wanted and then decided to call it a day once he got tired of it. This must have been the sort of story which the Europeans would still be narrating to their children and grandchildren.

But coming back to the negotiations in the 'Doha Work Programme', as I called it, the 'Doha Round' as some of my Western colleagues preferred to call it, or and the 'Doha Development Agenda', as was favoured by some of my developing country colleagues—they wore on. The schedule was punishing. The developed countries were pushing for its early completion with the next Ministerial Conference at Cancun as the target date for decision on all the major issues. I had another scrap with the others on who should be the next Chair of the group working on trade and investment, the most sensitive issue so far as my 'capital' was concerned, and against the inclusion of which successive Indian negotiators and Minister Maran had fought long and hard. Finally, we settled on Luiz Felipe de Seixas Corrêa, the Ambassador of Brazil, who later became a close and dear friend.

The public health negotiations

In Doha, I had come to realize that the public health issue was extremely important for the African group, spearheaded by the statuesque and dignified Ambassador of Kenya, Amina Mohamed, who had achieved great distinction in the academic field as well as in her career in international relations. She distinguished herself even further in later life, going on to become the Cabinet Secretary in charge of foreign affairs, initially, and later, education. India had not been particularly active in the negotiation on public health, but it was evident to me in Doha that Africa, battling all at once diseases and the non-affordability of patented medicines, lay great store by these negotiations. As a developing country faced with similar problems in the not too distant past, I could empathize easily with them.

I entered the health negotiation, therefore, enthusiastically. We used our resources at our Mission and in our capital to support the African cause. I myself virtually became a member of the inner council of the African group, and I frequented the Kenyan Mission almost as much as my own office. To the extent, in fact, that Amina once told me, 'I think I shall have to give you a room in my Mission.' The negotiation was acrimonious, particularly because the American pharmaceutical industry, protected by patents, wanted desperately to preserve high prices for their pharmaceutical products, which were critically needed by indigent Africans suffering from AIDS and other communicable diseases. The American pharmaceutical industry feared Indian manufacturers, whom they accused of reverse engineering drug molecules developed by them at huge costs and then selling them at low prices. The difference in price between the American and Indian drugs, molecule for molecule, was huge and the Africans wanted free access to cheaper medicine.

It would be relevant to understand the background to the issue of TRIPS and public health here. The TRIPS agreement had brought into the system a strict regime for intellectual property rights, particularly patents. The patent gave its holder the legal right to prevent third parties from making, using, offering for sale or importing a patented product without the holder's consent. Developing countries were, however, given time to adjust to the new regime, and in cases where they could not get access to patented products, the governments concerned could resort to compulsory licensing of manufacturing, subject to certain conditions, such as payment of adequate remuneration to the patent holder. The Nelson Mandela government in South Africa adopted healthcare legislations, which quickly resulted in an attempt by the

US and EU to resist it. Shortly thereafter, another complaint was filed by the US in the WTO against the compulsory licensing regime introduced in Brazil to deal with the increasing incidence of AIDS.

In the light of these incidents, developing countries in general and African countries in particular mounted a strong movement within the WTO for systemic relief. The issue was urgent as it was being discussed against the backdrop of the rapidly spreading HIV/AIDS epidemic across the developing world, especially Africa. Developing countries like India were able to produce the molecules constituting HIV drugs at a much lower cost than the price charged by pharmaceutical firms in developed countries. To contain the dreaded disease, Africa needed cheap drugs but patent laws and the TRIPS agreement prevented them from procuring supplies from pharmaceutical companies in countries with manufacturing capacities like India's. Meanwhile, human lives were at stake in some of the poorest countries of the world.

At the same time, developed countries, at the instigation of the pharmaceutical industry, started working towards an even stricter patent dispensation, particularly in their bilateral and regional trading arrangements. In the Doha declaration, submitting reluctantly to African pressure, the developed countries agreed that the TRIPS agreement 'should be interpreted and implemented in a manner supportive of WTO members' right to protect public health and, in particular, to promote access to medicines for all.'[6] Also, it affirmed the right of member countries to grant compulsory licenses on any grounds, not just in cases of national emergencies, even though the requirement to try to negotiate an agreement with the patent holder remained. Another significant achievement was that a developing country could produce drugs for other developing countries upon their request, provided that care is taken by the importing country not

---

6   Doha WTO Ministerial 2001: TRIPS, 'Declaration on the TRIPS agreement and Public Health', *World Trade Organization* (20 November 2001), https://www.wto.org/english/thewto_e/minist_e/min01_e/mindecl_trips_e.htm

to re-export it. Thus, Indian drugs could become available to African markets for HIV/AIDS, Ebola and the like at much lower costs than from Western producers.

This negotiation took a great deal of time and stretched the patience of developing countries to the utmost limit. The suggestion made was that Article 31(f) of the TRIPS Agreement, which stipulates that compulsory licenses may be issued 'predominantly' for the local market, may be waived. At this time, the window available to developing countries to import from cheaper sources such as India was rapidly coming to a close, as the patent regime had to be enforced by all developing countries by 1 January 2005.

I recall a fully attended meeting of the General Council on 20 December 2002. All countries agreed to the waiver of Article 31(f) except the US, which said that the waiver should be limited to HIV/AIDS, malaria, tuberculosis and a limited number of infectious diseases. The US was totally isolated at the meeting and the developing countries, including India, spoke strongly against that country's inability to understand the needs and problems of the indigent and the diseased worldwide.

The American ambassador was deeply embarrassed and she made every possible effort to try and persuade her industry representatives back home to take a more reasonable stance. Finally, one day, late in August 2003, just a few days before the Cancun Ministerial Conference, the Canadian Ambassador, Sergio Marchi, telephoned me in the morning saying that, after great effort, the Americans had agreed to some language which seemed to meet our requirements. He also said that the US was unlikely to go beyond what had now been agreed and that the situation might be beyond retrieval after the Cancun meeting.

Looking at the language now proposed and after consultation with other developing country counterparts, I came to the conclusion that this was the best that was achievable. The members agreed to legal changes which made it easier for producers of generic drugs under compulsory licensing to export more freely in packaged form to prevent re-export to developed countries, and urged importing countries to take 'reasonable measures within their means' to prevent re-exports. Most developed countries agreed not to make use of the provisions to import such goods and the larger developing countries agreed to make use of this provision only in cases of national emergency.

When the matter came before the General Council, at a meeting jointly chaired by the Ambassador of Uruguay, Carlos Perez del Castillo, and the Chairman of TRIPS Council, Vanu Menon of Singapore, I surprised everyone by strongly coming forward in favour of the proposed agreement. I had been one of the most outspoken critics of the United States in earlier meetings, and my turnaround was an important factor in moving the negotiation towards resolution. As the US diplomat Alicia Greenidge mentioned to me later, she was tearing up as I spoke. The Chairman of the General Council and of the TRIPS Council looked shell-shocked. The issue did not end at that meeting as some developing countries continued to express reservations. The Chairman of the General Council then suggested that the Ambassadors of India and South Africa may, later in the evening, meet with others who had concerns to resolve all issues and clarify doubts. We held a meeting accordingly in the evening, joined also by the Kenyan Ambassador, and a long-standing, festering issue thus came to a conclusion. Just before the General Council meeting the next day, the American ambassador came to me and requested me to say in my intervention that it is not India's intention to take commercial advantage of this agreement but to provide help and succour to countries that had serious public health challenges. I was only too happy to include this in my intervention as it expressed my country's deep concern for the problems faced by many other developing countries in respect of public health.

There was another reason why I wanted a resolution to the public health issue. The Cancun Ministerial Conference was just around the corner and I did not want this issue to linger on until then. The spotlight would then have shifted to this issue and, once it was resolved by the ministers, a sense of euphoria would be created among developing countries, which may have led them to take a less strident position on other, more important issues from our perspective, such as market access in agricultural and non-agricultural products, and the Singapore issues. The early resolution of the public health issue and the strong and supportive role played by India was recognized and appreciated by the African countries.

Agriculture, Singapore Issues and the Road to Cancun

'Let us never negotiate out of fear. But let us never fear to negotiate.'
—*John F. Kennedy*

While the dispute on public health dragged on, negotiations continued in other areas of serious concern to us, like agriculture. The Agreement on Agriculture was a painful relic of the Uruguay Round for developing countries. There were sharp divisions on approaches with regard to agriculture negotiations in the Uruguay Round and many interests competing with each other. There were the big two, the US and the EU, investing billions of dollars on income support for farmers and pushing their products out to other countries as food aid or as exports at highly subsidized prices. There were countries like some of the Latin American and Asian countries, and Australia and New Zealand, which were dependent on export

"

of agricultural products at remunerative prices but found themselves pushed out of markets because of subsidized exports. India and some other similarly placed countries had to perforce impose high tariffs and put quantitative curbs on imports to protect their small and marginal farmers. There were net food importing countries which had stakes in the continuance of subsidies in other countries so that they could get cheaper imports. There were countries depending on agricultural exports which enjoyed preferential treatment in the EU, in particular, and wanted that to continue. There were countries which wanted to protect particular sections of farmer populations, like Japan, which imposed astronomic rates of tariff on imports of rice. There were countries like Australia that blithely imposed non-tariff barriers, like phytosanitary standards, to keep out imports of certain agricultural products. Trade in agriculture was therefore a mixed bag of practices and to reach a solution acceptable to all was well-nigh impossible.

The Agreement on Agriculture that emanated from the Uruguay Round was by no means a satisfactory solution. It was primarily driven by the US and the EC. Their infamous Blair House Accord created the framework on which settlement was finally reached. The Blair House Accord was an agreement between the US and the EU to reduce subsidies to exporters and domestic producers with a view to extract concessions from other participants in the Uruguay Round negotiations. There were many countries left out in the cold that had to succumb to unrelenting political pressure. The final result of the Uruguay Round caused little change to the subsidy programmes of the developed countries. Food aid was exempted from any cuts so that developed countries could still siphon off excess production in the form of aid, giving them the capacity to offload their surpluses and at the same time gain political advantage. The device of 'decoupled income support' was invented to facilitate continuance of subsidies to farmers in the US and EU without linking it to production. This meant only that instead of giving farmers subsidies on the basis of quantum of production, they would be given similar or higher amounts on the basis of crops and acreage. Just an attempt to put old wine in a new bottle, in my view.

The outcome of the negotiations was not as expected. The total agricultural support in Organisation for Economic Co-operation and Development (OECD) countries, principally the US and EU, went up from US $271 billion in 1986–88 to US $331 billion in 1998–2000. As part of the Uruguay Round agreement, the concept of 'Green Box' was invented, consisting of income support and research expenditure. It was a relatively simple task to maintain and increase the level of subsidies to farmers by shifting existing subsidies to the green box and even enhancing them. It is estimated that US agricultural exports were valued 10 to 50 per cent lower than their cost of production in 2003. Prices received by OECD farmers in general were 30 per cent over world prices. There was no increase in the share of developing countries in agricultural exports, which remained at 36 per cent. Besides, as tariff cuts stipulated in the Agreement on Agriculture could be averaged out, some products continued to attract prohibitively high tariffs.

It was against this background, therefore, that negotiations on the Agreement on Agriculture started. India was negotiating to preserve its own interests, which was essentially to protect our millions of indigent farmers from the inflow of cheap imports of subsidized products from affluent countries. The EU also had self-oriented interests as they wanted to continue to pay huge subsidies to their farmers. They justified such subsidies on the grounds that they wanted to preserve the culture and ecology of their countryside. Initially, therefore, we joined the EU and many other countries to occupy the defensive position and protect the status quo.

Our joining the EU in taking a common position on agricultural negotiations caused a great deal of discomfort to many countries. The Ambassador of Brazil visited me in my office and expressed his deep disappointment. He said, 'We had expected India and Brazil to work together in these negotiations from the beginning to the end.' The US ambassador also expressed her deep concern at our action at a private lunch with me.

In February 2003, the chairman of the Committee on Agriculture, Stuart Harbinson, Chef de Cabinet to WTO Director General Supachai Panitchpakdi, produced a text of draft modalities. This was roundly criticized by all. The US wanted deeper tariff cuts and removal of export subsidies. The EU and Japan felt that there was not enough emphasis on export credits and food aid. Developing countries were of the view that the text was primarily intended to benefit richer countries.

The birth of the G20

The US and EU then sat together and attempted to impose another 'Blair House Accord' in August 2003. In the document which they put forward, they took care of each other's interests, leaving out the rest. India, which had backed the EU in the negotiation, found that our interests were seriously compromised. The US and the EU agreed between themselves on continued trade-distorting subsidies, a blended formula for tariff reductions in bands which could be self-selected; reductions in minimum crop-related subsidies allowed in the Uruguay Round; and an extension of the Peace Clause, according to which agricultural subsidies could not be challenged under the dispute settlement mechanism. There was hardly any mention of special and differential treatment for developing countries.

A special meeting of the Committee on Agriculture was scheduled one evening to discuss the US–EU paper. Just before the meeting started, representatives of international media came up to me and wanted to know my views. I said categorically, 'We cannot accept this paper as it does not take care of our interests.' I saw a headline in an Indian newspaper the next day, saying 'India says no', quoting me. The atmosphere in the meeting was tense and most of the delegates, including me, as ambassador of India, raised uncomfortable questions.

Used as they were to Blair House and their eventual capacity to prevail in a WTO negotiation, developing countries by and large felt distressed and unhappy. It was at this time that the Ambassador of Brazil, Felipe, came to me and said, 'The situation is getting out of control. We should think of working together in the negotiation.' Brazil and India had hitherto been in opposite camps in the negotiations. Brazil was a large exporter of agricultural products, while India had essentially defensive interests.

However, we agreed to having our respective counsellors working together to attempt a draft. There was a brilliant officer from the IAS Sikkim cadre, Rajesh Aggarwal, who was working on agriculture in our Mission. He sat together with his Brazilian counterpart and produced a text which fully took care of our interests.

Then began the campaign to find strong supporters. From my experience at Doha, I had realized that a weak alliance tends to fall apart under the slightest pressure from the strong economic and political forces of the world, notably the US and the EU in the WTO context. Brazil was, of course, a much stronger developing country with a significant presence in world trade. But we needed more allies with whom India and Brazil could forge a coalition that could match the influence of the big two.

The first port of call obviously had to be the People's Republic of China. Ambassador Sun Zhenyu and all his diplomats had become very close to me and my officers by then. I telephoned him and said I needed to see him urgently and that Felipe would also be joining us. Sun immediately asked me to come over and I asked Felipe to join me. I reached there first, and briefly mentioned the reason for my visit. By then, Felipe had also reached the Chinese Mission. Generally, China takes time to take diplomatic decisions; they wait until they have considered their position at length in Beijing and then respond. This time, however, the response was immediate and Sun at once agreed to join the budding coalition. Obviously, the Chinese had extensively discussed the US–EU initiative internally amongst themselves and with Beijing, and they felt a great deal of discomfort at the turn that the negotiations had taken. Felipe and I were taken aback by the swiftness of the Chinese response. As we returned to our respective cars, Felipe told me, 'This is a big coup.'

I then telephoned the ambassadors of South Africa, Egypt and Thailand. By a strange coincidence, all of them were in their respective capitals. They were able to immediately seek orders from their governments and join our coalition. Meanwhile, Felipe organized a meeting with the ambassadors of the Latin American countries, and several of them came on board. The coalition of countries, called G20, started initially as a group of thirteen countries and played a dramatic role in changing the dynamics of negotiation at the WTO.

The G20 put forward a paper on agriculture as an alternative to the US–EU paper. While calling for steep cuts in subsidies, it provided for strengthening the special and differential treatment for developing countries, identifying Special Products for exemption from tariff cuts and extending the Special Safeguard Mechanism introduced in the Uruguay Round to include more products of interest to the developing countries. The Special Safeguard Mechanism enabled member countries to put safeguard duties on some sensitive crops selected by them. Unfortunately, India did not select any crop for inclusion in the Special Safeguard Mechanism under the Uruguay round. Had we done this, some of our plantation crops would have been in a stronger position today.

In Delhi, Commerce Minister Arun Jaitley—who had taken over after the short tenure of Arun Shourie, following the demise of Murasoli Maran—called a press conference and announced the formation of the new coalition. At this point, I must acknowledge the great support that I invariably received from our government. We could work with freedom and courage in the Vajpayee era and take bold decisions. I never consulted the minister; I had the confidence that he would back me. As Jaitley himself is reported to have said, 'My role was only to give clearance [for the G20 paper] over the phone, the rest of the work was done by our delegation in Geneva.'[7]

Enormous credit must also go to Brazil and other agricultural exporting countries in the G20. They had huge offensive interests in agriculture and had been our adversaries in this sector for long but for the sake of unity among developing countries, they forsook their traditional position and wholeheartedly accommodated our defensive position. The agricultural exporting countries were members of the Cairns Group of agricultural exporters, headed by Australia; the formation of a different group, the G20, was reflective of the growing disillusionment of developing countries with it. 'Brazil had to reduce its ambition in market access in order to gather the support of India and China for its demands. It also had to emphasize the idea of proportionality of concessions to be made during the negotiations: developing countries were supposed to pay less than the developed ones in the agricultural negotiations.'[8]

After the formation of G20, the Brazil Ambassador offered the chair to India. I refused and asked him to chair it. Throughout my tenure, I preferred other countries to lead coalitions on issues of vital importance to us. This was a fallout of my experience in Singapore and Doha, where I had seen developing country coalitions, orchestrated and led largely by India, fall apart and crumble at the slightest sign of pressure from economically powerful countries. The G20 waxed and waned. Attempts were made to divide the group. Some countries went out and others came in. However, the group essentially held together and became stronger still after the Cancun Ministerial Conference.

---

7   Sidhartha, 'Our man at the WTO', Rediff.com (8 September 2003), https://www.rediff.com/money/2003/sep/08wto4.htm

8   Pedro da Motta Veiga, 'Brazil and the G-20 Group of Developing Countries', Managing the Challenges of WTO Participation: Case Study 7, *World Trade Organization*, https://www.wto.org/english/res_e/booksp_e/casestudies_e/case7_e.htm#fnt1.

Singapore issues

Before we turn to Cancun, there was another area in which India was at the forefront. Both in Singapore and in Doha, India had set itself up strongly against bringing new issues—trade and investment, trade and competition policy, government procurement and trade facilitation—into the agenda of the WTO. This was a protracted and arduous battle in which the US and EU inched forward, pushing India back little by little at both conferences. Our main objection was that we did not want the WTO and its ubiquitous dispute resolution mechanism to extend its reach to other areas of economic activity. We wished to retain freedom and not come within the constraints of binding multilateral rules at an early stage of development. While in the negotiations at Geneva between delegations, there was a measure of unity between several developing countries held together by India, we lost ground repeatedly at the Ministerial Conferences.

The main problem, so far as India was concerned, was related to trade and investment. The developed countries, particularly the EU, were extremely persistent in trying to bring investment into the WTO agenda and, consequently, making it subject to its dispute settlement mechanism. This would have resulted in giving foreign investors the right to entry and establishment and to operate in member countries without conditions, and the right to be treated on par with domestic industry. It would take away the rights of host countries to impose any restrictions or conditions, including fund transfers. This arrangement, as propounded by the OECD countries, was to apply to all kinds of investments, including foreign direct investment, portfolio investment, credit, intellectual property rights, non-commercial organizations and all sectors other than defence and security. By restricting the rights of host countries, developing countries were going to be denied the opportunity to offer reasonable protection to their own domestic industries in the earlier stages of development of the economy, a right which had been exercised by the developed countries in the past. This has now come to the fore once again in India through the 'Aatmanirbhar' or self-sufficiency programme, initiated by the present government. Had we succumbed to the pressure to include trade and investment in the WTO agenda, 'Aatmanirbhar Bharat' and other present production-linked incentives would have been impossible to implement.

So far as trade and competition were concerned, competition rules were still at nascent stages in most developing countries. They needed more time to evolve a structure of competition law. With respect to government procurement, it could have precluded national policies to support local industry, even though the initial focus was only on transparency. Today, as part of our Aatmanirbhar programme and our efforts to curtail trade from certain countries and to restrict imports of certain goods, an international agreement on government procurement would have constrained government policy. Trade facilitation was not really an issue which caused a great deal of difficulty to the developing countries, even though it was resisted as it came as part of the Singapore package.

In Doha, developing countries battled with a draft Ministerial Declaration sent from Geneva, which did not reflect the opposition of many developing countries. The Doha meeting was largely consumed by the Singapore issues, of which India was virtually the sole opponent. After many hours of deliberation, a final text came that negotiations would take place after the fifth session of the Ministerial Conference on the basis of a decision to be taken by explicit consensus at that session, on the modalities of negotiations. Finally, primarily to appease India, the Chairman of the meeting, the Trade Minister of Qatar, elaborated the 'explicit consensus' aspect in the following words:

Let me say that with respect to an explicit consensus being needed in these paragraphs for a decision to be taken at the Fifth Session of the Ministerial Conference, my understanding is that, at that session, a decision would indeed need to be taken by explicit consensus before negotiations on trade and investment and trade and competition policy, transparency in government procurement, and trade facilitation could proceed. In my view, this would also give each member the right to take a position on modalities that would prevent negotiations from proceeding after the Fifth Session of the Ministerial Conference until that member is prepared to join in an explicit consensus.[9]

This was the situation when I reached Geneva as Ambassador. In the beginning, India was the strongest opponent of negotiations in the working groups. We had the support of several African countries, a group of which presented a paper seeking continuance of the clarification process, rather than negotiations on these issues. The turning point, in my view, was a joint paper on trade and investment presented by India, China and three other developing countries. This paper was significant for two reasons. First, this marked the beginning of joint work by China and India, the two most populous countries in the world, accounting for one-third of the world's population. Secondly, the paper reversed the argument. The OECD paper had emphasized the rights of investors vis-a-vis the host countries. The India–China paper, on the other hand, sought rights for host countries vis-a-vis investors. The fact that India and China were acting together, and that any negotiation on investment would be difficult as the rights of host countries would also come into the equation, discouraged some of the proponents of the issue. The US had never taken a particularly aggressive position in favour of these issues; they had merely gone along with EC and Japan, the principal protagonists, in the hope that they would be able to get their support in areas of real concern to them. Once the India–China paper came to the table, they became even more cautious.

---

9   Doha WTO Ministerial 2001, A Historic Moment: '"May I take it that this is agreeable?" Gavel, applause, congratulations …', https://www.wto.org/english/thewto_e/minist_e/min01_e/min01_chair_speaking_e.htm

The Singapore issues and agriculture constituted the bulk of negotiations in Geneva. So far as tariffs on non-agricultural products were concerned, the negotiations had not made much progress. There was, of course, considerable pressure on India and other developing countries to lower tariffs that they had bound themselves not to exceed, as part of the Uruguay Round. India responded by constituting a group of eleven countries with like positions on non-agricultural products market access. The build-up to Cancun was punctuated with many meetings at the ministerial level in various places, including Geneva, Sharm-el-Sheikh, Montreal, Paris, Sydney and Davos. India was represented at these meetings either by Arun Jaitley or Arun Shourie. I got to know these ministers closely during the course of the negotiations.

Arun Shourie was a man of detail who liked to understand every issue thoroughly before each meeting. I recall one particular meeting in Davos with the minister. I had to drive up from Geneva, a journey of four to five hours, climbing the mountainside to reach snow-clad Davos. I was scheduled to have a meeting in the evening to brief Shourie and was a little late for traffic reasons. I recall the Indian ambassador in Berne calling me repeatedly, getting more and more nervous and telling me that the minister was getting annoyed. When I reached the minister's hotel, it was a pleasant surprise to see him actually come out of the hotel to welcome me. As soon as we entered his room, I said, 'Sir, you must forgive me but I need a cup of tea very urgently after my drive.' He immediately ordered tea for me through room service. Throughout my association with Shourie, which continues even to this day, his brilliance, his capacity to absorb information, his articulation and, above all, his great humility have always left a deep impression on me.

I also remember Shourie for his remarkable intervention at the Sharm-el-Sheikh meeting, which added a great deal of strength to my negotiating capacity in Geneva. On the first day of the meeting, the European Trade Commissioner, Pascal Lamy, launched a severe personal attack on my Kenyan counterpart, Amina Mohamed. I was sitting just behind Shourie while the Kenyan ambassador was seated next to me. The Kenyan minister was not present, and since this was a minister-level meeting, Amina could not defend herself. Shourie turned around to ask me whether Amina would like for him to speak on her behalf. Amina agreed immediately and gave me a list of points which Shourie could use.

Shourie then launched a vitriolic attack on Lamy, accusing him of trying to pressurize officials who did not agree with his position. As I recall, he spoke for nearly twenty minutes in this vein. The next morning, he renewed his onslaught, accusing Lamy of using 'pejorative' language against an official, knowing fully well that she could not defend herself in a meeting of ministers. The Kenyan minister was present on the second day but he chose not to speak about the incident at all. The result of Shourie's intervention was that India's stock amongst the African countries rose immensely.

We Win at Cancun

*'This is the art of courage: to see things as they are and still believe
that the victory lies not with those who avoid the bad, but those who
taste, in living awareness, every drop of the good.'*

—Victoria Lincoln

The stage was thus set for Cancun, Mexico, in 2003. The TRIPS and public health issue were out of the way, following the settlement in the General Council on 31 August of that year. Agriculture and the 'Singapore issues' were thus the main areas of discussion. There was considerable trepidation amongst the developing countries that, as in the Uruguay Round, developing countries would ultimately capitulate. Walden Bello wrote, 'One cannot discount that despite their deepening differences, the US and the EU may still pull together to coerce developing countries into approving new initiatives in trade and trade-related liberalization in Cancun.'[10]

---

10   Walden Bello, 'Why a Derailed Ministerial Is the Best Outcome for the South', Inter Press Service, *Global Policy Forum* (4 September 2003), https://www.tni.org/en/article/why-a-derailed-wto-ministerial-is-the-best-outcome-for-the-south

Combined with the deeply unfair negotiating process, the developing world has little chance at achieving fairer trade rules. The 'one member one vote' ideal of the WTO, so often cited by its defenders, collapses under the reality of the massive inequalities in negotiating strength. Indeed, there was no comparison between the sizes of delegations. The EU brought 651, the US 212, whereas China, India, Brazil, Argentina and South Africa brought only 235 delegates altogether. Civil society antagonism to the meeting grew stronger still when Lee Kyung-hae, a Korean farmer, climbed the police barricade around the venue of the meeting on 10 September, Chuseok day—the day for honouring the dead in Korea—and stabbed himself to death. He was wearing a placard that said 'The WTO kills farmers'.[11]

In India, too, there was a great deal of excitement. Thirty-five thousand farmers congregated in Bangalore, shouting the slogan, 'Either food and agriculture must be removed from the WTO, or India must quit the WTO'. An article published in *The Hindu* on 4 August 2003, while stressing the need for progressing forward in negotiations agriculture and other issues of concern to developing countries, cautioned that a US–EU pact on the eve of the Ministerial could prove to have a negative impact on developing countries and push them into agreeing on other issues which may later prove harmful to the interests of developing countries. They pointed out that 'a positive feature has been the India–China alliance at the WTO' and that 'it will not be easy to ride roughshod over a joint position by the two countries'.[12] Rediff, in a piece entitled 'Trade Can-Can at Cancun', summarized briefly the major issues in discussion and said, 'Now it remains to be seen how the Indian team weaves its way around the contentious issues at the

---

11   Najma Sadeque, 'How WTO Kills Farmers', *The Nation* (1 September 2013), https://nation.com.pk/11-Sep-2013/how-wto-kills-farmers.

12   C. Rammanohar Reddy, 'The importance of Cancun', *The Hindu*, 4 August 2003, https://www.thehindu.com/todays-paper/tp-business/the-importance-of-cancun/article27788392.ece

WTO.'[13] There was a huge contingent of Indian media and Indian civil society present at Cancun to capture each development in the ongoing drama.

The Cancun Ministerial meeting opened in salubrious surroundings. Situated in the south-east of Mexico, the city is on the shores of the Caribbean Sea and a major tourist destination. It is an ancient city with vestiges of pre-Columbian Mayan civilization still existing within and in its vicinity. There was unprecedented presence of civil society from all over the world, kept at bay from the venue of the Ministerial Conference. There was a great deal of nervousness and anxiety in all of us, notwithstanding the nonchalant demeanour that we assumed for public consumption. Before coming to Cancun, I had paid online to perform pujas at major temples in India during the conference. The Indian media, as usual, was diffident about India's ability to withstand pressure. There were murmurs, even among Indian diplomats, that India had come without a 'Plan B'. We are, as a nation, used to our 'Plan A' not finding support when push comes to shove. There was also little confidence in our coalitions in various sectors holding together. The US and EU, in particular, spread the canard that G20, our main coalition on agriculture, would break at any moment. The media representatives present repeatedly asked questions about this and we replied that the group was too strong to break. While there could be changes in the composition of the group, with some countries moving out and others coming in, the group itself would remain intact.

The Indian embassy in Mexico had wisely arranged for a hotel for our delegation with a large ground-floor room. This forethought proved to be of great advantage to us, as most G20 meetings were held in our hotel. The Indian delegation was led by Arun Jaitley, and though he showed some signs of hesitation in the beginning, he became one of the most dominant negotiators by the end. With his natural flair for

---

13   Rediff Business Bureau, 'Trade Can-Can at Cancun', *Rediff.com* (9 September 2003), https://www.rediff.com/money/2003/sep/09spec2.htm

making friends and expressing his views firmly but without creating ill will, he emerged a successful diplomat as the meeting progressed. In fact, his presence and his capacity to influence people resulted in G20 becoming a still more powerful entity with more countries in its fold.

However, pressures continued to be intense. Meetings on agriculture were held primarily between the G20 and the US and EU. The agriculture text for consideration by the Ministerial Conference was believed to be deeply flawed by many of us in the developing world. Despite a series of meetings, there was little progress on subsidies, domestic support and special and differential treatment for developing countries. The expectation that the US and EU would steamroll us was clearly belied. I must also mention here that the US–EU text was amended at the last moment to accommodate the needs of India. This would have meant deserting other developing countries like Brazil and China, which we considered a zero-sum game for India.

In fact, the developed countries, particularly the EU, had been circulating rumours, even in Geneva, of India breaking away from the G20 group. I had firmly scotched these rumours in a small group meeting in Geneva, where I said, 'The glamorous two have combined for a deal in agriculture. We have joined with others, less glamorous, but in whom we have confidence that they will remain with us till the end. We are very happy where we are and we have absolutely no intentions of changing our position.' There was no way in which we were going to repose faith in the EU any more.

As an aside, I must also mention a remark made by the DG (Trade) of the European Commission after a meeting in Geneva. He told me in a sarcastic tone, 'You have made a brilliant move by joining with Brazil and other countries. You will see the consequences here and at Cancun.' My friend, the Brazilian ambassador Felipe, was nearby when this incident occurred. He later told me, 'He was very nasty to you.'

The coalition against Singapore issues was aggressively and vociferously led by Malaysian Trade and Industry Minister Rafidah Aziz, who said unequivocally at a press conference jointly held with

Jaitley, 'We don't agree to launching any negotiations; there is no explicit consensus, and there is need for further clarification of these issues.' On the African countries' position, the Zambian Trade Minister said, 'The ministers in the African Union have said they don't want a launch of negotiations on these issues. More work is required. We also don't want linkage of these issues and other issues. Moreover, an explicit consensus is needed to launch negotiations, not an implied consensus.' On 12 September, India and Malaysia presented a letter on behalf of seventy countries against the Singapore issues to the facilitator of discussions on these issues, Pierre Pettigrew, Canadian Trade Minister, and Luis Ernesto Derbez, Mexican Foreign Minister and Chairman of the Cancun Ministerial, reiterating the same views.

Pettigrew and Derbez, however, chose to ignore the views of the majority of members. On 13 September, a revised Ministerial text appeared, popularly known as the Derbez Text. It provided for commencement of negotiations on trade facilitation and government procurement. In a convoluted way, it also provided for launching negotiations on the other two issues through the convening of special sessions, linking the results of negotiations on these issues with the single undertaking that would appear at the end of the Doha work programme, and also specifying that modalities allowing negotiations shall be adopted on an unspecified date. A footnote also provided that the date for adopting modalities shall coincide with the date for agreeing on negotiations relating to agricultural and non-agricultural products.[14]

This text created a furore among the developing countries and civil society representatives. A meeting of the Heads of Delegations was held on the evening of 13 September. I manoeuvred to get our minister placed fifth in the order of the speakers. I did not want him to make the opening speech but I wanted him to speak high in the order, so that other developing countries would be able to hear his views before the US

---

14   Martin Khor, 'The "Singapore Issues" in the WTO: Evolution and Implications for Developing Countries', *Third World Network*, 2007.

and EU ministers spoke. The hall was jam-packed as many civil society representatives also were present, along with members of delegations.

Jaitley made a fiery speech. 'We are disappointed,' he said, 'that the draft text ignores several concerns expressed by us and many developing countries. I note that the development dimension of the Doha agenda has finally been discarded, confirming the apprehension expressed by me at the plenary session that this is mere rhetoric.' He spoke of the continuing distortions in agriculture. 'How can we expect developing countries to reduce tariffs on a number of items to between zero percent and five percent when the distortions against which such tariffs are supposed to compensate, are sought to be enhanced?' On Singapore issues, he said, 'It represents an attempt made to thrust the views of a few countries upon many developing countries.' Expressing India's disappointment with the text, he said that it has 'arbitrarily disregarded views and concerns expressed by us'. He hoped that 'circumstances and environment will be created to enable us to participate constructively'.[15]

While the language was strong, Jaitley also had the gift of expressing himself forcefully. He was heard to the end in pin-drop silence. When he concluded his speech, for the first time in my memory of WTO meetings, there was thunderous ovation from all parts of the hall. After he spoke, several other ministers from other developing countries followed his lead and spoke strongly, thus transforming the atmosphere of negotiation conclusively. Later, in Geneva, the American ambassador told me that she could visualize Jaitley mesmerizing India's rural masses with his deep voice and his powerful articulation in remote villages lit by lanterns.

On 14 September, there was a Green Room meeting, attended by a few Heads of Delegations. Along with our minister, Commerce Secretary Dipak Chatterjee and I were present. There were about thirty

---

15 BBC Monitoring International Reports, 'Brazil, India Say WTO Draft Document One-Sided, Favours EU, US', *Institute for Agriculture & Trade Policy* (14 September 2003), https://www.iatp.org/news/brazil-india-say-wto-draft-document-one-sided-favours-eu-us

ministers, including representatives of the African Union, the Least Developed Countries and the African, Caribbean and Pacific Group of States. Derbez decided to start the meeting with the Singapore issues, proposing that negotiations may start on trade facilitation and government procurement but that the other two issues, investment and competition, may be dropped from the agenda. I saw this as an amazing development as all the work that we had done in Geneva had paid off and the most difficult issues—from the Indian perspective—were out of the agenda. As many developing countries still had reservations, a break was announced. The countries of the African, Caribbean and Pacific Group, the African Union and the Least Developed Countries met together separately and came back asserting their opposition to negotiations on any of the issues. Korea, on the other hand, said they would oppose the dropping of any issue. To our surprise, Derbez then decided to abruptly close the Ministerial Conference. We had expected that there would be many more painful discussions spread through the night. According to many, the Americans knew of this outcome even before Derbez had announced it, as they had packed and loaded their baggage, preparing for departure.

The conclusion of the meeting without result was greeted with loud cheers by civil society representatives of developing countries outside the premises of the conference. Jaitley became a national hero in India overnight. India's official delegation spent a happy day on the fifteenth at the Mayan ruins in Chichen Itza. I went back to Geneva and the Indian delegation left for Delhi. On its arrival at Delhi airport, there was a big crowd waiting to receive the minister, including the then Minister of State Rajiv Pratap Rudy. On 18 September, *The Baltimore Sun* reported:

A generation from now, analysts may look back at the World Trade Organization summit in Mexico as a turning point in the increasingly contentious globalization debate.

Why? Because for the first time in decades of globalization negotiations, democracy trumped narrow elite interests.[16]

In his article of 20 September 2003 in *The Telegraph*, titled 'Trading Places: India helped to keep developing nations together at Cancun', K.P. Nayar wrote:

The large function hall of the Mediterranean-style Cancun hotel was filled to capacity. If a vote had been taken among the non-governmental organizations present there to choose the most popular Commerce Minister attending the World Trade Organization meeting in Mexico last week, there would have been no doubt about the outcome. Arun Jaitley easily stood out among his WTO colleagues at the five-day meeting, which is now being hailed as a landmark in global politics in the new millennium.[17]

It was never India's intention that the Cancun deliberations should fail. The single undertaking that emerged after the Uruguay Round was skewed against the interests of developing countries. We had stakes in the negotiations following Doha in order to restore balance in global trade rules.

In the initial period after Cancun, there was a marked lull in the negotiations. There was considerable confusion, particularly about the Singapore issues, whether they would be totally dropped from the

---

16   John Cavanagh and Robin Broad, 'A Turning Point for World Trade?' *The Baltimore Sun* (18 September 2003), https://www.tni.org/en/article/a-turning-point-for-world-trade

17   K.P. Nayar, 'TRADING PLACES: India Helped to Keep Developing Nations Together at Cancun', *The Telegraph* (20 September 2003), https://www.telegraphindia.com/opinion/trading-places-india-helped-to-keep-developing-nations-together-at-cancun/cid/1018490

negotiations on the single undertaking or whether deliberations would continue in some other format. The EU position was particularly unclear. At the General Council meeting on 17 May 2004, the confusion continued with Ambassador Shotaro Oshima of Japan, then Chairman of the Council, saying that 'major questions of which of the issues, if any, should be within the single undertaking, and of what should be done with those issues to be put outside the single undertaking, are yet to be resolved'. However, there was no mention of reviving the working groups on three issues while trade facilitation was sent to a Deputy Director General for further discussion with delegations.

The delegations of Geneva then worked towards salvaging the detritus left by Cancun and to put the negotiations back on track. In the meanwhile, two major changes had occurred so far as we were concerned. First, on agriculture; to progress the deliberations, a group of five was formed, including the US, EU, Brazil, India and Australia. This was a significant development. Until then, the Quad, consisting of the US, EU, Canada and Japan, was considered to be the principal decision-making force in the WTO. The formation of the new group marked the emergence of developing countries in the equation. Secondly, in India, political changes took place with the BJP-led National Democratic Alliance government being replaced by a Congress-led United Progressive Alliance government. Kamal Nath became the new Commerce Minister of India.

The deliberations at Geneva finally led to what was popularly known as the July Framework Agreement in 2004. The agreement emphasized the need to progress the talks in select areas—market access in agricultural and non-agricultural products, development issues, trade facilitation and services. The inclusion of services in the main body of the agreement was another significant achievement for us. India had been single-handedly asking for inclusion of services in the main body of the text, rather than as an annex, which was the position in the first draft prepared by Ambassador Oshima in mid-July. Services negotiations were important for India in the context of the large number of Indians working in different parts of the world. Fortunately, the US

Trade Representative Robert Zoellick saw the fairness in my argument. For the first time ever, the Indian and US Ambassadors jointly wrote a letter to the Chairman of the General Council, seeking inclusion of services in the main body of the Agreement.

The Framework Agreement provided for continuance of negotiations in other areas in the Doha mandate. However, it stated explicitly on investment, competition and government procurement that 'no work towards negotiations on any of these issues will take place within the WTO during the Doha Round'. A broad framework on parameters for negotiations in agriculture was agreed to as an annex to the agreement.

The July Framework Agreement constituted an important step towards restarting the negotiations. As we passed each other after the meeting, Robert Zoellick came to me and thanked me for my role in restoring the negotiations. The WTO Director General, Supachai Panitchpakdi, called it a 'truly historic' achievement. EC Trade Commissioner Pascal Lamy remarked, 'the Doha Round is back on track'. Zoellick said, 'We have laid out a map for the road ahead. Kamal Nath was happy, too. He said, 'This more than adequately addresses India's concerns.' I learnt a great deal from my diplomatic experience, which concluded shortly after the July Framework Agreement, and I was posted back to Delhi as Revenue Secretary.

I had had many fears when I was posted as Ambassador to the WTO. The posting itself was the subject of considerable controversy with an unseemly and unnecessary conflict between the Ministry of External Affairs and the Ministry of Commerce, which put a greater load on me to prove myself in Geneva. I was also taking over from a formidable and much-feared predecessor, who had made a mark for himself in his tenure of five years. I had really no negotiating experience worth the name. I was not confident that I would be able to articulate India's position sufficiently well or strongly enough in the WTO. I was also taking over at a time when India was regarded as a pariah in the Geneva diplomatic community.

In retrospect, I consider my tenure in Geneva to have been the high point in my public service career. Looking back, I realize that the experience, skills and instincts I had and the sense of timing that came naturally to me were largely the result of my work in Kerala, which involved constant, sometimes acrimonious, interaction with politicians, trade unions, students and many others. In comparison, negotiations in Geneva seemed much easier. Each diplomat was listened to with respect, never interrupted by rude and loud-mouthed participants at meetings. There was never any animosity carried outside the meeting halls. I could have argued my position with no holds barred at any meeting with anybody, and after the meeting, my adversary and I could have had a drink and smoked a cigar together.

The Cancun Ministerial Conference marked a complete transformation in the dynamics of negotiations in the global arena. Kristen Hopewell has analysed this development in great detail in her dissertation. She said that the WTO had ceased to operate as a 'rich man's club', that it was dominated no longer by the Quad countries seeking to advance their interests at the cost of others. Developing countries were no more marginalized and Brazil, India and China emerged as significant players in the negotiations.

I am, however, disappointed that no further progress was made in the negotiations in subsequent years. India and other developing countries had a great deal to gain from the establishment of new multilateral trade rules. The proliferation of regional and bilateral trading arrangements in the past few years has made the multilateral trading system virtually redundant. There were many problems arising from the commitments made in the Uruguay Round that needed to be corrected and settled. The developed countries, with their insistence on continuance of agricultural subsidies, and the developing countries, with their reluctance to find common ground in a spirit of compromise, both contributed to the demise of the Doha work programme. The rise of the extreme right in politics in many parts of the world has further complicated the future of negotiations. Bloomberg News reported that then President Trump said about the WTO, 'If they don't shape up, I would withdraw from the WTO.'[18] Unilateral action by many countries, including the US and India, to raise import tariffs on a range of goods featuring in global trade and increase curbs on migration of skilled persons from developing countries to developed countries are indications of a major shift in the attitude of countries across the world to work in cohesion with each other.

As Arancha González,[19] Chief of Staff to then WTO Director General Pascal Lamy, put it in her collection of short essays titled *The Future and the WTO: Confronting the Challenges*:

> This is not a good time for international cooperation. This is not just a problem for the WTO. We see it too in climate change discussions, in negotiations over reform of the financial architecture, in macro-economic matters and in non-economic spheres as well.[20]

The situation has become a lot worse since then. If at all there has to be forward movement, it is necessary for each country to reflect on the changed power scenario in the global economic scene as well as the changes that have occurred within each country and in each region and lay out a fresh roadmap for the future, encompassing present realities. The need for progress has become even more urgent after the havoc wreaked by the pandemic.

---

18   'Donald Trump threatens to pull US out of WTO if it doesn't "shape up"', *The Economic Times*, 31 August 2018.

19   Arancha González was the first woman to serve as Chief of Staff to a WTO Director General, working in the Cabinet of Pascal Lamy from 2005 to 2013.

20   Arancha González, 'Is There a Future for Multilateral Trade Opening?', in *The Future and the WTO: Confronting the Challenges,* ed. Ricardo Melendez Ortiz, Christophe Bellman and Miguel Rodriguez Mendoza (Geneva: International Centre for Trade and Sustainable Development, 2012).

From Diplomacy to Regulation

'The income tax created more criminals than any other single act of government.'

—*Barry Goldwater*

When I returned from Geneva in October after completing my six-year tryst with diplomacy in Brussels and in the WTO, I was posted as the Revenue Secretary in the Ministry of Finance. Throughout most of 2004, rumours had been rife that I would be posted as Commerce Secretary in light of Arun Jaitley's open appreciation of my work as Ambassador to the WTO. It seemed a foregone conclusion at the time that the NDA government led by Vajpayee would be voted back into power with a sizeable majority. I had my doubts even then. I remember mentioning to the Cabinet Secretary of the time, Kamal Pande, that even though the newspapers and periodicals of the time waxed eloquent about the NDA cakewalking to victory in the 2004 elections, the political structure of the country and the results of elections in the provinces did not entirely point to an easy win for the ruling party. I recall that I had mentioned this also to the US Ambassador during an informal lunch at a restaurant overlooking the lake in Geneva. Later, she said, 'You were the only person predicting a possible change of government in India. All others said the ruling party will sail through.'

The change of government meant also that I would no longer become the Commerce Secretary. I was told by a friend that two senior officers, one of them a good friend, went to the PMO and convinced the Principal Secretary to the PM that a 'senior' Secretary should handle Commerce. And so Commerce was not to be, but strangely, I was given charge of the Revenue Department, which is much larger in size than Commerce.

Just before I left Geneva, the new Indian Prime Minister Manmohan Singh happened to pass through the city on his way back to India. Geneva is a city well-known to Singh, as he had spent a good four years in the South Centre there. He was visibly tired, but still blew out the candle on a cake arranged by my colleague, the UN Ambassador Hardeep Singh Puri, and participated in a little party. I recall telling him at the event that he had a rare chance to succeed as PM as he had raised no great expectations and made no promises that could not be achieved within his tenure. This was proven right and his first tenure was a decisive and productive one, obviously appreciated by the voters, who brought him back to power in 2009 with more strength in the Parliament.

The position of Revenue Secretary in the Ministry of Finance is an unusual one. It is by far the largest and most powerful position in the ministry, responsible both for direct and indirect taxes. The Enforcement Directorate (ED), the Financial Intelligence Unit, the Directorate of Revenue Intelligence and, of course, the Central Board of Direct Taxes and the Central Board of Excise and Customs—all reported to the Revenue Secretary. The formidable P. Chidambaram was the Minister. He had picked me once before as Joint Secretary in the Trade Policy Division when he was Minister of State in the Commerce Ministry. I am told the system has drastically changed under the present government and that ministers now have little to do with the appointment of officers; the decision travels top down from the Prime Minister's office.

Obviously, the fact that the present government has a sizeable majority in the lower House of Parliament gives the Prime Minister and his office the space to make appointments without consulting the ministers concerned. Whether this is good or bad is a matter of opinion. There have been cases of ministers conducting deep searches to find officials who will toe their line, whether right or wrong. On the other hand, there were ministers like Arun Shourie who told me once, 'I leave appointment of officers entirely to the Secretary. I tell him, "It is your responsibility to deliver results as I want and you are free to select your own team".' I am personally of the view that in a democracy, the sanctity of the Appointments Committee of the Cabinet should be maintained. The procedure of the Appointments Committee envisages a role for the Secretary of the Department, the Cabinet Secretary, the minister concerned, the Home Minister and the Prime Minister. The selection is made in the Civil Services Board, headed by the Cabinet Secretary, only after the Department Secretary has sounded the minister and ensured that he or she is also on board. Thereafter, through the Cabinet Secretary, the file goes to the Home Minister and then the Prime Minister.

Working with Chidambaram was no walk in the park. Intellectually very sharp, remarkably quick to understand and completely familiar with the tax law, he stood head and shoulders above most of us. During my tenure, India was admitted as an observer into the OECD committee dealing with tax law. On one occasion, he flummoxed OECD officers totally for close to an hour, delving deep into the intricacies of taxation. When they met me later, one of them asked, 'Is your minister a tax lawyer?' They seemed comforted when I told them that he was indeed adept in tax law.

My time in the Revenue Department was a period of learning for me. Before that tenure, I had worked primarily in developmental areas, international trade and commerce and diplomacy. In the Revenue Department, under a stern and demanding minister who could not be relied upon to support me in case I blundered somewhere, I got a taste of the regulatory world. I learnt also that tax law in India had been immensely complicated with a plethora of provisos, provisos to provisos and explanations that it was beyond the comprehension of even highly educated people, and understanding it required the support of batteries of lawyers and chartered accountants.

Any attempt to simplify the income tax law never came to fruition. I recall that there was a saying in the income tax department that any government that attempted to change the law would fall before the revised bill came to Parliament. Even during my time, several evenings were spent on trying to work out a simplified law, which came to nought. The present government also set up a committee when Jaitley was Finance Minister to formulate a direct tax code. This committee was headed by the cerebral Arbind Modi, whose knowledge of the law is unsurpassed and who has been associated with every previous attempt to reform the law. Working day and night and pushing himself to extreme limits, as is his wont, Modi finished the text on the last day before his superannuation and sought time with Finance Minister Jaitley to present the documents. Late in the evening, he was told that he need not meet the minister or present the fruits of his labour. One more attempt to clean up the law thus probably went down the drain. Hopefully, at some future date, these papers would be retrieved and put back into the Parliamentary process. Meanwhile, there could be a further multiplication of provisos, tying up the law into still more knots.

The Revenue Department can be an instrument both of facilitation and of oppression. Banking institutions, too, can likewise help or handicap entrepreneurs. Not too long ago, both the Revenue Department and banking institutions were transformed into tyrannical organizations, with the Income Tax Department conducting raid after raid, striking fear in the hearts of business persons everywhere. At the same time, banks became demonic in the name of non-performing assets, without regard to the fact that some assets cannot perform when the economy is down in the dumps or when the industry itself is struggling. In August 2019, the unfortunate suicide of one of India's boldest young entrepreneurs, V.G. Siddhartha, founder of the café chain Café Coffee Day, highlighted the need to approach economic policy cautiously and with understanding.

By giving up his life, Siddhartha left several messages which India must heed. He talked about his company being weighed down with debts from many different sources and his belief that he would not have been able to service them. This raises two issues. The first is probably that some of our young and growing companies need to be particularly wary of overleveraging in their quest for expansion. Sometimes, growth has its own momentum, which can mesmerize the aspiring entrepreneur and lead him to take more risks than an established and conservative business house would have taken. This is a lesson also for those in the government in charge of implementing projects to proceed more cautiously while advocating adventurism.

Another message was that the crusade against non-performing assets in banks has to be tempered by the needs of the economy. Inability to repay a debt in time arises not just on account of a deliberate and malicious intent to defraud the bank and society. In many cases, incapacity to repay in time arises out of the company running into bad times or getting caught up in an economic slowdown. A certain amount of flexibility has to remain with the banker to distinguish between a miscreant and a man genuinely facing temporary difficulty, who will meet his debt obligations if given a little leeway. It is necessary for the banker to be able to work with the well-intentioned entrepreneur and try and see him out of the woods. Any good and honest banker can make this distinction but not if he fears investigative and enforcement agencies breathing down his neck. Like most of us, the banker would then become a rigid adherent to the rule book, divorced from the realities of the economic situation. This situation has become far more concerning presently, as medium- and small-scale industries have been badly hit, both by the pandemic and by the fall in incomes, unemployment and the consequent sharp drop in demand during the two years preceding the pandemic.

Finally, there was also the message that Siddhartha left regarding pressure on him from the tax authorities. As Revenue Secretary, there were pressures on me to deliver higher revenues, which I, in turn, passed on to my officers. Hence, I can understand why the officers acted as they did. I recall that during my time, Amitabh Bachhan raised a big furore about having been served an income tax demand notice, even as he was going for emergency treatment to a hospital. The need to collect more money as taxes must never become an unbridled license to allow tax officials to torment taxpayers. It is a good thing that the present Finance Minister Nirmala Sitaraman recognizes the dangers of 'tax terrorism' and has endeavoured to rein in her officers and to eliminate direct interface between the assessing authority and the taxpayer.

There is another incident that comes to mind, related to my days with Chidambaram. The price of an important commodity had risen disproportionately and there was concern within the government that this was going to hit a range of developmental activities downstream. A meeting of manufacturers was called by Chidambaram. To my surprise, the manufacturers concerned told him off in no uncertain terms. I thought they were exceptionally rude and that there were ways in which tax departments could have dealt with them. I told the Finance Minister as much. He thought for a moment and then said, 'No, we don't deal with such things using our powers and our officials.' On reflection and introspection, I feel he was absolutely right. We could have used our machinery to put a few captains of industry in their places, but we would never have been able to prevent the same machinery from overreaching itself and creating mayhem in the economy. Controlling tax officials and ensuring that taxpayers are dealt with fairly and with dignity is as important as sniffing out the miscreants.

This is something which is not new to the government taxation machinery. Over the years, the effort has been to root out discretion and building systems. Today, the vast majority of income taxpayers have no direct interface with assessing officers. Our returns are fed into machines, which quickly assess what is due from us on the basis of our returns and information collected from many other sources, and tell us how much more we have to pay or how much has to be paid back to us. A risk analysis system and an electronic data interchange simplify customs assessment, while the introduction of GST has meant that indirect tax collection, earlier an impossible melange of central and state indirect taxes—the playground of officials—has become an increasingly self-driven, self-policing mechanism. It is important that the movement towards management of taxes through systems rather than individuals continues with vigour and that this process never lapses back into arbitrariness and harassment.

Several significant events happened during my days as Revenue Secretary. The presence and support of the learned Parthasarathi Shome, a tax expert with phenomenal knowledge of the sector, played a great part in making significant changes. The Enforcement Directorate became once again a powerful organization. The ED, when it was originally set up, had powers under the Foreign Exchange Regulation Act. With growing liberalization, it was felt that the Act was too harsh and Yashwant Sinha, as Finance Minister in the Vajpayee government, substituted it with the toothless Foreign Exchange Management Act. The Prevention of Money Laundering Act had been passed in 2002 but the rules had not been issued. This act was resuscitated and strengthened, and a whole range of offences under legislation relating to customs, child and bonded labour, environment protection, emigration, passports, foreigners, copyright, trademarks and information technology were brought within its competence. Significantly, even the Prevention of Corruption Act was brought within its purview. It is unfortunate that later amendments to this act have been so rigorous that the ED is armed today with immense powers that can be used indiscriminately and viciously. The Supreme Court is closely examining this law at present. Judicial intervention will hopefully lead to the law being remodelled so that it no longer remains on the statute books as a perennial weapon that can be used to bludgeon people into submission.

One major event during my early days in the Revenue Department was the Volcker report and its reverberations in Indian politics. Following Saddam Hussein's ill-advised invasion of Kuwait and the resounding pushback by the US, sanctions were imposed by the UN on Iraq, particularly on its oil exports. However, to ensure that this did not cause undue hardship to the Iraqi people, they were allowed to sell oil under UN supervision, under what was called the Oil-for-Food Programme, started in 1995. Under this scheme, Iraq could sell oil, the proceeds of which would be kept in an escrow account. A part of it would be used for war reparations to Kuwait, but the bulk of the amount could be used by Iraq to purchase goods that were not under sanction. There were many allegations of corruption and misuse of the system. On 25 January 2004, the Iraqi newspaper *Al Mada* published a list of individuals and organizations that had illegally benefitted from the scheme. The list included the Congress party and, more specifically, K. Natwar Singh, who later became Foreign Minister in the United Progressive Alliance government formed by Manmohan Singh.

In March 2004, an independent investigation was launched by UN Secretary General Kofi Annan, headed by Paul Volcker, former Head of the US Federal Reserve. Volcker submitted a 219-page report naming individuals and organizations that had benefitted from the scheme. Among the beneficiaries were the Indian National Congress and Natwar Singh.[21] This was taken to the Cabinet and in November 2005, an inquiry commission was appointed to look into the findings of the Volcker report, headed by Justice R.S. Pathak, former Justice of the Supreme Court and of the International Court of Justice. At the same time, senior diplomat Virendra Dayal was appointed to verify

---

21   Praveen Swami, 'Figuring out Volcker', *Frontline*, 2 December 2005.

the allegations in the Volcker report, then travelling to the UN and verifying their records as necessary. The ED, headed by one of the finest officers in the IAS, Sudhir Nath, also jumped into the fray to investigate violations of the Foreign Exchange Management Act. I was present at a Cabinet meeting late in the evening, which decided on the appointment of the Pathak Commission.

Natwar Singh was a senior minister and it was expected that he would emerge unscathed from the enquiry. He resigned, but his position was not filled up in the expectation that he would come back as Foreign Minister. The Ministry of External Affairs reported directly to the PM in the interim. As Revenue Secretary, the enquiry and the investigations fell under my jurisdiction. As the ED and Justice Pathak were both looking at the same issue, it became my responsibility to keep peace between them and to ensure that both had access to all the relevant papers. Justice Pathak submitted his report to the PM in August 2006, indicting Natwar Singh and his MLA son, Jagat, for helping Aditya Khanna, their kin, and Jagat's friend, Andaleep Sehgal, to get three Iraqi oil contracts, which were sold to foreign companies to get kickbacks amounting to US$146,000.[22] The letterhead of the Congress Party was used by Natwar to get the contracts from Iraqi authorities. However, the Congress Party was exonerated, much to the discomfiture of the BJP, which was the Opposition. 'On what basis was a carte blanche was given that Congress had no role to play?' asked the BJP spokesman, Ravishankar Prasad.[23]

Later, when I had the occasion to meet Sonia Gandhi, the subject came up in the course of conversation. The normally impassive Sonia showed a flash of emotion. 'He used the name of the Congress!' she exclaimed. In his book, *One Life is Not Enough*, however, Natwar claimed that he was made the fall guy to absolve the Congress. According to him,

---

22   'Pathak Panel Indicts Natwar, Son', *The Economic Times*, 4 August 2006.

23   'Why Has Congress Been Let Off in Volcker Issue: BJP', *Rediff.com* (4 August 2006), https://www.rediff.com/news/2006/aug/04volcker.htm

the Pathak Report—not made public—said that there was not enough evidence to show that Natwar received any benefit from the deal. The ED, however, initiated action against him and others, alleging that they got foreign exchange of about Rs 50 million in violation of the Foreign Exchange Management Act.

One of the great success stories of Indian federalism was the formation of the Council of State Finance Ministers. In the '70s and '80s, the taxation structure in India was a confused mixture of different rates imposed in different areas. It required patience and much cajoling by the Union Finance Minister to bring uniformity in indirect taxation and ensure freedom of movement of goods across the country. The climactic moment, of course, came with the introduction of the Goods and Services Tax across the whole country. This was possible only because of unceasing efforts by successive Finance Ministers to bring about change, little by little, with the cooperation of the states. There were many steps taken before GST. One such was the introduction of Value Added Tax (VAT). This happened soon after I took charge of the Revenue Department. Chidambaram convened a meeting of the State Finance Ministers. There was stout opposition at the start, as several State Finance Ministers were apprehensive of loss of revenue. Chidambaram passed a chit to us, saying 'Shall we create a fund of Rs 50 billion to offset whatever losses they make?' We agreed and the states, too, were satisfied. Thus, a significant step forward was taken on the road to create a uniform indirect tax structure in India, which led ultimately to the introduction of the GST.

The GST, brought into existence recently amidst great fanfare in the dead of night in the Parliament to signify the rebirth of India, was perhaps not thought through fully before its introduction. The GST has many advantages. It is conceived as a single, simple indirect tax, even though there are multiple rates in existence at present. By extending the principle of input tax credit across all indirect taxes across the country, encompassing both centre and states, it was expected that overall tax incidence would come down by eliminating cascading of taxes. It was intended also to reduce, if not eliminate, the degree of tax oppression that prevailed in commercial tax offices of the centre and the states and to create a system that is largely self-policing. It was intended to be a logical extension of the VAT system in place separately for the centre and the states.

The problems involved in introducing such a massive system across a federal country of India's dimensions were clearly underestimated. The fact that the technology platform created for the purpose may not be able to digest millions of transactions and match them for input tax credit was not fully understood. Today, we find increasing cases of fraudulent grant of input tax credit, and also millions of micro industries and petty traders struggling with the system. While, with the removal of check posts and entry restrictions, transport of goods across states has quickened, it is not certain that tax oppression has markedly declined because both the Central Excise officers and the State Commercial Tax officers can conduct inspections.

Several important products still remain out of the purview of the GST, the problems faced by small business entities remain largely unaddressed, the rather tangled system created for interstate movement of goods remains difficult to resolve and the lack of complete knowledge about how the GST system works has resulted in the continuance of cascading of taxes at many levels. The expected anti-inflationary effect is, therefore, yet to materialize. Besides, since the tax, being destination-based and not origin-based, would result in shifts in movement of revenue across states, growth patterns would obviously be affected.

There are many experts who believe that not enough homework was done before introducing the task. There are others, possibly including the central government, who believe that India is a 'last-minute country', which lacks the will to anticipate problems and take corrective action in advance, and that we will act only when confronted with crises. I recall, in this context, Manmohan Singh quoting the fabled P.N. Haksar, Principal Secretary to PM Indira Gandhi, that 'In India, reform is possible only by stealth'. The 'great leap forward', envisaged in the thought process that led to the GST, is yet to materialize but it does signify the success of collective thinking by the states and the centre, which started with VAT and has culminated in the GST Council.

The danger that lurks ahead is that consensual decision-making could be supplanted by a brute majority, which will ultimately weaken and loosen the bonds amongst the states and between the centre and states that GST has forged. The angry conflict that arose between the farmers of Punjab and Haryana and the Government of India could surely have been avoided completely had the same route of consultation and consensus-building been followed in Parliament and outside. Democratic systems should not be considered inconvenient enemies of reforms. Our best reforms have been facilitated by people's willing participation. It is good that the government understood the depth of feeling among farmers and withdrew the legislation before more bloodshed and violence occurred. There is a lesson to be learnt here: the importance of close collaboration between the centre and the states and the emergence of what Prime Minister Modi calls 'Team India'.

The GST came not too long after another extraordinary economic decision was taken by the Centre on an impulse—the decision to demonetize the 1,000-rupee and 500-rupee notes. Touted as a measure aimed at destroying black money, it resulted in the abrupt removal of 86 per cent of the money in circulation. Business came to a standstill, goods remained unsold, wage payments were delayed, industry ground to a halt and growth was arrested. Since, strangely, the effects of withdrawal of the 1,000-rupee note was sought to be mitigated by the introduction of a 2,000-rupee note, it was difficult to visualize how the capacity to store black money in cash was, in any way, reduced.

Later, after a long period of suffering for the common people, it was revealed that all the money that had been in circulation earlier had come back into the Reserve Bank of India coffers. If indeed there were huge amounts of black money stashed away as 1,000- and 500-rupee notes, the receipts of the RBI post demonetization should have been significantly less than the quantum of currency in circulation at the point of demonetization. All that has happened seems to have been the evolution of new channels and modes of corruption. There was a temporary side effect of a spurt in digital financial transactions, but this too has subsided to normal growth rates which India would have achieved with or without demonetization. A recent study[24] shows that while digital payments increased in volume by 44.8 per cent and in value by 14.6 per cent in the pre-demonetization period from 2011–12 to 2015–16, there was a spurt in the demonetization year of 2016–17 to 64.4 per cent in volume and 26 per cent in value. However, these figures declined to 44.7 per cent growth in volume and 1.94 per cent in value during the period 2018–19 to 2020–21. However, the value figure in the last period is not the same as in the first period as the Reserve Bank of India had changed the definition of digital transactions. It is clear nevertheless that demonetization per se has not resulted in increase in digitalization.

Politically, however, demonetization became a means for separating the grain from the chaff. Those who spoke up in defence of demonetization could expect favours from government. Those who spoke against this measure were obviously demons deserving to be crushed. Those who did not speak up for demonetization were also suspect to be watched very carefully.

---

24   Sunil Mani and Chidambaran Iyer (2022), 'Diffusion of Digital payments in India, 2011-12 through 2020-21, Role of its sectoral system of innovation', Working Paper No. 505, Thiruvananthapuram: Centre for Development Studies.

Reflections on Democracy and Dictatorship

'The best weapon of a dictatorship is secrecy, but the best weapon of a democracy should be the weapon of openness.'

—Niels Bohr

Regulatory institutions and investigative agencies can be sources of strengthening governance and nurturing the roots of democracy, but they can also be means to crush all dissent. Dictatorships have a tendency to start at a low ebb and then grow more and more unrestrained as challenges against it are dissipated. They tend to feed on hidden suspicions and the differences in society, blowing them out of proportion and creating deep fissures in the social fabric. Strangely, democracy is the feeding ground for potential despots. As Kalyani Mookherji puts it in her book, *20 Dictators of the World*, 'Another interesting trait about dictators from the modern history has been that many of them came to the power on the strength of the same institution—democracy—that they eventually subverted in the process of establishing their absolute authorities.'[25]

Adolf Hitler is, of course, the best known example. The deep sense of humiliation among the German people following their defeat in the First World War, the unreasonable demands made by the Allies of Germany after its defeat and the growing economic and political depression in the country together provided fertile ground for the emergence of a different line of thinking which emphasized racial superiority, stereotyped people perceived as enemies of German society and led eventually to the strangulation of democratic institutions. Hitler expounded the principle of Führerprinzip or unquestioning obedience of all subordinates to their superiors. Appointed in due course as the leader of the German Reich, Hitler and his Nazi cohorts rose to power on the ruins of a Parliamentary democracy, the Weimar Republic.

A demagogue who could rouse passions and generate powerful feelings of hate, Hitler also was quick to seize every opportunity that came his way. Shortly after Paul von Hindenburg gave him power in January 1933, there was a fire in the Reichstag, attributed to the Communists, but considered by some to have been engineered by the Nazis, the National Socialist German Workers Party. A crackdown on civil liberties followed and the space for democratic expression dwindled progressively thereafter. Fostered on hatred of particular segments of German society and delusions of racial invincibility, the German people were drawn into a kind of dream world from which they were rudely awakened only after suffering crushing defeats. The economy, paradoxically, flourished as Hitler stopped paying war reparations and invested in German companies, as huge public infrastructure development programmes were taken up, the army was expanded and

---

25 Kalyani Mookherji, *20 Dictators of the World,* (New Delhi: Prabhat Prakashan, 2016).

a supporting munitions industry sprang up. Jews and women were deprived of jobs, which were given to German men instead. However, the policy of autarky or German self-sufficiency, spearheaded by Hermann Goring, failed, and measures to reduce reliance on imports and to expand domestic production did not make headway.

More recently, the Chinese Cultural Revolution is another example of stifling opposition by creating divisions within society. Indeed, the Red Guards, initially—and interested bureaucracy, later—dug so deep into the entrails of society that children applauded, tears streaming down their cheeks, as their parents underwent corporeal punishment, even execution, for supposed insubordination to the leadership, based on what the little ones themselves had conveyed to bureaucratic overlords. The 'back to the countryside' movement saw a large forced exodus of millions of urban people to rural areas for 're-education'. The destruction of the 'Four Olds' (old customs, old culture, old habits and old ideas) led to widespread ruination of the ancient culture, philosophy and wisdom of China. The Red Guards, in their fervour for the Four News, ransacked homes, vandalized art treasures, destroyed ancient libraries and desecrated temples.

In April 1976, when tens of thousands of Chinese spontaneously poured into Tiananmen Square to mourn the death of the moderate Zhou Enlai, they were crushed mercilessly by the so-called protectors of the pure Mao Zedong doctrine. Millions are reported to have died all over China. The death of Mao and the subsequent arrest of the Gang of Four brought this period of state-sponsored militancy and misery to an end. Later, in June 1981, the Central Committee adopted the 'Resolution on Certain Questions in the History of Our Party since the Founding of the People's Republic of China'. The Resolution stated that the 'chief responsibility for the grave "Left" error of the "Cultural Revolution", an error comprehensive in magnitude and protracted in duration, does indeed lie with Comrade Mao Zedong.' It sought to exculpate him to a certain extent by affixing blame on Lin Biao and Jing Qiang. However, it stated unequivocally that the Cultural

Revolution brought serious disaster and turmoil to the Communist Party and the Chinese people.[26]

Nicolae Ceaușescu in Romania was another leader considered to be forward-looking and liberal when he started his political career. Very soon, the pattern of repression, destruction of institutions and accumulation of absolute power became his chosen method of consolidating his position. On the economic side, his authority manifested itself in building giant infrastructure projects too large for his country, which resulted in the state accumulating huge amounts of foreign debt. His answer to this problem was another colossal blunder. He ordered the export of his country's agricultural and industrial production in 1982, creating shortages and a humanitarian crisis within Romania.

Purging of all dissent and indescribable cruelty marked the short rule of Pol Pot in Cambodia. Three million out of a total population of eight million died during his infamous regime. Religion was outlawed and controls imposed on social practices.

Muammar Gaddafi in Libya and Saddam Hussain in Iraq thrived on repression of dissent. Ruthlessness, destruction of perceived or imagined enemies, creation of hatred and divisions within the populace were the hallmarks of the tyrannical regimes they created. The story has not ended. Nascent dictatorships and megalomaniac rulers are still to be seen, some full-blown, some in their infancy.

My digression to a discussion on dictatorships and their emergence is intended to stress the importance of institutions and balance of power within a nation to preserve its freedom and to

---

26 Wilson Centre Digital Archive, 'Resolution on Certain Questions in the History of our Party since the Founding of the Peoples' Republic of China', 27 June 1981. History and Public Policy Digital Archive, Translation from the *Beijing Review* 24, no. 27, 6 July 1981 (Para-4 and 22), https://digitalarchive.wilsoncenter.org/document/121344. pdf?v=d461ad5001da989b8f96cc1dfb3c8ce7

create an environment in which people can realize their potential without fear. India's strength essentially derives from the faith its founding fathers had in the fundamentals of democracy. We owe a great debt of gratitude to our first Prime Minister, Jawaharlal Nehru in particular, because he never wavered from his deep conviction in constitutional democracy and its innate ability to resolve problems through discussion and debate. The growth of democratic institutions prevented India from going the way of some of our neighbours, who had spells of democracy intercepted by periods of authoritarian rule, with the result that they failed to keep pace with India in social, economic and political growth. As Shashi Tharoor stated in his article, 'Nehru and Democracy':

> Nehru was never tempted by the argument to which so many fellow heroes of the anti-colonial struggle in other developing countries succumbed—that dictatorship was the only way for them to forge unity and direct development. For he was a convinced democrat, a man so wary of the risks of autocracy that, at the crest of his rise, he authored an anonymous article warning Indians of the dangers of giving dictatorial temptations to Jawaharlal Nehru.[27]

But for a brief period during the Emergency in the mid-'70s, Indian democracy has stood its ground. Indeed, it has deepened and grown roots that stretch to the rural areas in the form of panchayats and other forms of local self-government. The growth of democracy was facilitated by the elaborate system of checks and balances which effectively prevented overreach by regulatory institutions. The Revenue Department, which I headed at the official level for about three years,

---

27   Shashi Tharoor, 'Nehru and Democracy', *The Asian Age*, 18 November 2018.

contained within itself instruments which, in authoritarian hands, could be instruments of oppression—the Income Tax Department, the Enforcement Directorate, the Department of Revenue Intelligence, the Customs Department and the like. The effort was always to rein in overreach at the lower level.

Not that all was clean, all well-managed. There was corruption, there was misuse of authority. After a full day's work, I used to carry home six boxes of files. Three boxes contained files relating only to disciplinary actions against officials who sought to enrich themselves by corrupt means using the immense regulatory powers at their disposal. Not only in India, but in other countries too, governmental systems can be distorted to promote self-aggrandizement. Governmental systems can be abused to crush opposition and silence dissenting voices but the direction of government policy was always to check abuse. It would indeed be a major calamity for the country if regulatory mechanisms are consciously captured and used to promote authoritarianism. The temptations are many, the means exist and democracy could be uprooted and discarded by rulers who believe in control and direction, rather than in building consensus by listening to differing views and seeking to find acceptable solutions. Consensus-building is the essence of democracy.

Dr Manmohan Singh is a man who believes in democracy, in discussion and debate in taking decisions, leading, as far as possible, to consensus. He is a simple man, who rose from an academic background, through various rungs of the bureaucracy, to the highest position. When he was still an academic, a lecturer in Punjab, an Air Force officer who was regarded as an astrologer of sorts had taken a look at his astrological positions and told him, 'You will be the Finance Minister of India and, later, the Prime Minister.' This was mentioned by his wife, Gursharan Kaur, at one of her dinners. Both of them must have laughed heartily at this unbelievable prediction, but it happened. He entered the bureaucracy as Economic Adviser in the Commerce Ministry in the early '70s, thanks to then Minister L.N. Mishra. His rise up the ladder was meteoric. In just over a decade, he had become Finance Secretary and then Governor of the Reserve Bank. By the mid-'80s, he had spent four years in Geneva as Secretary General of the newly formed South Commission. His Chairman was the formidable Mwalimu Dr Julius Nyerere, revered all over the world as the apostle of South–South unity and inclusive growth. In its report of 1990, titled 'The Challenge to the South', the commission stressed the need for a rapidly expanding economy to satisfy the basic needs of the people, combined with a concern for social justice in the cultural context of each nation and a democratic framework. This was the kind of thought process that imbued the policies of Manmohan Singh as Finance Minister in the early '90s and later as Prime Minister.

Indeed, this unobtrusive, humble man would never have expected to become even a minister. Serendipity often throws up opportunities which would never ordinarily arise. When Narasimha Rao became Prime Minister in 1991—again a consequence of serendipity following the assassination of Rajiv Gandhi and the refusal of Sonia Gandhi to occupy the chair in his place—the economy was in dismal shape. Declining exports and burgeoning imports as oil prices soared at the start of the Gulf War led to a current account deficit of almost 13 per cent. Internal debt of the government had gone up to 53 per cent of the GDP. On top of all this, the Chandrashekhar government could not get its budget passed. Moody's downgraded India below investment grade and even short-term loans were not available to the country in the global market. The situation came to such a pass that we had foreign exchange reserves only to pay for another three weeks of imports. The government of the day had no option but to borrow more than 2 billion dollars from the IMF by ferrying 67 tonnes of gold reserves to the UK and to Switzerland as pledge for the loan.

It was at this critical moment that Narasimha Rao assumed office as Prime Minister. He was clear in his mind that there were no soft options. One of the first decisions he took was to entrust the Ministry of Finance to Manmohan Singh. With vast experience in foreign trade, economic policymaking and knowledge of monetary field to back him, and with an understanding of global development issues in the South Commission, there could be no better man to steer the economy out of troubled times. In normal times, it is unlikely that Manmohan Singh would have become Finance Minister. Finance is a highly prized ministry and the job would have generally gone to a senior political figure in the ruling alliance. The situation was such in 1991 that not many senior contenders would have been vying for the job. It required at that time a man of knowledge and experience not reluctant to take up an economic policy challenge.

Manmohan Singh rose to the challenge quickly, supported by Prime Minister Narasimha Rao, who turned out to be a leader capable of taking difficult decisions and managing them politically, even without a clear majority in Parliament. Presenting his first budget on 24 July 1991, Manmohan Singh said, quoting Victor Hugo, 'No power on earth can stop an idea whose time has come.' Then started a process of dismantling and reconstruction of a kind that was unimaginable. An economy that was closed to the outside world, a thought process attuned to the socialist rhetoric of the past several decades, suddenly underwent dramatic transformation. Taxes were reduced, structural changes took place, the Directorate General of Technical Development was abolished in one stroke, customs duties came down, the door was opened to foreign investment, technology began to flow in as intellectual property rights were recognized and strengthened, the areas reserved for the small-scale sector were sharply curtailed and the crusade against the growth of industry in the name of control over monopolistic power came to an end.

The significance of the reforms of 1991 was that it was a turning point in our economic history, comparable in its width and intensity to the first and second industrial revolutions in Great Britain and Europe, the Meiji Restoration of Japan, the age of Henry Ford and the rise of consumerism in the US, the sweeping reform of the Chinese economy that started with Deng Xiaoping in 1978, the fall of the Soviet Union and the end of extreme forms of socialist order. That this happened in a democratic country headed by a minority government led by men of no great distinction as political leaders; that it took place in a country accustomed to socialist rhetoric; that this happened virtually overnight—these constitute the stuff of miracles in history.

Years later, when I worked with Manmohan Singh as his Cabinet Secretary and he faced recurring attacks from a remorseless Opposition, I would often tell him that a hundred years later, history would recognize him and his comrades in arms during those exciting years of change as the saviours of India, the makers of modernity; people who brought about a sea change in the global balance of economic power.

Perhaps I would never have reached the top had Manmohan Singh not been the Prime Minister. He never sought or demanded shortcuts in public service; he believed in process and he had no goals other than to run a fair and transparent administration beneficial to all, more particularly, the indigent and the deprived. He believed strongly in democracy and spent a great deal of time in the Parliament whenever it was in session. Having been a bureaucrat himself, he understood the ways in which the Indian system works and attached a great deal of importance to integrity, openness and decision-making by building consensus. Indeed, some of the biggest reforms for the poor were initiated in his time as Prime Minister, including guaranteed rural employment, financial inclusion, right to food security and right to education, striking at the roots of the most acute problems faced by rural India.

The Road to the Top

'It's a bizarre but wonderful feeling, to arrive dead centre of a target you didn't even know you were aiming for.'
                                        —*Lois McMaster Bujold*

To reach the top of the civil service is, by and large, a bridge too far for the majority of civil servants. Most services cannot even aspire to the position. IAS officers have hitherto been appointed by virtue of faster promotions, there being more Secretaries from the IAS than other streams.

The content of the Cabinet Secretary's work varies from country to country and also changes from time to time. The only unchanging element of the Cabinet Secretary's work has been that of servicing the Cabinet, examining Cabinet notes received from different ministries and departments and ensuring they are in the format laid down by the Cabinet—that they lucidly state the subject and the points for decision, that all other ministries and departments concerned with the subject have been consulted. It is also the function of the Cabinet Secretary to study each note and to briefly present it before the Cabinet, indicating also differences of opinion, if any, between ministries. When the issue is contentious, and has evoked different views among ministries, Cabinet Secretaries also occasionally advise the Prime Minister on possible ways forward.

This is, however, only one of the many responsibilities that the Cabinet Secretary has to carry out. In the Indian context, the Cabinet Secretary is also the head of all the civil services in the country and, as Secretary to the Appointments Committee of Cabinet, becomes the last link at the official level in the chain that decides appointments of senior officers in the government. However, the major function of the Cabinet Secretary in India has been to coordinate the work of different ministries through the institution of Committees Of Secretaries.

Committees of Secretaries are not uniform, the composition varies from issue to issue and subject to subject. Through such committees, many differences between the various arms of the government are ironed out, and several programmes and projects are monitored. The Cabinet Secretary also becomes the decision-maker, handling emergencies of all kinds, whether they be natural calamities or man-made disasters, inclusive of terrorist action, militancy, even hijacking, particularly when the Home Ministry is not as active as it should be. The Cabinet Secretary also serves often as a point of contact at the official level between the civilian government and the military, even though the major responsibility for internal and external security presently remains with the National Security Adviser.

India adopted the system of having a Cabinet Secretary from the British practice. As stated in the web portal of the Cabinet Secretariat, during the Raj, all the work in government was carried out by the Governor General in Council. Later, as work diversified, the portfolio system came into existence, and work was distributed among members of the Council. Only more important cases came to the Council for collective decision. The Indian Councils Act of 1861 legalized this practice and formed an Executive Council. The Secretariat of the Executive Council was headed by the Viceroy's Private Secretary. The Private Secretary did not, in the beginning, attend Council meetings but this changed with Lord Willingdon. Officially, the Private Secretary was designated Secretary to the Executive Council only in 1935. The link between the Viceroy and his Council is the reason why the Cabinet Secretariat continues, to this day, to be housed in the Rashtrapati Bhavan. The humble beginnings of the position of Cabinet Secretary is probably the reason why the room of the Cabinet Secretary is markedly smaller than the rooms of Secretaries in charge of the various ministries and departments.

In 1945, Lord Wavell, as Viceroy, constituted a Coordination Committee for war resources and reconstruction. In his note of 22 October 1945 to the Secretary of State, Wavell stated,

Sir Eric Coates is setting up a small secretariat, which, I hope, may develop later into a real Council Secretariat capable of serving the Executive Council and its committees and also perhaps a committee of Indian Defence. Sir Eric Coates is to take over shortly as Secretary of the Executive Council in addition to his present duties, and the Secretariat will then become a proper Cabinet Secretariat, as was always intended.

When Coates was replaced by A.E. Porter as Council Secretary, the Executive Council's Secretariat became the Cabinet Secretariat.

There was apparently a difference of opinion between Nehru and Sardar Patel, with the former preferring a strong Prime Minister's Office and the latter a strong Cabinet Secretariat. This went to Lord Mountbatten, who left it to Nehru to decide. Ultimately, Nehru decided to retain the Cabinet Secretariat. Ever since, there has always been a sense of unease between the Prime Minister's Office and the Cabinet Secretariat. Which of the two has prevailed at what time has depended greatly on the authority of the Prime Minister and the perceived relative influence and capacity of the Cabinet Secretary and the Principal Secretary to the Prime Minister.

The Cabinet Secretariat in India has undergone significant change over the years. In the initial years after Independence, the status of the Cabinet Secretary was the same as that of other central government Secretaries and one rung below the Chiefs of the Army, Air Force and Navy. The position of the Cabinet Secretary in the work hierarchy was, however, on the ascendant.

Proximity to the Prime Minister, the acumen of successive Cabinet Secretaries and the fact that it had a role in selection of senior officials of all wings of the government gave the position increasing importance. Despite the coordinating role that the Cabinet Secretary had assumed over the years, despite the fact that central government Secretaries had begun to use the Cabinet Secretary as an accessible sounding board in respect of various problems that they faced from time to time, he still remained at the same level as other Secretaries. As the Fourth Pay Commission, headed by Justice Singhal, observed in 1986, 'The post of Chairman, Atomic Energy Commission, is the only civilian post at present on a pay of Rs. 4,000/-(fixed).'[28]

Sensing that the Cabinet Secretary had become a nodal position in administration, it was the Fourth Pay Commission that decided to raise the level of the post. The Commission stated: 'The Cabinet Secretary ranks highest among officers of the central government. He has a very important role as coordinator at the inter-ministerial level. In view of the importance of the duties and responsibilities of the post, we recommend the pay of Rs. 9,000/-(fixed) for it.'(Para10.511). This was the highest pay for any official at the time both in the Armed Forces and the civilian administration. Other perquisites, such as a dedicated bungalow in Lutyens' Delhi, staff to manage the house and its lawns,

---

28   Fourth Pay Commission Report, Part I, *CGS Publication India* (June 1986), http://www.cgspublicationindia.com/Pdf/Pay%20Commissions/ Fourth%20Pay%20Commission/4th%20CPC%20(Report,%20Part 1,%20Vol%20I%20to%20IV).pdf.

staff to manage the Camp Office of the Cabinet Secretary and the 'Z' category security status with its concomitant security personnel came later.

After Independence, the Cabinet Secretariat expanded and contracted its role several times and the content of its work at any point of time was merely a matter of circumstance. The subjects the Cabinet Secretary has to deal with are varied and motley. This can both be an advantage and a disadvantage. It is an advantage because it gives him the space to pry into all areas in which he is interested. It is a disadvantage because nothing is ever fixed and work can be taken away from him with the same facility as work can be entrusted to him.

Besides, if the work is too flexible and indeterminate, the element of continuity and stability in administration is lost. The Central Personnel Agency was created under the Secretariat in 1949 and an economic wing and an electronics wing were added the next year. The Central Statistical Organisation and later, the Department of Statistics, the National Sample Survey, the Director General of Resettlement, the Department of Personnel and Administrative Reform and the Bureau of Public Enterprises were all part of the Cabinet Secretariat at some point of time.

The Cabinet Secretary also coordinated matters of national security for many years. It was only in November 1998, when Atal Bihari Vajpayee was the Prime Minister, that the position of National Security Adviser (NSA) was created, with Vajpayee's Principal Secretary Brajesh Mishra becoming the first NSA in charge of both internal and external security. The possibility of confusion among roles in managing matters relating to security has existed since. The intelligence agencies and paramilitary agencies report on all operational matters to the NSA. The Research and Analysis Wing reports administratively to the Cabinet Secretary but operationally to the NSA. The agencies under the Home Ministry and armed forces intelligence do not usually brief the Cabinet Secretary on field issues, preferring to give the juicy bits only to the Home Ministry or the Defence Ministry or the NSA.

At the same time, without sufficient and timely information, the Cabinet Secretary is still required to deal with crisis situations, whether it be a terrorist attack or a hijack or militant extremism of various kinds. This arrangement is not conducive to effective management of crises. There were several occasions in my tenure when I worked virtually blindly, without complete knowledge of what had transpired and what the intelligence agencies knew. One such instance was 26/11, where prior knowledge would have certainly helped in dealing with the situation faster. Terrorist activity could also definitely have been controlled more effectively had intelligence been coordinated better. Likewise, lack of complete information also resulted in confused action when Anna Hazare and then Baba Ramdev launched agitations against corruption and black money.

The role and status of the Cabinet Secretary varies from country to country. The position of Cabinet Secretary in Australia was held by a sitting member of Parliament, until the position itself was abolished in 2017. In Canada, the equivalent position is called Clerk of the Privy Council. In Japan, again, the Chief Cabinet Secretary is of the rank of minister, as is the case in the Philippines. In Pakistan and Sri Lanka, however, the Cabinet Secretary is of the same rank as other Permanent Secretaries to the government. In the United States, there is a Cabinet Secretary within the Executive Office of the President which deals with the relations between members of the Cabinet and the White House. In the UK, the Cabinet Secretary initially carried out the functions of both the Secretary to the Prime Minister and the Head of Civil Service, but these positions were separated in 2005.

On 19 May 2007, I was summoned to the Prime Minister's house to meet him forthwith. He received me in his room and we chatted over a cup of tea. Manmohan Singh was a man of extreme humility, never projecting what he had achieved for the country, never displaying a trace of arrogance or pride. It was a hot summer day when we met and excessive perspiration has always been the bane of my life. My friend Vinod Rai used to tell me that I had the remarkable capacity to stand motionless at any place and have a pool of sweat form around my feet. I do not recall whether the air-conditioned room was cool enough to suppress my sweating or whether he thought I was excessively nervous or if I was having a heart attack. But he did ask about my health and whether I considered myself fit enough to hold the highest position in the civil service. As was usual with him, he had done his homework. He had asked a number of his colleagues and senior civil servants, people in whom he had faith and trust. This, I found later, was part of his stock in trade. On any issue, he would seek my opinion as well as that of some others and then make up his mind. Therefore, the opinions expressed by some others, who were never particularly close to him and definitely not a part of his inner circle, about his decision-making abilities and his dependence on the party chief are far from the truth and a deliberate attempt to tarnish the image of a good man whose contribution to the making of history will far outweigh the feeble efforts of his more aggressive peers.

The Prime Minister obviously thought I would be right for the job. Later in the evening, the Establishment Officer rang up, congratulated me and sought to come and personally give me the appointment order, as is the usual convention when Cabinet Secretaries are appointed. My appointment as Cabinet Secretary is another story of serendipity. I was among the top three in my batch and Ravi Sethi, my immediate senior in the batch, chose to resign from the civil services even before he completed the mandatory twenty years to qualify for pension. He became a highly successful entrepreneur in the field of real estate. Anuradha Mansingh, who had topped my batch, was a year older than me and had retired; seniority in a batch does not guarantee that an officer will reach the top position. Only one person in two or three batches could therefore aspire to be Cabinet Secretary. At that time, tenures of Cabinet Secretaries had also been fixed at two years. During the '90s, officers from the odd-year batches alone could reach the top—1961, 1963, 1965 and so on. Officers belonging to even-year batches had to perforce retire as Secretaries. I belonged to an even-year batch, 1970, and hence should have quietly retired into the shadows in 2008, when I reached the age of sixty. But then, serendipity or destiny or whatever one chooses to call it came into play.

Usually, Cabinet Secretaries, as a matter of happenstance, would assume office in the month of October and remain in office until October in the next but one year. Governments, again as a matter of electoral chance, assume office in June. In 2004, the unexpected happened. The Vajpayee government, expected to return to office easily, was toppled and a new Congress-led UPA government came to power. Manmohan Singh was the fortuitous head of this government, Sonia Gandhi having refused the chair. Kamal Pande was then the Cabinet Secretary. In the usual course, he would have continued until October that year and Manmohan would have had no problem with that, but he came under pressure from the parties forming the UPA to change the Cabinet Secretary. Hence, Pande could not complete his quota of two years and had to leave office in June. At that time, as one officer later told me, a 'beauty parade' of senior officers was held by the PM and he chose B.K. Chaturvedi, an officer with whom he had worked, who was not the senior-most. The senior-most officer was Dipak Chatterjee, who was later rewarded with the position of Indian Ambassador in Brussels as compensation for having been overlooked. The 'odd year' jinx was broken as Chaturvedi belonged to the 1966 batch.

But serendipity had not completed its mission. Chaturvedi should have finished his two-year tenure and left in 2006, and someone from the 1969 batch should have assumed office. I had no expectations, therefore, and only hoped that my colleague, Adarsh Kishore, then Finance Secretary, would become Cabinet Secretary, and I would have a shot at the office of Comptroller and Auditor General (CAG), which was falling vacant in 2007. At that point, I would have been the senior-most Secretary in the Finance Ministry and, therefore, would have a legitimate reason to be considered for appointment as the CAG. But then events took a strange new twist when top officers from the

1969 batch lobbied with ministers and cast aspersions on each other in the media. I was told by one of his private secretaries that the Prime Minister was perturbed by what was happening and he chose instead to give an extension of one year to Chaturvedi. When he completed his third year, I was the most senior among all officers to be considered for the top position, Anuradha having retired. Manmohan did look at some of the top officers available for appointment, but with my experience and record of work, he had no difficulty in selecting me. My way to the top was thus paved by a string of coincidences and unanticipated events, which, I now firmly believe, define life itself. In the words of Rossana Condoleo, author and life coach, 'When we tried to contain reality, to define it, to write down its laws, we failed. We should recognize the universe its right to be unpredictable.'[29]

---

29   Rossana Condoleo, *Happy Divorce: How to Turn Your Divorce into the Most Brilliant & Rewarding Opportunity of Your Life!*, CreateSpace Independent Publishing Platform, 2013.

Cutting My Teeth as Cabinet Secretary

'At first, they'll only dislike what you say, but the more correct you start sounding, the more they'll dislike you.'

—*Criss Jamy*

I must begin by saying that I do not exactly recall the sequence of issues as they occurred during my tenure as the Cabinet Secretary. The post of Cabinet Secretary was quite different from any other that I had held before. I was not reporting to a minister but directly to the Prime Minister and he was sitting in a different office or in his official residence. No longer did I need to consult with or get approval from other departments or ministries; instead, it was my role to settle differences between others. It was difficult in the beginning to adjust to a situation in which I was presiding over meetings attended by my friends and colleagues and taking decisions with which one or more of them may disagree. Indeed, it was embarrassing that one of the very first meetings I held was for reviewing the cadre of my home state, Kerala, because old colleagues from the state were present at the meeting and pressing for additional posts in the cadre, which I had to deny as Cabinet Secretary.

One of the earliest completed tasks in my memory is getting the Enron project going again. This happened in my first year, 2007. The credit for this goes largely to my predecessor, B.K. Chaturvedi, who had worked at it with bulldog tenacity, talking to technical people, the Ministry of Power, commercial banks, the Maharashtra government and the Empowered Committee of Ministers headed by Pranab Mukherjee. I observed in initial meetings that wrangling continued and new problems were constantly being raised. I decided, therefore, that a great deal of time had already been spent on trying to untangle the knots and that the immediate task at hand was to bring the matter to closure. Fortunately, the Empowered Committee of Ministers had also tired of this subject and at a meeting held late in the evening in South Block, final decisions were taken. Once high-level interest is taken in any matter, it is the practice of lower officials to push upwards every problem for resolution. I advised Pranab Mukherjee to discourage this and not to allow a committee of ministers to be treated like a board of directors. This was firmly conveyed by him and the project began to move forward under its own steam.

One other major issue that came to me in 2007 was the pricing of natural gas. The Ambani brothers, Mukesh and Anil, were at loggerheads at that time. There was a big dispute over property, settled ultimately by their mother, Kokilaben, with the help of top lawyers and finance experts, including P. Chidambaram. Anil felt that he had been short-changed in the process and, even as the properties were divided, resentment continued. The pricing of natural gas in the Krishna Godavari basin was a complicated issue, passed on by the Prime Minister to a committee of Secretaries, headed by me as Cabinet Secretary. This task was not easy as the Ambani brothers were influential at all levels.

The support of the knowledgeable Surya Sethi, Advisor in the Planning Commission, who had many years of experience in the energy sector and of my Joint Secretary, Atma Ram Sihag, both models of integrity, was invaluable to me.

There were many things wrong with the process of price fixation. While Mukesh was proposing a gas pricing formula that would yield a price exceeding $4.50 at the prevailing crude oil prices, Anil flaunted an agreement which the two brothers had reached, wherein Mukesh had agreed to supply gas to his younger brother's power plants at $2.34 per metric million British thermal unit (MMBTU). The significant fact was that this price of about two dollars had been discovered through an international tender initiated by the National Thermal Power Corporation (NTPC) in June 2004 for supply of 132 trillion units of natural gas annually to its power plants in Kawas and Gandhar. Reliance had won the bid against Petronas of Malaysia. However, they later reneged from the deal. The NTPC went to court but the case was not fought vigorously. There were many things wrong with the entire process of price fixation. The Krishna Godavari basin was to be developed as part of the New Exploration and Licensing Policy (NELP), whereby large stretches of land—discovery areas—were made available to private sector operators under the terms of a Production Sharing Contract (PSC) for exploration, production and sale at a market-driven, arms-length price. Reliance had acquired the rights to the D6 block, an area of about 7,500 square kilometres during the NDA regime in 2000. This itself was wrong, according to Surya Sethi, because the license was intended to be given only to upstream oil and gas sector companies with experience in exploration and production of natural hydrocarbon resources. Reliance had no such prior experience.

I spent an intense two weeks speaking to all stakeholders. At the end, I came to the conclusion that the price Mukesh was demanding was too high. Having agreed to a price of $2.34 both with the NTPC and with his brother, it looked suspicious that he now sought a higher price. Natural gas can only be traded across borders after massive investments in either the necessary pipeline infrastructure—including multiple high pressure gas compression stations—or by making equally large investments in liquefying natural gas and shipping the liquefied natural gas (LNG) in specially built cryogenic vessels and regasification by importers thereafter. Thus, unlike crude oil, a freely traded commodity in its natural form, there is no international price for natural gas.

The higher price was being defended on the basis of a formula developed by Reliance, linked to the price of crude oil. Such linkage was, as Surya Sethi argued, unique, unprecedented and without a parallel. The token 'price discovery' exercise done by Reliance was also flawed because only a select group of end users had been included. My point was that a cost-plus formula should be used and that the CAG should be involved in determining this price. Also, when Reliance had agreed to sell the gas at a price of $2.34, a price discovered through international bidding, I could not see any logical reason for justifying a price in excess of four dollars. A lower price, in my view, would be more beneficial to the country as it would lower the costs of downstream users, particularly the power sector and fertilizer industry, that together accounted for about 80 per cent of gas consumption.

There were other problems, too, with the deal. The NELP provision itself was worded in such a manner that the successful bidder can get the bulk of the revenue accruing from the lease in the initial years, with returns to government accruing only after the bidder had appropriated 2.5 times the capital cost. This allowed the bidder to gold-plate the initial investment and thus ensure that hardly any revenue would accrue to the government, for a natural asset that belonged to the people of India. My view was that the cost actually incurred needed to be concurrently audited, in order to ensure that deliberate inflation of costs and the consequent loss to government can be minimized, if not eliminated altogether. This was later confirmed in a CAG report, which observed: 'As per the PSC, more investments, especially in initial stages would mean more profit for the operator and less for the government. This structure gives inadequate incentive for operators to reduce capital expenditure and provides them with substantial incentives to "front end" capital expenditure.'[30]

I submitted the report to the Prime Minister and there was, at once, a huge uproar. As I was not entirely sure about the reliability and neutrality of some who attended meetings of the Committee of Secretaries, I submitted the report as a Cabinet Secretary's report. The immediate response was that the matter was referred to C. Rangarajan, then Chairman of the PM's Economic Advisory Council. An Empowered Group of Ministers, headed by Pranab Mukherjee, was also constituted. Rangarajan neither questioned nor rejected any of the arguments put forth by Surya Sethi. In fact, much of his report supported the stand taken by Sethi. Nevertheless, the dubious formula was accepted with minor tweaks, including a dollar-based pricing instead of the proposed rupee-based pricing.

The formula remained deeply flawed as it gave a price far in excess of prices prevalent in several other comparable countries, had no linkage to costs and conveniently ignored the fact that Reliance itself had bid a sale price of $2.34/MMBTU for seventeen years in response to an international tender floated by the NTPC to beat the bid made by Petronas of Malaysia that had quoted $2.79/MMBTU. Rangarajan's recommendations were accepted by the Empowered Group of Ministers, which, for form's sake, accepted a slightly lower price of $4.20/MMBTU.

I read a later interview of Surya Sethi with Prabir Purkayastha for NewsClick on 14 July 2011, in which he said that he had shown to the Empowered Group of Ministers how gas was priced in more than fifty countries, why it was wrong to fix prices of natural gas on the basis of Reliance's formula and the fact that—based on data submitted by Reliance to the Director General Hydrocarbons—the cost of production was not more than $1.43, at worst, and may even

---

30   Shishir Asthana, '10 Things You Should Know about the Reliance KG-D6 Gas Deal', *Business Standard*, 18 February 2014.

be less than a dollar. He said he placed these facts in writing before the ministers but Reliance's formula triumphed at the end of the day.[31] Indeed, the investment multiple and the formula for profit-sharing were efficiently used by Reliance right from the start. In their initial development plan, Reliance had projected a production of 40 million standard cubic metres of gas per day (mmscmd) for an investment of $2.39 billion.

In terms of the sweet deal signed by the NDA in 2000, every additional rupee of approved investment by Reliance by way of capex would give a return of Rs 2.5. In 2006, Reliance submitted a revised plan. They said they would produce double the quantity (80 mmscmd) at about four times the cost ($8.8 billion). As the increase in cost was disproportionate, the then minister demurred. He was promptly changed and given a less significant portfolio.[32] As expected, production was also well below projection at 27 mmscmd. The CAG, in its report of 2016, stated that Reliance had made excess cost recovery of $1.6 billion between 2012 and 2014.[33] It was also reported that in terms of the initial contract, Reliance was required to vacate acreage not in use after a stipulated period of time. The CAG reported that Reliance was still occupying about 832 square kilometres more than they were entitled to. Prima facie, it would appear from a perusal of facts reported by various news outlets that successive governments have enriched a company and an individual at the cost of the nation. The K.G. Basin episode did not stop with inflation of costs and loss of revenue to the

31   NewsClick, 'KG Basin deal: Murky valuation of gas prices & production costs,' 14 July 2011, https://www.newsclick.in/kg-basin-deal-murky-valuation-gas-prices-production-costs

32   Prashant Bhushan, 'Kya Congress Mukesh Ambani Ki Dukaan Hai?', *Outlook*, 27 January 2022, https://www.outlookindia.com/website/story/kya-congress-mukesh-ambani-ki-dukaan-hai/282815

33   PTI, 'CAG Red-Flags $1.6 Billion Excess Cost Recovery by RIL', *The Economic Times*, 2 August 2016.

K.M. Chandrasekhar with other probationary officers at the National Civil Services Academy, Mussoorie, 1970.

Author's collection

As Managing Director, Travancore Titanium Products Ltd, 1978.

Author's collection

The author and Ambassador Pradeep Kumar Singh meeting Romano Prodi, President of European Commission, in Brussels, 2001.

Author's collection

Speaking at the international conference of the Institute of Chartered Accountants of India, New Delhi, 2005.

Photo Division, Government of India

Attending the India-Brazil-South Africa Customs Cooperation meeting at Pretoria, 2006.

Author's collection

K.M. Chandrasekhar, assuming charge as the Union Cabinet Secretary, New Delhi, 13 June 2007.

Photo Division, Government of India

The author on a safari ride with family at the Rathambhore National Park in 2008.

Author's collection

Seen here with his wife at the Samadhi of Sri Sai Baba at Shirdi, 2009.

Author's collection

Former Prime Minister Manmohan Singh holding a meeting with the captains of Indian Industry to discuss the impact of the global recession on Indian economy in New Delhi, 28 March 2009.

Photo Division, Government of India

K.M. Chandrasekhar delivering the inaugural address, as the union cabinet secretary, at the SAARC Workshop on Government Performance Management, New Delhi, 30 March 2010.

Photo Division, Government of India

Seen here at the Nathu-La Pass in Sikkim, 2010.

Author's collection

Seen here attending a Civil Services Day event with former Prime Minister Manmohan Singh in April, 2010.

Photo Division, Government of India

K.M. Chandrasekhar addressing the annual conference of Chief Secretaries in New Delhi, 2010.

Photo Division, Government of India

Attending a Civil Services Day reception with the then President Pratibha Patil, Vice President Hamid Ansari and Chief Justice K.G. Balakrishnan, 2010.

Author's collection

K.M. Chandrasekhar holding a press conference on National e-Governance Plan (NeGP) and on various e-services offered under the programme in New Delhi, 16 July 2010.

Photo Division, Government of India

With former chairman of SEBI, U.K. Sinha, and its other members in 2011.

Author's collection

Attending the Kerala State Planning Board meeting with its then Chief Minister Oommen Chandy and other board members, 7 October 2011.

Public Relations Department, Government of Kerala

At the Planning Board Members' meeting with Oommen Chandy and the Planning Commission Deputy Chairman, Montek Singh Ahluwalia, in 2012.

Public Relations Department, Government of Kerala

Seen here at the launch of the Kerala Perspective Plan 2030 by Oommen Chandy on 13 July 2015.

Public Relations Department, Government of Kerala

K.M. Chandrasekhar at the signing of the concession agreement for the Vizhinjam International Deepwater Multipurpose Seaport by Gautam Adani and Oommen Chandy on 17 August 2015.

Public Relations Department, Government of Kerala

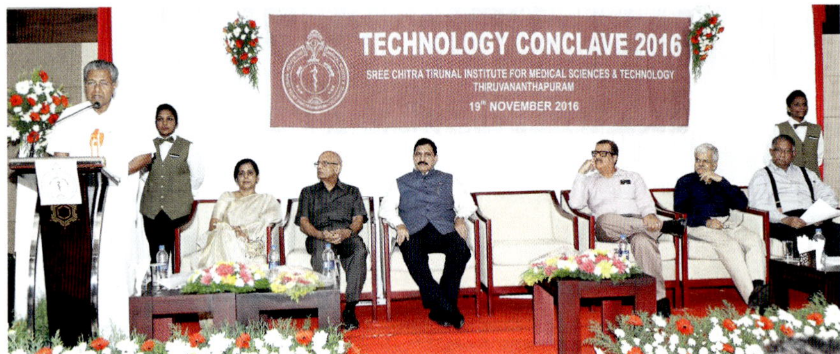

Attending the Technology Conclave at Sree Chitra Tirunal Institute of Medical Science and Technology, Thiruvananthapuram, on 19 November 2016.

Public Relations Department, Government of Kerala

Delivering a lecture to Kerala cabinet ministers at the Institute of Management in Government, Thiruvananthapuram, 2021.

Public Relations Department, Government of Kerala

government. Gas had apparently flown into the Reliance-owned block from the adjoining blocks under the control of the Oil and Natural Gas Corporation (ONGC). As the gas belonged to the state and not to the ONGC, it was the state that was the loser. The ONGC did not report the flow of gas into Reliance's field for six years. The Justice A.P. Shah Committee, appointed by the Ministry of Petroleum and Natural Gas in 2015, after going through the rules and the contracts, and after hearing the stakeholders out, concluded that 'RIL's actions of producing and selling the gas migrated from ONGC's blocks to its block amount to unjust enrichment' (Para 8.1) and that 'the Government of India, and not ONGC, is entitled to claim restitution from RIL for the unjust benefit it received and unfairly retained' (Para 10.2.7).[34] The quantification of the claim to be made on Reliance was left to the government. The government accordingly made a claim of $1.55 billion, but this claim was turned down by an arbitration panel.

The story of gas pricing did not end there. In 2013, the Cabinet approved the doubling of the well-head price of gas to $8.40/MMBTU, based on the recommendations of another committee headed by Rangarajan. In a lead op-ed in *The Hindu* dated 18 January 2013, titled 'Making a Mockery of Domestic Gas Pricing', Surya Sethi asks:

'Can the committee identify any significant independent conventional gas field in the world that receives or has received this high a well head price for dry natural gas year after year on arms-length basis?'

He emphatically made the point that nowhere in the world is the well-head price of natural gas laid down on the basis of a formula linked to an adjusted price of natural gas at an international gas hub or a basket

---

34 'Report of the Committee on Dispute Regarding Oil and Gas Blocks in KG Basin', Minsitry of Petroleum and Natural Gas (29 August 2016), http://petroleum.nic.in/sites/default/files/KGReport.pdf

of adjusted prices at a number of international gas hubs. Gas prices that various international gas hubs follow vary widely across the world and, perhaps, the only transparent, market-based discovery of natural gas prices is in North America, which allows competitive pricing in an independently regulated market with multiple suppliers and consumers wherein supply and demand are well-balanced.

The elections of 2014, however, put paid to the implementation of this Cabinet decision. The new NDA government re-examined the pricing of natural gas recommended by the 2013 Rangarajan Committee and came out with an improved formula in October 2014 that yielded a gas price of about $5.55/MMBTU against the then prevailing gas prices between $4.2–$5.25/MMBTU. Some of the elements of the new Rangarajan formula, such as the high weightage given to Japanese and Indian LNG-linked prices, were discarded, and better markers were used for calculating well head prices, of the US, Russian and Canadian gas. Also, the new formula shifted to the international norm of pricing based on gross calorific value.

With the fall in the prices of oil and gas worldwide, the price of natural gas also came down as the link prices declined. Now the government has come out recently with a new policy called HELP, Hydrocarbon Exploration and Licensing Policy. This replaces the New Exploration and Licensing Policy. This applies to all hydrocarbons, including shale oil and coal bed methane. On the face of it, this is simpler as it seeks to replace the existing, complicated investment multiple-based formula through revenue sharing. It also simplifies price discovery. As Amitav Ranjan puts it in his article:

Promoters will now be encouraged to develop their deep sea finds as their ceiling price would be lowest of the (i) fuel oil import landed price (ii) weighted average import landed price of substitute fuels (coal, fuel oil and naphtha) and (iii) LNG import landed price. This formula would result in an 85 per cent jump in rates to $7.08 per million British thermal units from the government-regulated \$3.15 per mBtu that comes into effect from 1 April.[35]

The saga of 'heads I win, tails you lose' continues.

Another major issue that came up in my early days was the Sethusamudram issue. The Sethusamudram shipping canal was a pet project of the DMK, a close ally of the Congress and important partner in the UPA. The project involved digging an 83-kilometre channel in the sea connecting the shallow Palk Strait with the Gulf of Mannar. The idea, developed by A.D. Taylor in the mid-nineteenth century, was intended to create a navigable passage through the shoals called Adam's Bridge between the southern tip of India and Sri Lanka, so that ships would not have to circle around Sri Lanka to reach India's eastern coast. There was a big controversy as the BJP and other Hindu groups opposed cutting the shoals, mythically stated to have been built by Sri Rama for the movement of his soldiers into Lanka. To them, Adam's Bridge was Ram Setu, a bridge created by Lord Rama. Under enormous pressure from the Tamil Nadu government and the DMK, the project was launched with great fanfare by the UPA government. Immediately, the matter was taken to court and a huge controversy arose on an affidavit filed by the Archaeological Survey of India under the Ministry of Culture, which seemed to question the historicity of Rama and of the epic Ramayana.

The Hindu groups and the BJP were up in arms while the DMK was equally adamant. Manmohan Singh, in the middle of the spat, was searching for a way forward. I spent countless hours wading through maps and talking to lawyer Minister Kapil Sibal, to the ubiquitous man for all seasons, Pranab Mukherjee, and technical experts and oceanographers. We tried to work out alternative routes avoiding

---

35   Amit Ranjan, 'Profit Share to Revenue Share, Multiple Windows to Single: HELP for Explorers', *The Indian Express*, 16 March 2016, https://indianexpress.com/article/explained/profit-share-to-revenue-share-multiple-windows-to-single-help-for-explorers/

Adam's Bridge. The existence of an oceanic biosphere on the east coast further compounded the problem. The intensity of the dispute was so great that, once, Manmohan asked me whether I thought the government would fall under the weight of Sethusamudram.

As my relationship with Minister T.R. Baalu, confidante of the Tamil Nadu Chief Minister, was good, I managed to keep a link with one of the warring sides even as the battle went on. Ultimately, the Supreme Court asked the government to consider another possible route for the canal, which we had considered earlier in our discussions and found unfeasible. However, the Supreme Court's query gave us hope of a way out of the burgeoning crisis. I suggested the formation of a committee headed by the eminent environmentalist R.K. Pachauri to examine the feasibility of the route suggested by the Supreme Court. Baalu thought well of Pachauri and agreed, but asked me to speak to him to give the report within weeks. Pachauri, expert scientist that he was, said that he needed a full year to study the seasonal movement of tides and currents. In 2015, Solicitor General Rohinton Nariman told the Supreme Court that the Pachauri Committee did not find the alternative alignment feasible as it could 'potentially result in ecological threat that could pose a risk to the ecosystem in the surrounding areas and in particular to the biosphere reserve (Gulf of Mannar)'.[36] Finally, in 2018, in response to a petition filed in the Supreme Court by Subramaniam Swamy, the government said that it would not touch Ram Setu and would explore other possibilities.

36 Anupam Chakravarthy, 'Sethusamudram Alternative Route Not Feasible', *Down to Earth* (2 July 2012), https://www.downtoearth.org.in/news/sethusamudram-alternative-route-not-feasible-report-38606

India and the Great Recession

'Economics, politics and personalities are often inseparable.'
—*Charles Edison*

The global financial crisis of 2008 was the single most important emergency that tested the capacity of Manmohan Singh in his first tenure to weather difficult situations. The crisis started in the United States in 2006–07 in the sub-prime mortgage market and grew into a full-fledged global phenomenon that engulfed India, among other countries. The prelude to the crisis was a prolonged period of calm, stability, sustained growth and low inflation in the global economy over many years. A mild recession sparked off a series of interest rate cuts by the Federal Reserve, as many as eleven times, from 6.5 per cent in May 2000 to 1.75 per cent in December 2001, thus substantially injecting liquidity into the market. With so much cheap money sloshing around, banks and financing institutions chose housing mortgages as the favoured channel for funnelling credit, particularly since affordable housing had become a prime policy objective of the federal government. 'In the US, benign macroeconomic conditions sparked off a housing boom funded through an increase in mortgages originated by banks and non-banks.'[37] This also induced speculation as real home prices rose by 85 per cent from 1997–2006. The underlying expectation was that real estate prices would continue to rise and rise, and that the upward growth spiral would be unlimited. It was also expected that if at all the bubble burst, the bits and pieces would be picked up by government institutions and the Federal Reserve.

This seemed to be too good an opportunity for big finance to pass up. Housing debts were repackaged with other high-risk debts and sold to eager financial investors, creating financial instruments called Collateralized Debt Obligations or CDOs, a form of mortgage-backed derivative. The risk was thus passed on manifold through derivatives trade. The entry of big finance into the mortgage market was on the back of high leveraging. Derivatives trade in financial markets, supported by low interest debt of a high order, replaced genuine house buying and selling activity, thus making the bubble grow and grow, until it inevitably burst. As Alan Greenspan, former Governor of the Federal Reserve and a votary of animal spirits in the economy put it, 'The very nature of finance is that it cannot be profitable unless it is significantly leveraged … and as long as there is debt, there can be failure and contagion.'[38]

In early 2008, a major US investment bank, Bear Stearns, was sold on an emergency basis. The second largest US investment bank, Lehman Brothers, went bankrupt. Another big investment bank, Merrill Lynch, merged with a commercial bank. The capital adequacy

---

37   Adarsh Kishore, Michael Debabrata Patra and Partha Ray, *The Global Economic Crisis through an Indian Looking Glass* (New Delhi: Sage Publications, 2011), p.16.

38   Gillian Tett, 'An Interview with Alan Greenspan', *Financial Times*, 25 October 2013.

of Fannie May and Freddie Mac, home mortgage companies created by the US government, came under increasing pressure. The financial markets were in turmoil and the contagion spread worldwide, affecting severely global capital flows, global trade and global growth. As credit became increasingly vulnerable, deleveraging took place almost in a panic mode and a huge credit crunch enveloped the world. National stimulus packages became the order of the day in all major economies.

The years before the crisis had been great years for India. India had become a US$1 trillion economy in 2007–08. The rate of growth of per capita income had accelerated to more than 7 per cent in the previous five-year period as compared to 3 per cent to 4 per cent in the preceding two decades. Despite the conservative stance of the Indian monetary policy for years, the malaise was sure to affect a large and growing economy like India, whose global interface had been increasing steadily since the sweeping economic reforms of 1991. Liquidity seemed to disappear overnight from the market. The call money rate rose dramatically from 9 per cent on 8 September 2008 to about 20 per cent a month later.

'In responding to the crisis, it is essential for public policy to resist the temptation to excessively focus on measures recommended by international institutions and ignore the unique features of the Indian economy.'[39] For India, the answer lay in the Government of India and the Reserve Bank, then led by D. Subbarao, acting in sync with one another. It was a test of complete harmony and cohesion between the fiscal and monetary policies—mutual coordination and support between two great arms of policy in the economic sphere. In later years, I watched with consternation a developing conflict between the Reserve Bank and the government, as Reserve Bank Governors immaturely fought with the government for 'autonomy', regardless of the needs of

---

39   Kishore, Patra and Ray, *The Global Economic Crisis through an Indian Looking Glass*, p.143.

the economy and the people of India, and I could not help but reflect on the unity of action displayed by them in those difficult days.

Montek Singh Ahluwalia, then Deputy Chairman of the Planning Commission, prepared the first stimulus package aimed at revving up the economy and stimulating certain affected sectors like automobiles. I worked with him to add a few elements like an across-the-board cut in excise duties. Dr Manmohan Singh, who was holding charge of the Ministry of Finance at the time, asked me to discuss the package with Pranab Mukherjee and P. Chidambaram, then Home Minister, formerly Finance Minister. I recall that Chidambaram asked me in particular whether overall cuts in excise duty were necessary. I told him that a clean cut across all products was better than sectoral cuts, as otherwise we would be battling with problems of duty inversion for a long time. The package contained a slew of measures aimed at stimulating consumption, promoting investment and exports and specific measures to support hard-hit sectors like housing, automobiles, textiles and small and medium industries.

The first stimulus package was announced on the evening of 7 December at a press conference by Montek, jointly with Ashok Chawla, then Secretary (Economic Affairs), and me. Before the press conference, Montek requested me to call Subbarao and see if the Reserve Bank could come out with a supportive package on the same day. Surely enough, an hour after the fiscal policy package was announced, Subbarao announced further measures to ease liquidity. The combined effect was electric.

The Reserve Bank played a major role in containing the crisis in India. The bank rates were reduced significantly, the Statutory Liquidity Ratio and the Cash Reserve Ratio were cut, financial markets were given confidence and many other measures were taken to infuse liquidity. I, on my part, encouraged commercial banks to convert the easing of liquidity announced by the Reserve Bank into more investment and more consumption, through greater outflow of credit. Along with Montek, I also endeavoured to make statements intended to revive confidence in the market. I held several meetings with industry associations to bolster their confidence. I had a colleague and friend, an outstanding officer, who, in the later years of his career, developed a great fascination for the media. Whenever he saw any group of media persons, particularly those with TV cameras, he would be magnetically drawn towards them. The media could ask him any question on any matter and pat would come his answer, regardless of whether he knew anything about it or not. He saw a great media opportunity in the crisis and promptly announced that half a million jobs had been lost. I had to ring him up perforce and tell him that our role was to talk up the economy, not to create more alarm.

Another fiscal stimulus package was announced a few weeks later. The net result, as stated by Stephen S. Roach, Chairman, Morgan Stanley Asia, was that 'India sailed through the Great Crisis of 2008 without barely missing a beat.'[40] However, it is my belief that the stimulus package, intended to serve a particular purpose at a particular period of time, could have been withdrawn in phases earlier than it actually was. This is the problem with all concessions. Once given, there are political constraints against their withdrawal.

Every crisis, political, economic or military, has its lessons to teach. For the US, as Janet Yellen, later Governor of the Federal Reserve and presently the Treasury Secretary, said, 'New financial tools, which the Federal Reserve developed to respond to the financial crisis and the Great Recession, are likely to remain useful in dealing with future downturns.'[41] It would have been great if India had learnt three lessons from this crisis. First, let us not be guided in our policy responses by what we hear from international agencies or experts sitting abroad.

40   Stephen S. Roach, '2008 Crisis a Wake-Up Call for India', *The Economic Times*, 2 June 2010, https://economictimes.indiatimes.com/opinion/et-commentary/2008-crisis-a-wake-up-call-for-india/articleshow/6000712.cms

41   'Janet Yellen's Speech to Jackson Hole: Full Text', *Financial Express*, 26 August 2016.

They do not know India and Indians. We are enthusiastic people; we quickly respond in full measure to action that is being taken. The recent experiment with demonetization shows that our people are willing even to pay for the mistakes of their leaders, provided they believe these actions were performed in good faith. The second lesson is that there is nothing that we cannot overcome if all the arms of governance—and here, I include the Reserve Bank—work in unison towards a common goal that is material to the country. The third lesson is that measures taken to deal with a crisis must be unwound when normalcy is restored. This is something we failed to do in the years following the crisis. In her book, *The Lost Decade: 2008–18*, Puja Mehra distinguishes four different phases in those ten years.[42] The first was 2008–09, when the economy had to undergo a severe shock, imposed by the global effects of the sub-prime crisis that rocked the financial sector in the US. The author speaks of the unrelenting faith of the then Governor of American Federal Reserve Alan Greenspan in the capacity of the market-based capitalist system to correct itself. In a House Congressional Hearing in the US, Greenspan admitted that he was in a state of 'shocked disbelief' after the collapse of Lehman Brothers, the forced merger of Merrill Lynch with the Bank of America and the billions and billions of dollars the Federal Reserve had to cough up to keep the economy afloat. When a Congressman asked him whether he had miscalculated, he said, 'No, that's precisely the reason I was shocked, because I've been going for forty years or more, with very considerable evidence that it was working exceptionally well.'[43]

India boldly put in place a rescue plan consisting of two main segments, monetary easing and the pumping of liquidity into the system by the RBI, and a fiscal stimulus package announced by the

---

42   Puja Mehra, *The Lost Decade: 2008–18: How India's Growth Story Devolved into Growth without a Story* (New Delhi: Penguin Random House, 2019).

43   Harry Binswanger, 'Alan Greenspan vs. Ayn Rand and Freedom', *Capitalism Magazine*, 7 November 2008.

government. According to Mehra, 'Much of the 7 December package had been prepared when Chidambaram was in the finance ministry …', but I can say that this is not factually accurate as I myself took the package to show Home Minister Chidambaram upon the instructions of Dr Manmohan Singh after the original proposal, received from the Planning Commission, had been discussed with External Affairs Minister Pranab Mukherjee and the Prime Minister.

Mehra acknowledges in her book that India handled the crisis well. 'India's success,' she says, 'was that the shock was prevented from becoming a crisis.' Despite the fall in share prices, the financial markets functioned in an orderly manner. The RBI had placed restrictions on the use of bank loans for purchase of land, which prevented the emergence of a real estate bubble. 'The confidence with which the 2008 crisis was managed was in stark contrast to the 1991 crisis that had brought the economy to its knees.'

The next phase, 2009–12, she characterizes as the 'recovery destroyed'. This phase corresponds largely to the period when Pranab Mukherjee was Finance Minister. According to her, the first mistake made by Mukherjee was the announcement of a third fiscal package in February 2009 when the two earlier ones had already worked and the economy was on the mend. Mehra writes that this was done without consulting the Cabinet or even the Prime Minister. She quotes Pranab Mukherjee from his memoirs, *The Coalition Years*, 'I and Manmohan Singh had differing views on economic issues.' Mukherjee, according to her, was cast in the pre-1991 dirigiste mould and caused much damage to the economy through excessive social sector spending.

The tax cuts and spending boosts, given during the 2008–09 crisis, were not reversed in time, with the result that inflation went up to 8.7 per cent in 2010–12 as against an average of 5.4 per cent in the entire decade of 2001–10. The current account deficit went up, as did the fiscal deficit. The amendment of the Income Tax Act to retrospectively tax Vodafone, after the Supreme Court had ruled in the company's favour, damaged business confidence. This was further exacerbated by the general anti-avoidance rules proposed by the Revenue Department. This period also coincided with the CAG reports on 2G and coal, and excessive Supreme Court intervention, which sent the economy into a tailspin.

The third phase, 2012–15, was, according to Mehra, a period of 'slow recovery again'. By then, Pranab Mukherjee had become President of India and the Prime Minister and then Chidambaram took charge of the Finance Ministry. A slew of reforms was initiated to make the government look more business-friendly. The period was, however, too short to pull back the economy. The inability of the government to release procured food stocks into the market led to relentless food inflation. The 'taper tantrums', fear of the US Fed tapering out its easy money policy and raising interest rates, resulted in outflows of foreign portfolio funds, 'bringing the currency, equity and bond markets under pressure'. Chidambaram succeeded in improving the fiscal deficit figures even in this situation, 'although the quality of the fiscal deficit numbers he reported was hardly enviable'. India was out of the 'Fragile Five' and had managed a significant macroeconomic turnaround.

The last phase, according to Mehra, was 2016–18, 'another recovery destroyed'. The public sector banks, which had given loans irresponsibly and resorted to 'evergreening' to keep their financial statements in order, were compelled by the RBI to recognize non-performing assets. In the initial period, there was a flurry of activity, presentation after presentation before the Prime Minister and tension amongst officers. The lack of a clear focus, excessive centralization with the Prime Minister's Office and random ill-considered decisions on the economic front had adverse effects on the economy. The Planning Commission was abolished all at once without serious thought on what would take its place. The NITI Aayog, which came in its place, has become, over time, a sidelined organization with no specific role or purpose. Initiatives like 'Make in India', which promised much for reviving manufacturing in India, were never followed through consistently.

Then came demonetization, an ill-conceived and impulsive measure, which left lingering effects on the economy. Rahul Gandhi's accusation of this being a 'suit-boot ki sarkar' apparently struck home and focus turned almost entirely towards populist schemes. Even positive action, such as the insolvency code, failed to deliver for want of an adequate support mechanism. Without planning and without direction, the economy started floundering.

Oilmen's Strike and 26/11

'*Everyone's worried about stopping terrorism. Well, there's really an easy way: stop participating in it.*'

—Noam Chomsky

Towards the end of 2008 and early in January 2009, officers of oil companies of India decided to go on strike and paralyse the country. About 55,000 of them below the level of Deputy General Manager, employees of fourteen public-sector companies, including ONGC, BPCL, HPCL, GAIL, Oil India, Balmer Laurie and Cochin Refinery, comprising the Oil Sector Officers' Association, decided to go on strike for higher salaries. The NTPC Executives Association resolved to support the cause. Heading the strike was the Oil Sector Officers' Association's President Amit Kumar, who revelled in the publicity that this irresponsible act gave him. The loss was estimated at Rs 20 billion per day. The strike was in clear violation of the Home Ministry order of 1982, declaring the oil sector an essential service.

The strike started on 7 January 2009. The then Petroleum Minister Murli Deora tried to negotiate but failed to make headway. The strike started and I started holding meetings twice daily with Secretaries to manage the crisis. Petroleum Secretary R.S. Pandey—now a BJP MLA in Bihar—the Home Secretary, all other concerned Secretaries, the Chiefs of Staff, the Director of the Intelligence Bureau (IB) and others attended the meetings, as did Sarthak Behuria, Chairman of Indian Oil Corporation (IOC). I was also in regular contact with Chief Secretaries. If the issue had not been handled sternly, the city of Mumbai would have gone without power and water and, indeed, the whole country would have come to a standstill. We decided to get very tough. 'Tough', said Murli Deora, 'is an understatement.' 'Firm action is being taken and will be taken', said Home Minister P. Chidambaram.

On the morning of 9 January, I held a meeting where I made it very clear that the law book would be thrown at the striking officers. I said that the officers would be booked for sedition since the strike was patently an anti-national act, aimed at the vitals of the country, no better than what the Pakistani marauders had done in Mumbai on the fateful evening of 26/11. The State Chief Secretaries rose to the occasion and showed how tough determined governments could be. There was a colony for oil sector officers in Gujarat. The state officers, acting under firm directions of the Chief Secretary, gave the striking officers a choice: 'Either you go to the refineries and start work or you go directly to jail.' By the evening of the ninth, the strike had crumbled. Amit Kumar was in tears, but a grave danger confronting the country had been averted. 'Government "strikes" back', screamed the headlines of a Delhi paper on the next morning. Later, I took meetings to consider the grievances of the officers. I overruled opinions that there must be some equation between salaries of government officers and those of public sector employees. I always held the view that we would get the right kind of officers to man public enterprises only if we establish some parity with comparable officials in the private sector. Comparison with grossly underpaid government officers would further undermine the quality and competitiveness of government-owned companies.

The first decade of the twenty-first century had been marked by bomb explosions in different parts of the country. An abortive attack on the heart of Indian democracy, the Indian Parliament, took place in 2001. In 2002, there was the attack on the American Culture Centre in Kolkata; the Jaunpur train crashes of 2002 and 2005; the attack on the Akshardham temple in Gujarat in 2002; train and bus bombings, as well as the August bombings and communal conflagration in Mumbai in 2003; the Delhi bombings in 2005; synchronized bomb explosions in Varanasi and the Malegaon incident in 2006; the Samjhauta Express bombing in Rajasthan and the Ajmer Dargah bombing in Rajasthan in 2007. Then, in 2008, there were serial bomb blasts in Ahmedabad and localized incidents even in the eastern parts of India in Agartala, Imphal and Assam.

There was militancy aroused by other causes also, such as the resurgence of left-wing extremism over a wide swathe of forests, straddling Bihar, Jharkhand, Andhra Pradesh, Madhya Pradesh, Chhattisgarh and Maharashtra, with some militants holed up even in the Western Ghats in the south of Maharashtra. Therefore, terrorism had, unfortunately, become a staple in the news diet of every Indian. We had learnt to live with terror, which could strike at any place and at any time, just as we are now beginning to learn to live with unending waves of the Covid-19 pandemic.

Of all these incidents, the one I remember best was the attack on Delhi in October 2005. I was living in Delhi at the time, on Satya Marg, close to Sarojini Nagar Market. I had planned to walk to Sarojini Nagar Market to buy something. Sarojini Nagar Market, at that time, was to middle-class consumers what Amazon is today—a place where a range of commodities are available at prices that will not hurt one's pocket too much. I dressed up to leave, but then my dog, Sandy, got very restless for a walk. Sandy and I had been walking partners for long. We walked miles and miles in Trivandrum, Delhi, Brussels and

Geneva. As his need was urgent, I decided to take him for a short walk around our line of flats. After the walk, I deposited him back home and then set out for Sarojini Market.

I watched with curiosity as a large number of fire engines moved southwards along the main road, Africa Avenue, parallel to the little by-lane I used for my walks to the market. I was halfway there when I got a frantic call from my daughter in Bangalore, telling me of bomb attacks in Paharganj and other places in Delhi, asking me to go back home at once. I had been lost in my own thoughts while walking, not too conscious of my surroundings. When I looked up after her call, I saw a thick cloud of smoke over the market. There was nothing to do but to turn back and return home. A bomb had exploded in Sarojini Nagar Market as in other locations in Delhi, killing seventy and throwing the city into turmoil and a state of panic, from which it took days for citizens to recover.

I have often wondered what would have happened had Sandy not insisted on a walk. I would have reached the market a lot earlier and would have been there when the bomb went off. I may not have been at the place of the explosion, but then I could also have been there at the precise spot—it was entirely a matter of chance. Sandy, having lived for a full nineteen years and travelled with us to many places, now lies buried in a corner of the kitchen garden adjoining the lush lawns of the Cabinet Secretary's then dedicated house on Prithviraj Road.

The date 26 November 2008 is written forever in the history of India in letters evoking terror and gore. This was the day on which we saw mankind stoop to the lowest depths of depravity and inhumanity. A day on which the flames of hatred so consumed certain people in our neighbouring country that they had no compunction in sending rivers of blood flowing through Mumbai for a momentary feeling of exultation. A day on which a group of young men, heavily indoctrinated both by the Inter-Services Intelligence (ISI) and its allied organizations, performed a dance of death on the streets and in prime locations all over the city, mutilating and killing scores of hapless, innocent, unarmed citizens. This was also the day on which India learnt important lessons about the nature of terror, the weakness of existing intelligence and security systems and how the tenets of religion can be twisted and contorted to make men heartless beasts delighting in extinguishing innocent human lives.

The story by itself has been told and retold several times in different media in varied forms. It does not bear repetition here, particularly since it is a gruesome one. We know how ten heavily armed young men, trained and incited by the Lashkar-e-Taiba (LeT) and the ISI of Pakistan, came across the seas from Karachi in a captured Indian fishing boat, landed on our shores, hired taxicabs and then set off on their trail of destruction. We know the venues of their attacks: Chhatrapati Shivaji Terminus, Mumbai Chabad House, the Oberoi Trident, the Taj Palace and Tower, Leopold Cafe, Cama Hospital, Nariman House, Metro Cinema, a lane behind *The Times of India* building and St. Xavier's College. We know of the explosion at Mazagaon, in Mumbai's port area, and in a taxi in Vile Parle. We know also that Operation Black Tornado, unleashed by the National Security Guard (NSG), finally flushed out all the terrorists. Only one miscreant was captured alive, Ajmal Kasab, who was unrepentant to the end and was finally hanged in 2012. The story of the attack was extracted partly from him, partly unravelled, thread by thread, from many other sources, including foreign intelligence agencies.

It was around 5.30 in the evening when I received information regarding violence in Mumbai. I was in touch with Johny Joseph, Chief Secretary of Maharashtra, my main point of contact in the city. Johny, I must say, was very active and led the situation from the front. There was little clarity regarding the nature of the violence that had broken out and still less clarity on whether this was a crisis that could be handled by the Mumbai Police.

When I first spoke to the Maharashtra Chief Secretary in the evening of that fateful day, the scale of the attack was not known. The presumption then was that this attack was similar to the ones that had agonized many parts of India in the last two decades. I informed the Prime Minister and the Home Minister, who, at the time, was the gentle, benign, nattily clad Shivraj Patil. I was also in touch with the Special Secretary (Internal Security) at the Home Ministry. Madhukar Gupta, the Home Secretary, was himself in Pakistan on an official visit. He was due to return on the twenty-sixth but had rung me up that morning to say that he would stay another day in Islamabad as the talks were not complete.

The entire evening was occupied with a flurry of telephone calls with the Chief Secretary, the Home Ministry and the PM. In fact, my last call to the PM was as late as 2 a.m. on the morning of the twenty-seventh. For me, it was a sleepless night. The theory of a string of explosions as in Delhi was given up late in the evening and I was then told that it looked more like gang warfare. Meanwhile, it became clear to the Maharashtra Police that they could not handle the crisis on their own. Johny Joseph told me he needed the support of the naval commando force Marine Commandos (MARCOS). I rang up the Naval Chief, a bewildered Suresh Mehta, who had not heard of the developing crisis in Mumbai. He obliged at once and MARCOS were made available to the Maharashtra government. At the same time, I telephoned J.K. Dutt, Director of the NSG in Manesar, Haryana, to be ready to proceed to Mumbai, should the Maharashtra government need further help. Dutt was an enthusiastic and energetic leader who was able to bring about synergy and effectiveness to the NSG. The force itself is constituted by two diverse streams from the Army and the Police and requires a strong leader to maintain cohesion and unity of purpose.

As the night wore on, it became increasingly clear that the Mumbai Police and the Marine Commandos would not be able to deal with the situation on their own. I suggested to Johny Joseph that we move the NSG to assist local police. He accepted my suggestion and also agreed to provide logistic support to ferry the NSG commandos from the Mumbai airport to the locations at which the terrorists were holed up. In law and order situations, the state government is in command and central forces can move in only on their request. We had no time for formal paperwork, as is required in bureaucracy. All the orders were, therefore, issued by word of mouth and all credit must be given to Johny Joseph and his team and Dutt and his force for the way in which they responded with alacrity to the crisis.

The NSG force proceeded to Mumbai in the wee hours of the morning. The Home Minister chose to accompany them and, on landing in Mumbai, immediately took Dutt to the Raj Bhavan for a meeting while the rest of the force proceeded to Taj Hotel in Colaba, which had become the central point in the terror that had overtaken Mumbai that day. The rest, as they say, is history. The NSG proved its mettle. Dutt proved his leadership. I was in constant contact with Dutt and his confidence was amazing. By 8 a.m. on the twenty-ninth, Mumbai was free of terror and a period of high tension for the country came to an end. Unfortunately, the NSG lost two precious lives, Major Sandeep Unnikrishnan in the Taj complex and Commando Gajender Singh Bisht in the battle at Nariman House. Mumbai Police lost some lion-hearted officers; many citizens as well as foreigners visiting Mumbai were mowed down by a hail of bullets fired by remorseless people carrying state-of-the-art weaponry.

Immediately after the event, Foreign Secretary Shivshankar Menon came to me and spoke of retaliation against Pakistan. The Air Force Chief Fali Major was all ready to strike Pakistan. Obviously, any such decision was far, far above my pay grade. The Pakistanis were clearly concerned and repeatedly contacted the Indian government at various levels. The scale of the attack and the cruelty and barbarism that had been displayed was such that a retaliation seemed imminent. In his book, *Choices: Inside the Making of Indian Foreign Policy*, Menon talks of several discussions involving NSA M.K. Narayanan on possible responses. Indeed, it is difficult to imagine the evil in the minds of the men who planned and perpetrated this horrific crime. This was not a war or a battle, but cold-blooded murder of innocent people; people unrelated to the political dispute that had triggered the invasion. The fact that religion was used to inflame young people to commit such crimes on humanity further exacerbates the gravity of their crime.

On cold assessment, the government decided to use other means to deal with the situation. Menon himself goes on to say, 'But on sober reflection and in hindsight, I now believe that the decision not to retaliate militarily and to concentrate on diplomatic, covert, and other means was the right one for that time and place.'[44] Taking into account all factors, including the possibility of its slipping into a widespread conflagration with probable use of nuclear weapons and the effect of such a war on our economy and on our people and the diplomatic initiatives mounted by other countries, the government would have been dissuaded from any precipitate military action. Whether we should have flexed our muscles immediately after the incident is a subject that has been debated for long and will continue to dominate political discourse in future electoral battles. In the present combative atmosphere in the country, the answer would be clear and in favour of immediate retaliation. But times are changing, the world is changing and very soon, hopefully, we will move into a problem-solving mode in all parts of the world. Indeed, the statements made by India in the aftermath of the war in Ukraine point to a more pacific view on handling international disputes.

Two days after the crisis, on the twenty-eighth, the Delhi elections took place. Coming so close to the terror strike, I expected a vote against the Congress. But Sheila Dikshit and her government sailed through with ease. In 2009, in the national elections, the Congress returned to power at the centre with greater strength of numbers. Significantly, all the Parliamentary seats in Mumbai were won by the Congress. The people obviously did not consider the government to have messed up

---

44   Shivshankar Menon, *Choices: Inside the Making of Indian Foreign Policy* (Washington, DC: Brookings Institution Press, 2016), p. 62.

seriously in handling the crisis or failing to retaliate, regardless of the noise made by the media.

The incident was, no doubt, gruesome in itself but even more disturbing were the lacunae in our security systems that it revealed. India is a large country, a subcontinent with miles and miles of land borders and open seashores both on the west and east coast. Until 26/11, the focus was essentially on land borders. In 1947, 1962, 1965 and 1971, pitched battles had taken place all along the borders with Pakistan and China. Both our major neighbours have substantial nuclear arsenals. Pakistan matches India in nuclear strength, while China is far ahead of us, both in terms of strength of conventional armies and nuclear power. Even our land borders with Bangladesh and Myanmar were exceedingly porous. Gorkha militant leaders found refuge in Bangladesh, particularly when that country was ruled by regimes unfriendly towards India. There was constant movement of cowherds and villagers between Bangladesh and India, particularly since there were Indian villages in Bangladesh and Bangadeshi villages in India. One of the achievements of the Modi government has been to redress the anomalies created by the Radcliffe Line on the India–Bangladesh border by exchanging such villages.

Northeast militants, particularly Naga extremist leaders, operated from the forests of Myanmar adjoining the Indian border. The sea border, too, was always under threat, particularly when there was brisk Tamil militant activity in Sri Lanka. We lost a former Prime Minister in a ghastly assassination orchestrated from across the seas. A border dispute has now erupted even with Nepal, following the construction of a border road through Uttarakhand which could facilitate movement of pilgrims from India to Kailash Mansarovar without having to touch Kathmandu and restricting travel within China to only a few kilometres. Nepal was also used as a transit point and safe haven by Pakistani militants. Thus, in all ways, our borders are difficult to protect and if conventional warfare deteriorates into use of nuclear weapons—which could happen, particularly with Pakistan, since it has inferior conventional military strength—there will be unimaginable havoc across the subcontinent. So far as China is concerned, 1962 has taught us the lesson that discretion is the better part of valour, which recent incidents in Doklam and Ladakh have further confirmed. The solution, obviously, lies in a determined political effort to settle all borders but this seems a distant dream in a country in which jingoism is a dominant factor in electoral politics, and the existence of institutions in neighbouring countries, like the Pakistani army and the ISI, which will have no raison d'etre unless the conflict with India is kept on the boil.

The 26/11 attacks also exposed weakness at the highest level in decision-making in a grave emergency. For many years after Independence, internal security was looked after by the Cabinet Secretariat. Obviously, the Cabinet Secretariat was not the ideal location to house all security matters as its mandate was too wide and its responsibilities too multifarious. The creation of the position of National Security Adviser was, therefore, a step in the right direction, but instead of going all the way, the government chose to distribute responsibilities and power between the NSA and the Cabinet Secretary. We also had the Ministry of Home Affairs (MHA) in the same area of internal security and there was the Department of Revenue dealing with enforcement in the financial area. The IB, the NSG and the Central Paramilitary Forces worked under the MHA. Administrative matters relating to the Research and Analysis Wing (R&AW) were dealt with by the Cabinet Secretariat, but as my batchmate and friend, Ashok Chaturvedi, the Director of R&AW, clearly told me at our very first meeting, no operational details would be shared with me, as those belonged exclusively to the domain of the NSA and the PMO. The Special Protection Group, looking after the security of VVIPs, nominally reported administratively to the Cabinet Secretariat, but no operational information was ever shared with the Cabinet Secretary. Besides all these organizations, there was military intelligence, encompassing all three wings of the Armed Forces, which functioned separately as a world in itself.

There was also no real coordination mechanism in place. There was a National Crisis Management Committee, but its mandate was limited to natural calamities. The Cabinet Secretary was the Chairman and it had as its members, Secretary to Prime Minister, the Home Secretary, Secretary (MCD), Director (IB), Secretary (R&AW) and Secretary (Agriculture and Co-operation). There was a co-opted member, an officer of the Cabinet Secretariat who acted as Convenor. There was another committee of secretaries called COSAH, set up in the wake of the Kandahar hijack of the Air India plane, but its mandate was limited only to such an event and it contained officers from the Air Force, IB, Ministry of Civil Aviation, NSG and others.

When a real crisis blew up on 26/11, therefore, there was no real clarity on who was to do what at the central level; confusion confounded by the fact that law and order is a state subject under the Indian Constitution and that central intervention can only be at the request of the state government concerned. I waded into the crisis and its handling as is my wont but I had no background information, no Intelligence inputs, not even full knowledge of what was actually happening in Mumbai until late in the night. I had no knowledge about the dimensions of the crisis and the capacity of the state government to handle the crisis on its own either, as normally happens in all such events. I could have called a few Secretaries and officers together in my office and held a committee meeting. I deliberately chose not to, because I thought they would be able to work better with the facilities available in their individual offices, establishing contacts and gathering information, instead of bottling them all up in the conference room of the Cabinet Secretariat without access to the facilities that they needed to function independently and to communicate more effectively with me, with each other and with their counterparts and informants in Mumbai.

The event clearly showed up gaps in our intelligence gathering and information systems. In his book, *26/11: The Attack on Mumbai*, Vir Sanghvi says that enough information was available to various intelligence outfits to have anticipated the attack.[45] R&AW, according to him, had provided several intercepts from signals intelligence over the last three months on a possible terror attack on a Mumbai hotel. On 18 September, R&AW computers are said to have intercepted a satellite phone conversation between a known LeT asset and an unknown person, stating specifically their intention to attack a hotel near the Gateway of India, using the sea route to approach it. Another satellite conversation was recorded on 24 September that possible hotels for attack could be Taj Gateway, Taj Lands End, Marriott or Sea Rock.

R&AW's computer also is stated to have recorded another satellite phone conversation. This time, the LeT asset identified the hotels that were being considered for the attack by name. They were the Taj, the Marriott, the Lands End and the Sea Rock, with a possible attack on the Juhu airfield (used by a flying club). All these hotels have one thing in common: they are easily accessible from the sea. Sanghvi writes that on 19 November, R&AW intercepted another satellite phone conversation which mentioned that attackers would reach Mumbai between nine and eleven. All this information, clearly pointing to an intended attack, was apparently passed on to the centralized group under the NSA since the R&AW cannot operate within the country. I cannot vouch for the authenticity of this information as it was never conveyed to me before or after the event, and as no subsequent enquiry was held on possible failure to act in a timely manner on available intelligence.

Sanghvi's book also includes an article by Prem Shankar Jha, titled 'How the Plot Was Lost'. It says that eight LeT fidayeens were located in the sea as early as March 2007 by a Coast Guard ship, and they were traced and arrested later in Jammu after the IB came to know of the episode. Another group of operatives was arrested by the UP Police in February 2008, which had infiltrated into the country apparently to

---

45   Vir Sanghvi, *26/11: The Attack on Mumbai* (New Delhi: Penguin Random House, 2009).

blow up the Stock Exchange. The UP Police recovered maps from them of the Fort area in Mumbai, referring particularly to Oberoi Hotel and the Chhatrapati Shivaji terminus. On 19 November, it is stated there was another input, probably from American sources, picked up from the sea south of Karachi that the 'cargo' was on its way and four days' sailing from Mumbai. Prem Shankar Jha observes in the article that had the available information been effectively shared between the agencies and the political system, the crisis could have been averted.

This was an episode that had been planned over years. The Pakistani American David Headley had made many visits to India between 2002 and 2009. He was also a member of the LeT and had collected every possible detail. He was stated to have been given $25,000 by one Major Iqbal of the Pakistani ISI. He built connections in Mumbai, collected detailed information on possible targets, built a model of the Taj hotel to help the terrorists move around and helped set up a communications strategy. He was a double agent, working also for the US Drug Enforcement Administration, a fact that caused some problems for Indian investigators to gain access.

The fact that so much information was apparently available and still we could not put the pieces together and prepare ourselves clearly points to serious gaps in our intelligence systems at that point of time. The message was clear: we needed to quickly look at our systems and rectify them to the extent we could.

Another major lesson that the event taught us was the thorough irresponsibility and callousness of the news channels. The way in which they reported events as they unfolded showed brutality and insensitivity of the highest order, besides cavalier disregard for preserving the secrecy of security operations. It has been reported that terrorists inside Taj obtained information on the movements of security from television sets in hotel rooms. In the words of Vir Sanghvi in his article, 'The Medium Is the Mess', 'One problem with much of the TV coverage—and the principal reason why people are so angry—was the complete misjudgement of tone. At times of national crisis, we don't need hysterical reporters telling us how bad things are. We can see the pictures for ourselves.'[46] The attempt to exaggerate and sensationalize the event was quite out of sync with the mood of the country, which was angry and, at the same time, united by the cause. The media did not cover themselves with glory during this period and acted in a manner that seemed actually inimical to national interests.

Soon after the crisis was over, a senior minister told me that I would have to conduct an inquiry on what went wrong and who was responsible. This never materialized but a national committee for strengthening maritime and coastal security against threats from the sea was formed with the Cabinet Secretary as Chairman, consisting of the Chief of Naval Staff, Secretaries of the MEA, Defence, Revenue, Shipping, Fisheries, Petroleum and Natural Gas, Deputy NSA, representatives of security organizations and Chief Secretaries of coastal states as members. We met several times to discuss measures to strengthen coastal security. Another issue that was causing great concern at the time was repeated hijacking of commercial vessels of various nationalities, including Indian vessels, by pirates of Somalian nationality. This, too, featured in the discussions.

We held several meetings, the Chief Secretaries and Chiefs of Police of states generally joining through video conferencing. We decided on creating an NSG hub close to Palam airport so that quick movement is facilitated. NSG hubs were also to be opened in a handful of other strategic locations. The Navy was given primary responsibility for maritime security. Areas of responsibility of the Navy, the Coast Guard and the State Police were delineated. Marine police stations of the state police were to be strengthened and more patrol boats provided to them. The Coast Guard was to be beefed up and a coastal radar surveillance system put in place. A decision was taken to set up State Maritime Boards to coordinate the work of state governments, the Coast Guard

---

46   Vir Sanghvi, 'The Medium is the Mess', *Hindustan Times*, 14 December 2008, https://www.hindustantimes.com/india/the-medium-is-the-mess/ story-Ezs3NfNFfQwcnEwEiCtMDK.html

and the Indian Navy. Besides setting up and strengthening marine police stations, states would also set up rapid action commando forces which could serve as the first line of defence against any future attacks. Measures were put in place to develop closer communication between the coastal states, the Navy and the Coast Guard and to improve intelligence gathering and sharing.

It was recognized that fishermen and fishing boats would play a key role in identifying intruders. The Navy ran a training programme for fishermen on the east coast. Kerala set up 'Jagrata Samitis' in fishing villages to quickly pass on information when they noticed suspicious activity in the sea, an initiative that was adopted by other states also. In many places, two-way communication was established between fishing boats and control points on the shore. The Department of Shipping was authorized to devise a scheme for registration of fishing vessels and the Department of Animal Husbandry and Fisheries to issue identity cards to fishermen. We worked on ways in which Indian fishing boats could be identified even from the air and through Radio Frequency Identification (RFID) systems. We discussed also an approach paper on Integrated National Maritime Domain Awareness at the meeting held on 20 April 2010.

Regular meetings and interaction with states were helpful in solving many problems and creating new interfaces. This was an ongoing effort, which continued even after I had left the Cabinet Secretariat. Subsequent reports show that the measures initiated have begun to bear fruit. Writing in *Mail Today* on 26 November 2019, Commodore Srikant Kesnur said, 'We have come a long way since 26/11.' The Indian Navy was put in overall charge, and the Flag Officer Commanding-in-Chief of all four naval commands were put in charge of coastal security. A 24/7 Joint Operations Centre was set up with all the major players represented. The Sagar Prahari Bal, equipped with a fast interceptor and intermediate support vessels, was established. There is now an extensive network of Navy and Coast Guard monitoring stations, radars, electro optic cameras and electronic systems. A new state-of-the-art Information Management and Analysis Centre at Gurugram presently receives and analyses information from multiple sources for the Navy. Information exchange agreements have been signed with other countries in the Indian Ocean region. Thus, as Commodore Kesnur puts it, 'We can confidently say that our Maritime Domain Awareness is of a very high order; higher than it has ever been. Structures have been created to enhance "jointness" among military, law and order, and intelligence agencies.'[47]

In the states, too, much work was done. Marine police was strengthened with the establishment of more police stations on the coast, providing them with fast motorboats, equipping and training marine police. Shipping agencies and fishing boats are actively involved in passing on information regarding suspicious activity to the controlling authorities. CCTV cameras have been set up, fishing boats provided with automatic identification systems and there is a great deal more coordination and joint exercises between stakeholders. We are certainly better prepared, but can we say we are impervious to attacks?

The 9/11 attacks happened in the most technically advanced country in the world. There have been terror attacks in the UK, various parts of Europe, Australia and New Zealand—all of them technologically advanced. India has porous borders both by sea and by land. Terror attacks can be carried out by a few individuals with little resources. However, the influence of Pakistan and the military aid that it used to receive regularly during the years of the Cold War and those of the US action in Afghanistan have declined. On the face of it, the ISI seems to be less active as Pakistan too has begun to feel the impact of terrorism in its own country and is currently in a deep hole with its finances at sixes and sevens and its political stability under serious threat.

---

47   Commodore Srikant Kesnur, '11 years of 26/11: Lessons learnt from Mumbai terror attacks', 26 November 2019, DailyO, https://www. dailyo.in/politics/2611-mumbai-attacks-indian-navy-national-security-guard-navy-marine-commandos-indian-coast-guard-32217

It is obvious that the work started in response to that eventful day in November 2008 has paid off in good measure. At the same time, the Home Ministry made far-reaching changes under its then newly appointed minister, P. Chidambaram. He quickly realized that the main problem lay in the inability or reluctance of intelligence organizations to talk to each other. He started the practice of holding meetings every day, where they would share whatever information they had. He realized the need for a dedicated organization to monitor terrorist and militant activity. The National Investigation Agency (NIA) Act was legislated. The NIA was given concurrent jurisdiction which empowered it to investigate terror attacks in any part of the country. It could investigate all challenges to the country's sovereignty and integrity, bomb blasts, hijacking of aircraft and ships and attacks on nuclear installations. Subsequent amendments extended its scope to economic offences, including smuggling of High-Quality Counterfeit Indian Currency—under the definition of a terrorist act aimed at damaging the monetary stability of the country. The object of the act gave it a wide mandate to 'investigate and prosecute offences affecting the sovereignty, security and integrity of India, security of state, friendly relations with foreign states and offences under Acts to implement international treaties, agreements, conventions and resolutions of the United Nations, its agencies and other international organizations and for matters connected therewith or incidental thereto.'[48] He also appointed as its first Director Radha Vinod Raju of the Jammu and Kashmir IPS cadre, a man who had already made his mark several times over as one of the great crime investigators of the country.

Chidambaram was also the person who, as Home Minister, conceived of the National Intelligence Grid (NATGRID), an idea that is being pursued by the present government. NATGRID was based on the perceived lacunae in our databases and the lack of communication

---

48   Government of India, The National Investigation Agency Act, 2008,
      https://legislative.gov.in/sites/default/files/A2008-34.pdf

between agencies that allowed terrorists and other miscreants to escape unscathed, even though information on their activities was available in some database or the other. David Headley, one of the principal architects of the 26/11 attack, came many times to India after 2002. This information was available in immigration records but was perhaps not known to the IB or not followed up by it. Movements of money could often send warning signals about emerging terrorist and militant activity. Here again, details would be available with banks but intelligence services would not have access to it. If any agency had suspicions about any individual or organization, it could never collect all the information that it needed to confirm its suspicion or to trace such movements with the required speed and efficiency. The information was available in the country but it was scattered across diverse databases. NATGRID was an endeavour to use electronic means to facilitate access to different databases by any agency pursuing a lead.

There was resistance in the Cabinet and in the media to NATGRID when it was first mentioned. The belief was that this would mean that the Home Ministry could accumulate data about individuals and organizations to harass them. We saw the same opposition to the use of the harmless Aarogya Setu application in recent times. With regard to NATGRID, I had to hold a meeting of Secretaries and technical experts to understand the process myself. It was only when I assured the Cabinet that the intention was not to accumulate data in the Home Ministry but to provide electronic means for any agency investigating a suspected crime to access related databases that approval was finally given. The Opposition parties, however, continued to raise an uproar against it and, when the government fell in 2014, the whole scheme fell apart. It is good to know that now, once more, the realization has come that an information access system is an integral part of national security.

It was again during Chidambaram's tenure as Finance Minister that the Financial Intelligence Unit (FIU) came up. The offices of the unit were inaugurated by him. The FIU, headed by the brilliant Arun Goyal, who had worked with me earlier at the Commerce Ministry, was charged with the task of collating and analysing movements of large money in banks. The bank branches had to report all out-of-the-ordinary, unusually large or suspicious transactions. As it was humanly impossible to monitor every single transaction in every branch, we hit upon the idea of weekly reports from banks and a random selection of branches to examine transactions in greater detail. Our admission into the International Financial Action Task Force gave us the means to exchange information with multiple countries and gain access to more information.

Thus, brick by brick, a foundation was laid for launching a crusade against threats to the country, both financial and in terms of militancy and terror.

Corruption or Something Else?

'When orators and auditors have the same prejudices, those prejudices run a great risk of being made to stand for incontestable truths.'
—Philibert Joseph Roux

It is generally accepted that the fall of the UPA II Government took place on account of the proliferation of corruption issues and the incapacity of the leaders of the government at that time to defend themselves effectively. The repeated performance audits carried out by the CAG provided a great deal of material on the basis of which the credibility of the ruling government reached its nadir. Civil society, in particular, was up in arms and in the first half of 2011; movements initiated by Anna Hazare and Baba Ramdev attracted much public support. It is a different matter that the movements which they initiated have still not yielded the results that were expected, despite a change in government in 2014.

2G: The CAG strikes

The avalanche of protest against the government was triggered by the CAG's report on 2G, perceived corruption in the conduct of the Commonwealth Games, wrong dealings in the allocation of coal and the general perception that the government could not be trusted. The 2G issue came to public attention a few months after I had taken charge as Cabinet Secretary. I was not directly involved as the deliberations took place within the Telecom Department, in the Telecom Commission and through direct correspondence between the PMO and the department. However, there was much furore in the media and a number of allegations of corruption and malpractice in the award of 2G spectrum. I recall asking the Central Vigilance Commission (CVC), the CAG and the Central Bureau of Investigation (CBI) to look into the allegations so that if, indeed, there was some malpractice, it would be nipped in the bud before it blew up. Only the Director, CBI, tried to seek some information, but he could not make much headway.

On the 2G issue, a minister, a Government Secretary and an MP were in jail for months on end awaiting trial on the basis of the CAG's performance audit report. Finally, a court of law found no evidence and acquitted all the accused. I have gone through the court's voluminous judgment. The issue is interesting because it contains several elements of relevance to public administration. First, the CAG concluded that there was great loss to the public exchequer, deviations from existing procedures and unearned profit to particular private players. On the basis of this report, particularly the higher figure of loss of about Rs 1.76 trillion as estimated by him, there was widespread consternation articulated through the media. The inability to defend the case effectively resulted in government being increasingly pushed on the back foot, finally giving it an image of high corruption, which contributed to its ultimate defeat in 2014. The intervention of the

Supreme Court resulted in the cancellation of licenses already given which, in turn, caused turmoil in the telecom industry.

The CBI filed a case against Minister A. Raja, the Secretary, Department of Telecommunications and several others. The case was heard by a Special Judge of the CBI Court, who went through thousands of pages of documents and countless witnesses, before coming to the conclusion, after seven years, in a 1,552-page judgment, that no case had been established against the accused. In the meanwhile, Raja and others had already undergone imprisonment, while on trial, for almost one year. The case is important also because it created a great deal of uncertainty in the administration which resulted in what was called 'policy paralysis'.

2G: The court strikes back

The Special Judge went into all the allegations against A. Raja and others in the 2G case. The main allegation, which created much sensation, was that the public exchequer had lost heavily on account of the entry fee for spectrum allocation being retained at the 2001 level of pricing. The CAG himself gave three different figures of losses to government revenue, varying from about Rs 600 billion to Rs 1.76 trillion, based on three different modes of calculation. The CBI, in its case, gave a more conservative figure of about Rs 310 billion based on the growth in the Adjusted Gross Revenue per Megahertz per year during the period between 2002–03 and 2007. The CAG and the CBI also pointed to various deviations from procedure adopted by Raja and others.

Was there an actual loss to the people of India?

On the main allegation of loss to the exchequer, the Court went into the details of the background against which it had been decided to retain the entry fee at the rate of Rs 16.58 billion. It was pointed out that the prevalent policy called the New Telecom Policy of 1999 stated specifically that spectrum utilization should be reviewed from time to time, 'keeping in view the emerging scenario of spectrum availability, optimum use of spectrum, requirements of market, competition and other interests of public'.[49] In other words, gain to the exchequer was not to be the sole criterion for allocation of spectrum. In fact, if one looks at the history of telecommunication, particularly mobile communications, it is quite evident that government policy has resulted in huge reduction in tariffs. The creation of competition in the telecom field over the years has thus ensured gain to the consumers, rather than to private service providers. Any measure that would significantly push up telecom tariffs may result in gains to the government but only at the cost of consumer interests. The New Telecom Policy specifically provided for keeping consumer interests and the needs of the economy as the primary factor in deciding spectrum prices.

The New Telecom Policy also provided for seeking the recommendations of the Telecom Regulatory Authority of India (TRAI) before taking decisions on allocation of spectrum. In the 2G case, the TRAI recommended no cap on the number of access service providers in any area and stated specifically that even though there is a case for revision of entry fee on the basis of unprecedented growth of the telecom sector, it did not recommend allocation through auction as service providers were given spectrum in the past at different times and the amount of spectrum thus allocated also varied.

Therefore, deciding a cut-off date after which spectrum is auctioned in the 2G bands (800, 900 and 1,800 bands) would be difficult and would raise issues of the lack of a level playing field. In its recommendation dated 27 October 2003, the TRAI had specifically stated that 'the Authority is not in favour of high spectrum pricing, since such a regime will make the services more expensive and desired

---

49   Government of India, New Telecom Policy, 1999, para 3.1.1, Department of Telecommunications, https://dot.gov.in/new-telecom-policy-1999

growth will not take place in telecommunications'.[50] The Court also found that the fact that spectrum entry fee was being retained at the 2005 level was known to the Prime Minister, the Finance Minister, the External Affairs Minister, the Law Minister and the Attorney General. Hence, the Judge could find no evidence of conspiracy to do a criminal act by hiding relevant facts from various related authorities. The Judge also did not accept the view that availability of spectrum had not been assessed before deciding on the number of licenses to be given in each service area. He pointed out that 'mathematical precision' was not required in the assessment of availability of spectrum and that there was sufficient material in relevant government files to indicate that enough spectrum could be made available through better coordination and future vacation of spectrum by the Armed Forces.

The Court did not agree with the prosecution's contention that the first-come-first-serve policy hitherto followed had been violated. After going through all the files, the Judge came to the conclusion that the issue of grant of license was separate from the allocation of spectrum. The allocation of spectrum was separately done by the Wireless Planning and Coordination (WPC) Committee on the basis of applications filed by license holders. There were cases in the past, too, when license holders had to wait for a year or more for allocation of spectrum. The Judge did not agree with the view that the imposition of cut-off dates for processing of applications was unreasonable or illegal as it was clear that too many applications had been received. On the question as to whether two of the companies had offloaded the license to foreign parties at huge gain to themselves and corresponding loss to the exchequer, the Court held that there was lack of clarity on whether the shares had been offloaded or fresh equity issued and also that, even otherwise, there was nothing in the guidelines that specifically prohibited such action.

---

50 Government of India, 'Recommendations on Unified Licensing', para 7.33, TRAI, 27 October 2003, https://www.trai.gov.in/sites/default/files/Recomodifiedfinal.pdf

The Judge ruled that the Secretary, Telecommunications, in his letter to the Central Vigilance Commissioner on 18 December 2007 had clearly stated Government's intention 'not to bring changes in the existing policy and not to invite bids for grant of UAS licenses'.[51] The same position was maintained in reply to an unstarred question 1810 in Parliament. The revision in entry fee was not discussed at the Telecom Commission meeting on 7 December 2007, at which the Finance Secretary was also present. Thus, it would appear that a conscious decision had been made to adhere to the existing policy and not to revise the entry fee.

Role of performance audits

This brings us to the interesting point as to whether the CAG has the authority to question a policy laid down by the government through a 'performance audit'. It is very necessary to clarify exactly what a performance audit is required to do, the circumstances under which such an audit can be conducted and the areas which it may cover and those which it may not. I have looked at some literature on this subject. Pat McCarthy, representing the Washington State Auditor, had stated,

> Performance audits evaluate the efficiency and effectiveness of government programs with the goal of making them work better. These audits compare what an agency is currently doing against what's required by law and recommended by leading practices to look for improved outcomes that could include money saving methods or better processes for service delivery. By detailing problems and offering solutions, performance audits improve

---

51 CBI Court Judgment on 2G Spectrum Cases, https://www.hindustantimes.com/static/ht2017/12/CBI%20Vs.%20A.%20Raja%20and%20others.pdf

public services and provide valuable information to the public, program leadership and elected officials.[52]

This point is made also by Ohio Auditor Dave Yost, who has said that performance audit involves examination of the economy and the efficiency and effectiveness of government programmes and functions. Yost further emphasizes that performance audits will work only if there is collaboration with the government organizations being audited at all three phases of the audit: planning, fieldwork and reporting.[53]

The CAG of India, in his Guidance Note on Types of Audit, also seems to hold the same view. The note says, 'Performance auditing is focused on improving good performance in public administration by examining whether public programmes and services achieve the principles of economy, efficiency and effectiveness, and identifying conditions or practices that hamper performance and enable the auditor to make suitable recommendations.' All these statements seem to emphasize the audit of performance rather than the audit of policy or law. It is evident that performance audit is intended primarily to put in place more efficient and cost-effective methods of implementation of programmes and services.

This is better done in collaboration with governments rather than as a fault-finding mission initiated by the CAG. Of course, it is within the rights of the auditor to point out the manner in which the policy or law itself can be changed for the benefit of the government or the consumers of public services, but I doubt whether quick performance audits can be used as substitutes for a regular financial audit. As performance audits have been repeatedly resorted to by the CAG, both at the central and the state level in India, and quick

---

52   Pat McCarthy, 'About Performance Audits', *Office of the Washington State Auditor*, https://sao.wa.gov/performance-audits/about-performance-audits/

53   'Ohio Performance Team', *Ohio Auditor*, https://ohioauditor.gov/performance.html

reports have been furnished without exhaustive study of all aspects of policy, it is very important to be clear about its role in the future. The CAG's dramatic findings through performance audits may have high publicity value but the credibility of the institution itself will be eroded over time if they are seen to be based on insufficient data and incorrect understanding.

Can the CAG 'presume' losses when procedures are in consonance with accepted government policies?

The CAG's right to question policy, lay down prescriptions for another policy and calculate 'presumptive losses' on the basis of that policy are themselves wrong. If the issue of 'presumptive losses' is brought into audit, every budget, every finance act can be questioned. Reduction of taxes can be considered a 'presumptive loss' to the government; lowering prices or giving subsidized food grains to the poor or providing healthcare or education—all these can be brought within the ambit of 'presumptive losses' and astronomic calculations—pleasing to the media—can be made. In the face of sustained uproar by the Opposition parties, which even led to the abandonment of a Parliament session, a Joint Parliamentary Committee (JPC) was formed. The then Governor of the RBI, Subbarao, who had been Finance Secretary when the 2G issue was at its peak, was summoned from Mumbai as a witness. I was summoned from Trivandrum and grilled for about four hours.

In its final report, the JPC quoted both of us as follows:

In the course of evidence of Shri D. Subbarao, former Finance Secretary when asked about the loss that may have been caused to the exchequer in the above context, he stated that, 'If in the view of the government you want to give spectrum and licenses and sacrifice some revenue in the expectation that this would increase the tele-density and maximize welfare, then I believe, that you cannot attribute a financial loss to that. So, to say that there was a loss, to calculate loss you have to have reference points. So, it is not clear where the balance lay between welfare maximization and revenue maximization.' On the same question, Shri K.M. Chandrasekhar, former Cabinet Secretary, added that 'The issue to be considered here is whether there has been "atonement of revenue". My own interpretation would be that the "revenue" in this case relates to revenue that accrues by way of implementation of existing policies. The existing policy prescribed a particular entry fee for spectrum. If the Department of Telecommunications had allocated spectrum below the prescribed entry fee, there would have been "abandonment of revenue". The concept cannot, in my view, be extended to revenue that may have been obtained had the policy been different.' (Para 7.47)[54]

I also told the JPC that the Prime Minister had asked me to study the issue before the Telecommunications Department issued licenses and that I had reported to him that, under prevailing conditions in the economy and the telecom market, it would be possible for the government to secure more revenue. Obviously, the government, after consideration, decided to continue with the existing consumer-oriented policy designed to enhance competition in the marketplace.

A similar view was expressed by the former Director General (Audit) of Posts and Telegraph Department, R.P. Singh. The JPC quoted his testimony as follows in Para 7.48 of its report:

Justifying deletion of audit observations relating to policy, Shri R.P. Singh stated during evidence: 'Even today, I do not subscribe

54   Joint Parliamentary Committee (JPC) Report, 'To Examine Matters Relating to Allocation and Pricing of Telecom Licences and Spectrum' (Fifteenth Lok Sabha), New Delhi: Lok Sabha Secretariat, (October 2013), http://loksabhaph.nic.in/writereaddata/InvestigativeJPC/InvestigativeJPC_63561253547547737.pdf

to the theory of calculating losses on the basis of presumptions because that will touch upon the boundaries of a sort of policy prescriptions, in my view. That is it. Therefore, I deleted them and I retained whatever portion which I was satisfied that I should report in my version'. On being asked whether there was gain by the consumers as a consequence of the low price, Shri R.P. Singh replied: 'The presumption is that, had we allotted these licenses and issued spectrum directly, that much money would have come into Government coffers. Obviously, any burden or any extra cost, that would have been passed on by the service providers to the consumers. Normally the people would have ended up paying more or at a higher rate.'

The role of institutions

The next issue relates to the role of the judiciary. It is important that the judiciary must examine issues in detail before intervening in economic issues in particular. The reports of Constitutional authorities, like the CAG, cannot be considered to be final and complete, and judicial decisions based on such reports can cause incalculable harm to the economy.

The procedure laid down in the Constitution is to be considered before the Court begins to exercise authority in such cases. The Constitution clearly lays down that the CAG's reports are to be examined by the Legislature. It is after examination by the Public Accounts Committee (PAC) of the Legislature and its acceptance of the recommendations of the PAC that action has to commence. This has been recognized by the Supreme Court itself in several cases. In the case of Bajaj Hindustan Ltd. vs Sir Shadi Lal Enterprises Ltd. (November 2010), the Supreme Court set aside a decision of the Allahabad High Court, observing, inter alia, that, 'It is settled law that in the areas of economics and commerce, there is far greater latitude available to the executive than in other matters. The Court cannot sit in judgment over the wisdom of the policy of the legislature or the executive.'[55]

In an earlier 1997 judgment (M.P. Oil extraction vs State of MP 1997(7) SCC 592), the Supreme Court, referring to the executive authority of the state to frame a policy for administration, stated:

Unless the policy framed is absolutely capricious and, not being informed by any reason whatsoever, can be clearly held to be arbitrary and founded on the ipse dixit of the executive functionaries thereby offending Article 14 of the Constitution or such policy offends other Constitutional provisions or comes into conflict with any statutory provision, the Court cannot and should not overstep its limit and tinker with the executive function of the State.[56]

To sustain and nourish democracy, responsible reporting by the media is imperative. It is easy to create a major sensation by projecting a worst-case scenario, ignoring all other aspects of the case. In the 2G case, for example, the CAG had given three separate figures of 'presumptive loss' but the media picked on the highest figure to create the maximum adverse impact. Ultimately, such reporting would lead to defensive administration both at the political and administrative levels, resulting in a progressive inability to take bold and timely decisions. This gives another opportunity to the media to sensationalize 'policy paralysis'. We are therefore led to a zero-sum game which causes great harm to the

---

55   Supreme Court of India, Judgment on Civil Appeal No. 5856 of 2005, Para. 22, M/s. Bajaj Hindustan Ltd. vs Sir Shadi Lal Enterprises Ltd. & Anr (2005), https://main.sci.gov.in/jonew/judis/37198.pdf

56   Tarun Jain, 'Economic Policy beyond Judicial Determination: Supreme Court', *Law-in-Perspective* (7 December 2010), https://legalperspectives. blogspot.com/2010/12/economic-policy-beyond-judicial.html

economy. In this context, the enactment of stronger defamation laws and a law on privacy is necessary for protecting the rights of individuals.

The 2G case, therefore, teaches many lessons in public administration and, for that reason, deserves special attention. The judicial scrutiny of this case will probably continue through the appellate mechanism. Perhaps there could be more changes, more surprises and different findings on the same facts. The important point is that it gives the administration, the polity, Constitutional, statutory and regulatory authorities, and the judiciary a unique opportunity to evaluate their own approaches and work out appropriate mechanisms for the future.

The CAG strikes again on a 'presumed' coal scam

The so-called 'coal scam' is another such issue that created much furore. The incident erupted only after I had left the government. The story is explained vividly and in detail by a later Coal Secretary, Anil Swarup, in his fascinating and highly readable book *Not Just a Civil Servant*. The first point made by Anil is that the calculation of losses by the CAG was wrong. The CAG calculated a financial benefit of Rs 295 per tonne by taking the average selling price of coal mined by Coal India and deducting from it average cost of coal mining and financial cost. He then multiplies it by 'extractable reserves' of 6,282 million tonnes and comes to the conclusion that the financial gain to government would be Rs 1.8 trillion.

As in the 2G case, this is another presumptive figure which does not take into account factors such as wide variations in the cost of mining, the stripping ratio and the cost of transportation. Hence, while flaws in the process of allocation were rightly described as 'non-transparent' and 'discretionary', the estimation of financial loss to the exchequer was wildly exaggerated. It is true that auctioning of thirty-one blocks in 2015 yielded Rs 1.96 trillion but this, according to Swarup, was the result of irrational bidding in the light of perceived future shortage of coal and 'some allottees went to the court with a view to somehow wriggle out of the hole they had gotten themselves into'. In 2016, when nine blocks were put out for auction, 'there were hardly any takers'.

Anil Swarup summarizes the consequences of the CAG's findings as follows:

The CAG came up with numbers without going into the details. It was these numbers that created a 'Tsunami', got noticed and acted upon. Had it been amore precise mine-specific analysis, it would not have caused so much damage to the economy, bureaucratic 'psyche' and to honest civil servants like Mr Parakh himself [former Coal Secretary, in his book *The Coal Conundrum*] who blames the judiciary but not the one who started it all. Let us now look at the consequences of the CAG report: Officers refrained from committing themselves on the files. They were playing 'safe'. It was evident during the examination of bids when the officers conducted the auctions subsequently. The concrete recommendations on the bids were initiated at the level of the Secretary. It was conjectured that the coal production would increase if the blocks were auctioned. This was not so. In fact, post-auction, the coal production from auctioned mines was well below the estimated amount. The coal situation in the country eased because of unprecedented increase of coal production by Coal India Limited that had nothing to do with the CAG or its report. The CAG report led to the conviction of officers that enjoyed a spotless image. The then Prime Minister who in his role as Coal Minister had approved the proposals to allocate coal blocks conveniently dissociated himself from the process. The CAG obviously cannot be blamed for all of this, but he set the tone for devastating consequences.[57]

---

57   Anil Swarup, *Not Just a Civil Servant* (New Delhi: Unicorn Books, 2019).

This was not really the end of the story. The cancellation of licences meant that many thermal power plants which had concluded Power Purchase Agreements with state governments based on coal prices assumed on the basis of coal linkages suddenly found that they had been rendered totally unviable. There are multiple stranded assets today strewn across the country, which, in turn, led to non-productive assets in banks.

Later, after my retirement from the government, when I was on the Board and on the Credit Committee of an enterprising and forward-looking private bank, I found that colleagues, experienced bankers all, were adamant about not financing any part of the power sector, even if it was only a small increase in working capital limits of a distribution company which had never defaulted on any loan. When we talk of the proliferation of non-productive assets in banks and try to suppress them with an iron hand, blaming everyone from Nehru to Manmohan Singh for the 'woes' of the banking sector, let us not minimize the role played by the regulators, the CAG, investigative agencies and the judiciary, and the singular lack of understanding shown by them.

The end result of the action initiated by the CAG and accepted as gospel truth by the judiciary without analysing the matter more deeply and hyped by the media, eager in search of minute-to-minute sensations, was the charge-sheeting of the then Coal Secretary, H.C. Gupta. I did not know him very well and had not worked with him. When three other former Cabinet Secretaries, who knew him well, decided to make a last-ditch appeal to the government to bail him out, I had no hesitation in joining them. Anil Swarup knew Gupta by reputation, having worked in the same cadre with him. He further wrote in his book:

Questions were asked of me when, as Coal Secretary, Government of India, I chose to defend Mr H.C. Gupta, an IAS officer of 1971 batch and ex-Coal Secretary, who had been charge-sheeted along with others in several cases relating to

Coal Block auctions. A variety of questions emanating from those who hardly had any knowledge of the facts and from my well-wishers who questioned my desire to stick my neck out. Well, first of all, I firmly believed that Mr Harish Chandra Gupta was not wrong. No Secretary could/should be held responsible for not verifying facts that were not apparently erroneous on the face of the record. If this is mandated in administration, all decision making would come to a grinding halt. Secondly, I was convinced that there was no malafide or criminal intent in any of the allegations levelled against him. This was also borne out in the judgements against Mr Gupta. In one of the judgements, it was clear that neither it was alleged by the prosecution nor any evidence was made available to show that Mr Gupta obtained allocation of a coal block for the accused company by any corrupt or illegal means. Finally, I did it because Mr H.C. Gupta had enjoyed a spotless reputation as an officer, and I was a witness to it. Moreover, my personal belief is that if we hound the honest, the society and the administration will be left with either dishonest performers or deceitful non-performers. The decision to stand by and support Mr. Gupta was a personal one, born out of convictions and, hence, I was not bothered about the price to be paid in this regard. I was not sure whether I paid a price for being forthright and upfront in going the distance but felt contented that I did my bidding as per my conscience.[58]

The Commonwealth Games

Another issue with which I was closely involved was the Commonwealth Games of 2010, about which, again, there are tales of corruption, many of them not far from the truth. The seeds of the confusion that characterized the organization of the games had been laid much earlier,

---

58   Swarup, *Not Just a Civil Servant*, 2019.

in the period from 2003 to 2006. The scale of the effort was probably not known to Vajpayee's Cabinet when it approved entering into a Host City Contract with the Commonwealth Games Federation on 11 September 2003. It involved a whole host of activities, including development of sports infrastructure, consisting of competition and training venues, development of the Games Village to house athletes from 110 countries, and building of the international broadcasting centre, the main Press centre, the central logistics centre, the central accreditation centre and host broadcasting. Besides, it was expected that there would be a flood of tourists into Delhi and this meant augmentation of city infrastructure and tourist accommodation. A similar event had been organized in Delhi in the early eighties, the Asian Games, but then there was one man to call the shots and push all systems in the same direction, and that man was Rajiv Gandhi, son of a powerful Prime Minister, himself later a Prime Minister who won an election in 1984, virtually decimating the Opposition. I still believe that Rahul Gandhi lost an opportunity to establish himself in the political firmament by not taking control of the Commonwealth Games the way his father had.

The organization of the Games saw in the early years a pitched battle between Sports Minister Sunil Dutt and Chairman of the Indian Olympic Association Suresh Kalmadi, himself a Congress politician, who had been Member of Parliament both in the Rajya Sabha and the Lok Sabha, and had even served as Minister of State for Railways in Narasimha Rao's Council of Ministers. At the initial meeting held by the Core Group of Ministers, headed by Arjun Singh in October 2004, it had been decided that the Organizing Committee of the Games would be headed by the Sports Minister. Yet, for some reason, this was amended to an 'apex committee' in the minutes issued by the Cabinet Secretariat.

Meanwhile, Kalmadi exerted pressure to make himself the Chairman of the Organizing Committee and the Indian Olympic Association passed a resolution in November 2004 electing him as Chairman. This made Sunil Dutt very angry. The dispute continued and, finally, in

December, the PMO conveyed that Kalmadi would be the Chairman. This was the first mistake made in the organization of the Games, as Kalmadi did not have the capacity or the stature for organizing an event of this magnitude. Also, the conflict with the Sports Minister continued even with Sunil Dutt's successor, Mani Shankar Aiyar. Aiyar's successor, M.S. Gill, a former bureaucrat and Chief Election Commissioner, was confident initially of building bridges with Kalmadi, a misplaced confidence that evaporated a few months before the start of the games, when there was a genuine threat that the arrangements for the games would be incomplete by the scheduled start date.

It is not my intention to narrate the sequence of events leading up to the Commonwealth Games. This story has been told in books, in articles, and above all, in reports prepared by former CAG V.K. Shunglu at the behest of the Union Government; in the CAG's report and in the 347-page report presented by the Public Accounts Committee (PAC) in April 2017 to the Parliament. I will confine myself to my role and my learning in this process. In the organizational hierarchy approved by the Prime Minister in December 2004, the Cabinet Secretary had a limited role. There was a Group of Ministers headed by Arjun Singh, Human Resource Development Minister, to 'monitor and oversee the preparations of the Games',[59] an Empowered Committee headed by the Sports Minister to look after the construction of stadiums and infrastructure facilities, an Organizing Committee and an Executive Board, both headed by Kalmadi, for the conduct of the Games and a Committee of Secretaries, headed by the Cabinet Secretary, whose role was confined to 'implementation of the decisions of the Group of Ministers which do not fall within the purview of the Empowered Committee and the Organizing Committee'.[60]

---

59   Government of India, XIXth Commonwealth Games 2010, Public Accounts Committee (2016-17), 74th Report, Loksabha Secretariate, New Delhi, http://164.100.47.193/lsscommittee/Public%20Accounts/16_ Public_Accounts_74.pdf

60   Ibid.

Yet, when I took over as Cabinet Secretary, an explicit direction from the PM was that I should pay particular attention to the successful coordination of the games. This became necessary because GOM meetings were few and far between, and ministers really did not have enough time to focus on the nitty-gritty of organizing an event of such large dimensions. At the same time, the Organizing Committee, registered as a society under the Societies Registration Act, was treated by Kalmadi as his personal fiefdom and it never assumed the role of the prime driver of the games. On the other hand, eventually, despite the government appointing senior civil servants to strengthen its work capacity, it was recognized as the organization that gave the games a bad name. The PAC concluded that the government should have removed Kalmadi from his entrenched position as Chairman of the Organizing Committee. The Committee observed:

> In short, the Committee feel that had the government so desired, they could have easily ensured the resignation of Shri Kalmadi from the Presidentship of the Indian Olympic Association/ Commonwealth Games Association. Since the Government did not do so, Shri Kalmadi was able to manipulate the system in unauthorizedly setting up the OC and becoming its Chairman and subsequently engaging in profligacy and unlawful activities untrammelled.[61]

I could not devote full attention to the games as I had many other responsibilities to look after. It was difficult even to find time to hold meetings in 2008 and 2009, as we were battling an economic crisis and, at the same time, preparing for the national elections in 2009. Yet, it was fun working like a District Magistrate. In the last few months,

---

61   Government of India, XIXth Commonwealth Games 2010, Public Accounts Committee (2016-17), 74th Report, Loksabha Secretariate, New Delhi, http://164.100.47.193/lsscommittee/Public%20Accounts/16_ Public_Accounts_74.pdf

I had to visit every stadium under construction, every venue, every supporting facility, personally.

The construction of the new terminal of the Delhi airport by the infrastructure giant GMR was a major challenge and, at the same time, a stupendous success. The idea was to build it before the games started and it was no easy task to coordinate the work of fifty-eight departments and institutions of both the central government and the Delhi government. Yet, it was done and the best-ever airport in the nation came up in record time, with Mumbai following shortly thereafter. During all my visits abroad in the previous two decades, I used to marvel at fabulous airport terminals at Schiphol, Singapore, Frankfurt, Heathrow and Paris. Now, at last, across the country we have airports which rival those in other parts of the world and I am happy that I had the opportunity to be associated with the first such airport terminal in the country.

I was happy also that, through a grinding process, meeting after meeting, the stadiums and other infrastructure facilities also came up. The Delhi Chief Minister, the late Sheila Dikshit, was a human dynamo. She had the capacity to stimulate her officers to almost superhuman levels of performance. The Barapullah flyover was a significant achievement. In her book, *Citizen Delhi: My Times, My Life*, she wrote:

I remember how challenging it was to get the nearly 4.3 km-long Barapullah elevated corridor ready in time for the Games in exactly two years—the foundation stone was laid in September 2008. The PWD-executed project, the first of its kind in India, would drastically cut the travel time from the Games Village in East Delhi to the Jawaharlal Nehru Stadium and Thyagaraja Stadium.[62]

---

62   Sheila Dikshit, *Citizen Delhi: My Times, My Life* (New Delhi: Bloomsbury Publishing, 2018).

Indeed, it was an amazing piece of work, which she visited repeatedly and, I too visited at least two or three times a week, late in the evening, taking a detour on my way back home.

Different stadiums and, different training centres under multiple organizations and departments without a single full-time authority to control it meant that, by 2010, a great deal of work had piled up. The Sports Minister Gill and Delhi Chief Minister decided to fix firm dates for the inauguration of various infrastructure works. A series of inaugurations took place which undoubtedly helped to speed up construction. I was reasonably confident that we were on track. 'Commonwealth Games Federation President Michael Fennell said on Thursday that he was happy with the progress made in the preparations of the Commonwealth Games though the Organizing Committee still needed to do a lot of work,' wrote Jasleen Kaur in *Governance Now* on March 11.[63]

The situation changed dramatically over the next few months. We got hit from a direction which we least expected. The construction of the Games Village and its readiness to house and care for the athletes was the responsibility of the Delhi Development Authority (DDA), directly under the Lieutenant Governor (LG) of Delhi. Repeatedly, at meetings of the Group of Ministers, the LG had assured ministers that the construction of the village was well under control. Construction had been entrusted to a private developer, Emaar MGF, who in turn, had subcontracted the work to Ahluwalia Contracts. There were many allegations regarding the choice of the developer. The Central Building Research Institute had pointed out several deficiencies in the construction in several reports between 2008 and 2010. The DDA, however, failed to supervise the construction. The buildings were flawed in many significant ways.

---

63   Jasleen Kaur, 'You will hear a lot from us: CWG's Fennel tells Kalmadi', *Governance Now*, 11 March 2010, https://www.governancenow.com/news/regular-story/you-will-hear-lot-us-cwgs-fennel-tells-kalmadi

A few weeks before the games were to start, we found that it was in shambles. The DDA was required also to provide flats in Vasant Kunj for housing coaches and other officials of the games. This, too, was nowhere near ready. On top of all this, the Organizing Committee had failed to arrange for the 'overlays' in various stadiums, such as ticket counters, chairs, shelters and other facilities. And it rained and rained; Delhi had never seen such rains. It rained continuously and heavily until 24 September, slowing down all work. At that time, I was completely downcast. All the work that had been done during the past three years seemed to have come undone. I told the Principal Secretary to the Prime Minister and the National Security Adviser that if the games did not take place as scheduled, I would take personal responsibility and resign.

The Cabinet Secretariat backed me wholeheartedly. In particular, I had the support of my Joint Secretary, Dr Taradutt, who has himself written a book in which he has described at length his experiences in the Cabinet Secretariat, especially his role in the Commonwealth Games. Finding me depressed and unhappy, he came and told me one evening, 'Sir, you have to perk up. If you are yourself looking so upset, what would be the effect on the rest of us?' The Chief Minister of Delhi and I worked together shoulder to shoulder. Daily visits to the Games Village became the normal practice. She was a bit embarrassed because the village fell within the domain of her boss, the LG, in his capacity as Chairman of the DDA. I told her we had no time to look after bureaucratic niceties, we just had to get the job done. Almost every evening, we would be there, taking on-the-spot decisions. She brought in workers from all over to clean up the premises and to set things right. Her daughter, who worked in ITC Maurya, came with her team and virtually managed the hospitality arrangements.[64]

---

64 Government of India, XIXth Commonwealth Games 2010, Public Accounts Committee (2016-17), 74th Report, Loksabha Secretariate, New Delhi, http://164.100.47.193/lsscommittee/Public%20Accounts/16_ Public_Accounts_74.pdf

Meanwhile, at a meeting of the Prime Minister on 14 August 2010, barely six weeks before the event, the entire charge of organizing the event was given to me. A press release was accordingly issued but there was no government order. I sat with the sincere and hardworking Sports Secretary Sindhusree Khullar, and we decided that we will appoint competent senior officers at the Additional Secretary/Joint Secretary level to expedite work at each venue. This was something I had suggested six months ago to the Group of Ministers, but then I was vetoed on the ground that the Sports Authority of India would be able to manage construction of the venues. The officers went to the venues allotted to them and they put their heart and soul into the job. They hardly went home, working like manual labourers, inspiring and driving the workforce. If the Commonwealth Games finally took off, a large measure of the credit must go to these dedicated officers. As the PAC observed: 'Needless to say, this emergency mechanism of positioning senior government officers, albeit late, at the behest of the Prime Minister, ultimately saved the day and proved that government intervention can bring crisis management.'[65]

Meanwhile, the media, particularly news channels, went to town on the failures and shortcomings in the conduct of the games. This made the sports contingents from other countries delay their departure for Delhi. A group of Commonwealth High Commissioners, led by the Australian High Commissioner, came to see me. The President of the Commonwealth Games, Michael Fennell, called on me, together with Kalmadi. Displaying confidence that I really did not feel, I told them that we were absolutely on top of the situation and that all was well. They believed me and the contingents started trooping in from all over the Commonwealth. The delegations that came in earlier had

---

65   Government of India, XIXth Commonwealth Games 2010, Public Accounts Committee (2016-17), 74th Report, Loksabha Secretariate, New Delhi, http://164.100.47.193/lsscommittee/Public%20Accounts/16_ Public_Accounts_74.pdf

to be temporarily accommodated in hotels as the village was not ready. Before the event started, however, we were fully prepared.

The date of 3 October dawned bright and clear. In the evening, my wife and I wended our way to the Jawaharlal Nehru Stadium, the venue of the opening ceremony. As we drove along the newly renovated, bright-looking roads of Delhi and as we saw the beautiful new buses ferrying the athletes to the stadium, I had a lump in my throat. My country had overcome adversity and this was the moment of our triumph.

The Group of Ministers had spent hours planning the opening ceremony, sitting with Bharat Bala, who orchestrated the opening and closing ceremonies. The crowning glory, which set it apart from other such ceremonies, was the giant aerostat on which was projected from all sides snippets from the history of India, visible to all spectators from all sides of the stadium. The opening ceremony also caused some political problems. The Commonwealth Games are opened everywhere by the Queen of England or her representative. The Indian President's office, however, insisted that the games should be opened by the Rashtrapatiji. Some language was found to keep the President reasonably satisfied and Prince Charles opened the games while the President declared that it was open.

The opening ceremony was a resounding success. A jam-packed stadium expressed their approval with loud roars. Until that opening ceremony, the favourite game of the media was to compare most unfavourably our own preparation and work with that of China, who had organized the Olympic Games in 2008. The Chinese were ready with their arrangements a year before the Olympics started. As is the practice in India in most things, we were 'last minute' people. Even if we had taken many more months to put in place a more complete system, we would still have been in the same state of preparedness, or lack of it. We are 'jugaad' people, we improvise as we go along.

In her book, Sheila Dikshit has described the 'great sense of relief as well as anxiety' that she felt at the opening ceremony attended by

60,000 residents of Delhi. Relief, because the 'nightmarish run-up to the Games' had been overcome and anxiety that the huge applause that she received on mention of her name would 'attract the envy of others and sooner or later would land me and the Congress state government in trouble'.[66]

It is instructive to note that a prominent leader like Sheila Dikshit felt apprehensive about her popularity as displayed in the stadium that day and the effect that it might have on other leaders present.

The games, too, were flawlessly executed. The CAG, no friend of the games or of the government, said, in the conclusion of his Performance Audit Report:

It is acknowledged that India hosted the largest and among one of the most successful Commonwealth Games in Delhi in October, 2010. It is indeed a remarkable commentary on the nation's managerial and sporting capabilities that despite a multitude of adversities leading to the actual conduct of the games, India emerged successful both as hosts and as competitors.[67]

I never attended any of the sports events. However, I went to the well-appointed dining hall of the Games Village, replete with food representing every country and every region of the Commonwealth. Foreign athletes were all praise for the arrangements we had made. Indian athletes said they had attended many events in different cities all over the world and they had never come across any event that was better organized. Our athletes were very proud of what we had achieved

---

66   Sheila Dikshit, 'Why Sheila Dikshit was "Saddened" by CWG Probe', *Rediff.com* (17 February 2018), https://www.rediff.com/news/special/why-sheila-dikshit-was-saddened-by-cwg-probe/20180217.htm

67   Government of India, Audit Report on XIXth Commonwealth Games 2010, Comptroller and Auditor General of India, 2010, https://cag.gov.in/webroot/uploads/download_audit_report/2011/Union_Performance_Civil_XIXth_Commonwealth_Games_6_2011.pdf

and showed their appreciation in no uncertain manner with their best-ever display in any international event.

While the event was a great success, there were many mistakes from which we had lessons to learn. The main failure obviously lay in not creating a sound governance structure. As the PAC put it:

> To conclude, the Committee observes that crucial delays at critical junctures in the planning process for the organization and conduct of the CWG-2010 coupled with the opaque system followed in the appointment of the Chairman, OC, who subsequently engaged in high handedness and corrupt practices in the award of contracts, undermining the institutional mechanism, almost took the country to the brink of national shame but for the effective intervention by the government at the last moment.[68]

There were court cases thereafter; Kalmadi spent some months in jail and was dismissed from the Congress Party. In 2016, however, the Indian Olympic Association made Kalmadi its 'honorary life president' along with Om Prakash Chautala. This decision had to be reversed later on account of stern opposition from the government.

---

68   Government of India, XIXth Commonwealth Games 2010, Public Accounts Committee (2016-17), 74th Report, Loksabha Secretariate, New Delhi, http://164.100.47.193/lsscommittee/Public%20Accounts/16_Public_Accounts_74.pdf

Experiments in Public Administration in India

'Quality in a service or product is not what you put into it. It is what the customer gets out of it.'

—*Peter Drucker*

All over the world, starting with the Thatcher government in the UK in the mid-'80s, a number of productive exercises have been carried out to reform public administration. This took the form of 'New Public Management' in the UK, adopted enthusiastically by Australia and New Zealand in particular, bringing about sweeping changes in the entire structure of administration, making officials responsible for defined results. Even developing countries like Malaysia undertook administrative reform, spearheaded by the Performance Management and Delivery Unit (PEMANDU, which, in Malay, translated to 'the driver'). New public management morphed into new public governance later, bringing in less rigid and more welfare-oriented systems. This, too, was overtaken by the digital revolution.

Economic reform in India has, in its wake, brought about administrative change but this has been partial and limited to some sectors. The introduction of digital forms of governance has undoubtedly simplified many procedures. In the Income Tax Department, for example, the nexus between the assessing authority and the taxpayer was cut through the digitization of returns and their central processing. The GST system, now under introduction, is predicated on a digital network. The digitization of railway reservations has made life simpler for travellers. The introduction of competition in the airlines sector and the opening up of the car manufacturing sector has given the consumer more options.

Prime Minister Manmohan Singh, shortly after he assumed office in 2004, created the Second Administrative Reforms Commission, headed by veteran politician Veerappa Moily. I had met Moily many years ago when I was Finance Secretary in Kerala and Karunakaran was the Chief Minister. Moily was then CM of Karnataka and there was a meeting of Southern Chief Ministers and Finance Ministers to discuss taxation. Karunakaran, at that time, was flying high and was considered to be among the senior-most in the Congress Party. He played a significant role in the anointment of Narasimha Rao as Prime Minister and was considered to be not far from the top position himself.

Manmohan Singh believed in the centrality of administrative reform. Addressing civil servants on the second Civil Services Day on 21 April 2007, he said:

I view the reform of government as a means of making citizens central to all government activities and concerns and reorganising government to effectively address the concerns of the common people. This requires 'out of the box' thinking. It requires innovative thought backed up by a mechanism to implement new ideas. We live in a world characterized by unprecedented social, economic and technological change. An efficient management of change should be a key concern of a dynamic and well-functioning system of public administration.[69]

Expressing the importance of process change in an archaic administrative system, he stressed the importance of the delivery of outcomes.

Dr Prajapati Trivedi, a practical economist, whom I knew from my days of training in the Indian Institute of Management, Calcutta, met me several times after I had assumed charge and explained his idea of a performance management in the central government which could extend over time to autonomous institutions under various ministries. I was aware of Prajapati's work in the public sector in India, which resulted in the introduction of an MoU system, whereby the government and the enterprise concerned agreed on performance outcomes. Despite its stated shortcomings, it had introduced a certain degree of autonomy and flexibility in the performance of public sector enterprises.

The Administrative Reforms Commission called me for a meeting to discuss my ideas regarding the manner in which public administration could be reformed. I pitched strongly for a performance management system. Chapter 11 of the Tenth Report of the Commission was entirely devoted to the introduction of performance management systems in India. In its recommendations, the commission, after full examination of similar processes introduced in other countries, stated that, 'Annual performance agreements should be signed between the departmental minister and the Secretary of the Ministry/Head of Departments,

---

69   Government of India, Dr. Manmohan Singh, Speeches, 21 April 2007, New Delhi, https://archivepmo.nic.in/drmanmohansingh/speech-details. php?nodeid=507

providing physical and verifiable details of the work to be done during a financial year'.[70]

Shortly thereafter, the then President of India, Pratibha Patil, announced in her address to Parliament the government's resolve to 'establish mechanisms for performance monitoring and performance evaluation in government on a regular basis'.[71] Meanwhile, when a vacancy arose in the Cabinet Secretariat for a Secretary-level officer to manage our relationship with the Organisation for the Prohibition of Chemical Weapons (OPCW), I managed to get the Prime Minister's approval to bring in Prajapati, who would also look after the introduction of performance management in India.

The system introduced in the public sector in India was, in effect, the precursor of the Performance management and Evaluation System in Government. Under this system, an MoU was signed between the head of the public sector unit and the ministry concerned. About 50 per cent weight was given to financial performance, the remainder to other objectives specific to the organization in the light of the country's needs. The bonuses of public sector personnel were linked to profitability. This resulted in significant improvement in the performance of many public enterprises.

For long, administrative reform in India essentially meant incremental changes in particular areas of administration. These were driven principally by individual initiative or in response to specific needs and public demands in certain areas of governance. The advent of technology also created its own imperatives in governance reform when the realization came that the demands of the people could be met more easily through the electronic route, in many cases bypassing

---

70   Government of India, 'Second Administrative Reforms Commission: Reports, Department of Administrative Reforms and Public Grievances', (New Delhi; November 2008), https://darpg.gov.in/sites/default/files/personnel_administration10.pdf

71   Pratibha Patil, Address to the Parliament on 4 June 2009, http://pratibhapatil.nic.in/sp040609.html

traditional official–client relationships and procedures. The experiment with results framework documents in the year 2009 and thereafter for some more years marked a departure from the incremental method of administrative reform and held out a promise of systemic change.

Results Framework Document (RFD), at the highest level, is essentially a record of understanding between a minister representing the people's mandate and the Secretary of a department responsible for implementing the mandate. The RFD can be distributed down the line in a hierarchical set-up, thus creating a pyramidal structure for achievement of results and their evaluation at each ascending level. At the ministry level, the RFD sought to lay out the ministry's main objectives for the year, actions proposed to achieve these objectives and the manner in which progress was to be monitored. Based on these overarching considerations, the RFD was divided into six sections:

Section 1: Ministry/department's vision, mission, objectives and functions

Section 2: Inter-se priorities among key objectives, success indicators and targets

Section 3: Trend values of the success indicators

Section 4: Description and definition of success indicators and proposed measurement methodology

Section 5: Specific performance requirements that are required from other departments and are critical for delivering agreed results

Section 6: Outcome/impact of activities

The RFD was prepared by the ministry or department on the basis of proposed budgetary allocations and reviewed by an independent group of non-government experts. It was based on general agreement of the minister concerned on the objectives and key result areas of the ministry. The RFD was approved by the High Power Committee consisting of the Cabinet Secretary as Chairman, Finance Secretary, Expenditure Secretary, Secretary (Planning Commission) and Secretary (Performance Management). These were put up on the websites of each ministry. The performance was reviewed after six months and adjustments made to the RFD as required. At the end of the year, a report was prepared on achievements against targets, which was to be placed before the Cabinet for information. The reports were given scores based on agreed target values and agreed weights for different performance indicators. The average performance was then calculated.

The Indian experiment suffered from several serious shortcomings. It was never driven from the top by the political executive, as was the case in other countries which had effectively introduced systemic changes through New Public Management and other similar mechanisms. No Prime Minister or Cabinet Minister or Cabinet collectively took any interest in the initiative. At its early stages, there was irresponsible media reporting by a couple of journalists who wanted to create sensation and controversy. The journalists reported that the Prime Minister intended to introduce a marking system for ministers. This resulted in a complete hands-off approach by the PMO and this important administrative reform measure was treated as no more than a hobby horse of the Cabinet Secretary.

The system, as it was introduced in India, seemed to hang in the air as it was not linked to any structural reform, particularly financial reform. The results achieved by any ministry or department or organization never amounted to anything as it was not linked to a system of rewards recognizing performance. The feeling also grew among top bureaucrats that the system could be manipulated, targets kept low and results magnified. Without top-level backing, there was never any hope regarding its long-term future, even though it found a certain measure of appreciation and acceptance in neighbouring countries and in some Indian states. RFDs provided at best a beginning, but the beginning also proved to be the end.

Prime Minister Narendra Modi saw merit in an organized governance system when he visited Malaysia in November 2015. An MoU was signed by India with Malaysia during his visit for cooperation in the field of performance management, project delivery and monitoring in respect of government programmes. Modi said on the occasion, 'I have personally interacted with PEMANDU, and I am pleased that our NITI Aayog will work with them.'[72] In order to achieve comprehensive and lasting administrative changes, it is necessary to adopt this route of a self-sustaining, self-perpetuating and self-correcting total system. However, nothing significant has emerged from this connection with PEMANDU, and administrative reform continues to languish at the bottom of the priorities of government.

In fact, as Prajapati Trivedi points out in an article he wrote for *Business Today*:

> The present government started with the advantage of having a system in place as well as close to 1200 recommendations made in 15 reports by the Administrative Reforms Commission. The area of major administrative change was thus low hanging fruit which could have been easily plucked by the new government.[73]

The existing system, with its perceived shortcomings, could have been further developed and perfected. Instead, the system collapsed and no alternative system was put in place. Prajapati, after his retirement from government, joined the Commonwealth Secretariat. I recently learned from him that fifty-three Commonwealth countries have seriously

---

72   *The Indian Express*, 'Modi diplomacy in Malaysia: Cyber security, defence dominate talks', 23 November 2015, https://indianexpress. com/article/india/india-news-india/modi-diplomacy-in-malaysia-cyber- security-defence-dominate-talks/

73   Prajapati Trivedi, 'Administrative Reforms Must for Nation's Long-Term Growth', *Business Today*, 4 January 2015.

taken up performance management along the same lines as it was developed in India.

Reflecting on my own experiences in this area, I can only conclude that administrative reform is considered to be an unimportant endeavour in India, not taken seriously at the highest levels. Immediately after the re-election of the UPA government in 2009, I called on the Prime Minister and said, 'Sir, this is your victory, a statement of support for strong administration and unwavering decision-making. This is the time to introduce solid administrative change that could change the face of India.' Dr Manmohan Singh had agreed, saying, 'Yes, we must think of new ways of doing things.' However, my effort to have a joint meeting to promote the RFD system in India at the highest level did not succeed and the Prime Minister himself did not take personal interest in performance management in government. Sadly, even the present Prime Minister shows no inclination to reorient public administration to make it result oriented.

New public management, new public governance, the Malaysian system, the RFD—all these constitute efforts to make fundamental systemic changes in administration. Very often, the failures and shortcomings of public administration are attributed to the incapacity of officers manning the system. There is the fond expectation that if civil service officers are replaced by others, drawn from the private sector or government companies, there will be magical changes. This is a mistaken belief. Civil servants are recruited from the same stock as corporate employees. They have been trained in IIMs, IITs, medical colleges and the best institutions in the country and abroad. During their careers, they are given many opportunities at government expense and on government time to expand their skills. We have even experimented with 'lateral entry' in the past, we still sporadically undertake such experiments, but none of them have made a significant impact or proven to be substantially more effective than home-grown civil servants.

Public administration is far removed from corporate management. Corporate managers have a clearly defined objective: the bottom line of the company, its profitability and stock value for investors. In public administration, civil servants have to chase multiple objectives, which vary as governments change. Many of these objectives are not sharply defined and priorities suddenly change without warning. In public administration, we deal with people, not with buyers or profitability figures.

Whenever this discussion on civil servant versus corporate manager in public administration comes up, I am invariably tempted to quote Arun Maira, who distinguished himself at different periods in his life as corporate manager, consultant and public administrator in the capacity of Member, Planning Commission. In his book, *An Upstart in Government*, he writes:

I must admit that it is much harder to get tangible results in the Government … I have to also explain that the scope of the government's responsibilities is much larger than that of any private sector company. To produce outcomes that are equitable, and not only efficient, in providing health services to all citizens, for example, is more difficult than selling medicines to only those who can pay the price that covers their cost of discovery and production. The government's job is not to make a profit, it is to improve the world for everyone.[74]

The fact that there are at least four former civil servants in the Union Council of Ministers and that the PMO is manned largely by civil servants is an acknowledgement of the fact that their contributions are valued by the present dispensation. The Prime Minister, with fifteen years of prior experience as Chief Minister and five years as Prime Minister, is surely the best judge of what works for him and what does not.

---

74   Arun Maira, *An Upstart in Government: Journeys of Change and Learning*, (New Delhi: Rupa Publications India, 2015).

This is not to say that every position has to necessarily be filled by generalist administrators. To a great extent, the requirement of specialist personnel is met by specialist services within the administrative system. There still remain certain positions of a technical nature where induction of persons from outside the system with the required background would certainly help, but we must accept the fact that public administration itself is a specialist area in which skills acquired through many years of experience cannot be whimsically replaced.

The problem of administration is not really one that can be dealt with by wholesale change of personnel. It is the system that needs fixing. Writing in *Financial Express* on 10 October 2018, on the battle royale in the CBI in that year, Lord Meghnad Desai said, 'Even before this happened, I have argued that the administrative system needs drastic reform. The British have reformed their system at least twice in the last fifty years.' The way forward is to change the system, make it performance-oriented. Nothing will be achieved by a wholesale change of personnel. Of course, there are black sheep in government, but there are black sheep everywhere, not least in politics or in the private sector. Black sheep have to be dealt with differently, and a strong result-oriented administrative system can also weed out undesirable elements.

An innovation I started as Cabinet Secretary was to take the Central Secretaries to the states. We would go as a group to the weaker states, with a group of Secretaries accompanying me. While the Home Secretary, Defence Secretary, the Director of the IB and I would be discussing security-related matters with representatives of the Armed Forces and the Police, Secretaries of other departments would discuss pending issues with their counterparts in the states. There would then be a larger meeting with all the officers, including, in many cases, District Magistrates. Most of the pending issues would have been resolved at the Secretary-level discussions. I would help find solutions for the remaining issues. We also called on the Chief Ministers and Governors, many of whom entertained us with lunches, dinners and cultural programmes. I still recall an unforgettable dinner that Omar Abdullah hosted for us in Srinagar and the dinner Pawan Chamling hosted at Gangtok. I visited only the weaker states: J&K, the North-eastern states, Jharkhand and Chhattisgarh. For the stronger states, I organized interactions between Central Secretaries and State Secretaries at the Cabinet Secretariat. I also started the practice of having regular annual meetings of Chief Secretaries of states in which Central Secretaries also participated. The Prime Minister used to host a dinner for the Chief Secretaries and Central Secretaries at his house on these occasions. The whole idea was to open a new channel of communication between the states and centre to facilitate and speed up work in all parts of the country. Thanks to the understanding shown by the Central Election Commission, developmental work did not stop even during the 2009 elections.

The Cabinet Secretary, as Secretary to the Appointments Committee of the Cabinet and as Chairman of screening committees for empanelment of officers at various levels, played a big role in the appointment of officers at the centre. At that time, there was considerable pressure on the part of officers to come to Delhi because they would have an uninterrupted tenure of five years in a ministry. The minister concerned and the Home Minister also had a say in the appointment of officers. Today, interest in Delhi postings has waned because there is no longer security of tenure. Ministers also apparently have no role, with all decisions coming down from the PMO.

We had in place a meticulous system for empanelment of officers based on their performance over the years. This has been replaced by some retired officers and others sitting in committees, telephoning people, both officers and people outside government, and taking arbitrary decisions affecting the future progress of officers. This is the famous 360-degree system, which the Second Administrative Reforms Commission had rejected because they considered it unfeasible for India. Central deputation, therefore, does not loom large in the calculations of officers these days.

One of my ambitions was to introduce a sound performance appraisal system, which took into account the actual achievements of an officer rather than impressions of his work as encapsulated in the reports of their seniors. The replacement of a narrative system of performance appraisal by a numerical system by my predecessor was not an idea that yielded concrete results. We found to our horror that it had spawned a generation of superhuman officers, all of them scoring ten out of ten or close to ten out of ten on every parameter. It was thus difficult to separate the grain from the chaff. We thought of many alternatives, such as reintroduction of a simplified narrative form of reporting, based on actual achievements, including also a confidential section in the report that would not be shown to the officer concerned. We thought of formation of small committees which would assign points to officers in a batch based on reports and actual achievements, strictly adhering to a bell-shaped distribution, with no more than 20 per cent of officers in a batch at the higher or lower end. We thought also of using the last phase of in-service training of officers to assess them in terms of actual achievements. None of this worked out and I must confess that I was disappointed. My attempt to amend the conduct rules of officers to make them more realistic also failed to gain traction. I am happy that this has been done by the present government.

On all my visits to the states, I made it a point to talk to younger officers. I was inordinately impressed by the enthusiasm and energy they showed, the level of technical skill they displayed and the innovations they introduced in administration. India is safe in their competent hands. However, visits to Uttar Pradesh were particularly disappointing. Mayawati was then the Chief Minister and it was her practice to transfer officers frequently and remorselessly. Officers would proceed to a district headquarters to take charge only to find someone else already in occupation of their seats and their own orders cancelled. Three months was considered a long time then in UP for a district posting. Officers would leave their families behind in Lucknow and go to the districts with just a suitcase as there was no certainty as to how long they would remain in their posts. With so much of politics entering the realm of administration, both in the states and at the centre, and nepotism being rampant everywhere, I sometimes wonder whether the age of the professional administrator is finally over.

Administrative reform has to be integrated into the fabric of administration and led from the top. An authority on good governance, headed by the Prime Minister at the central level and the Chief Minister at state level, can make reform a continuing and productive process that can bring about a period of transformation to buttress and strengthen economic growth and meet the rising aspirations of our people.

Back to Kerala

'I am proud to represent the capital of Kerala, a state that in so many ways is a trailblazer for India's progress, though in other respects, it seems to have been left behind in the race for 21st century development.'

—Shashi Tharoor

After handing over charge in Delhi, I returned to Trivandrum with my wife and my dog in July 2011. While I was still working as the Cabinet Secretary, a political change had taken place in Kerala. As had been happening every five years with unfailing regularity, the Left Democratic Front (LDF) government, led by the Communist Party of India (Marxist) (CPI(M)), had been replaced in the elections by the Congress-led United Democratic Front (UDF) government. As Cabinet Secretary, I had tried to help ministers in the ruling government as far as I could in untangling procedure on matters important to them. I got along well with the aged but energetic and zealous Chief Minister V.S.

Achutanandan and I was impressed by the work done by their Health Minister Sreemathy Teacher and the Industries Minister Elamanam Kareem. One of my objectives during my tenure in Delhi was to be of help to all states and I had several interactions with Governors, Chief Ministers and ministers of various states besides, of course, keeping in close touch with Chief Secretaries.

The UDF electoral victory had been spearheaded by Oommen Chandy, whom I knew well from my days as Industries Secretary in the early '90s, when he was the Finance Minister of the state. Oommen Chandy was an unusual minister. His office was an open house for anyone who wanted to see him and was generally crowded with people. There were no appointments, no limitations of time for anyone. As Secretary, I, as well as all my colleagues, could walk in any time into his room with or without our ministers and get his attention on anything we wished to discuss. Another extraordinary feature of his personality was his complete equanimity and unfailing courtesy. I had seen him hold four meetings at a time within his room with the minister flitting from one corner to the other, retaining his calm demeanour at all times, despite the fact that the state was in dire financial distress at the time.

The victory of the UDF was a hard-fought one. Achutanandan, who led the Left, was a towering political personality, firmly wedded to Left philosophy of unrelenting "struggle" and a man of absolute integrity. The electoral battle hung in the balance until the very end when the UDF forged ahead with a narrow margin. I telephoned Chandy and congratulated him. Two days later, he rang me back and asked whether I would come back to Kerala as Vice Chairman of the State Planning Board. I said I would speak to the Prime Minister and get back to him. At that time, there were many rumours afloat regarding post-retirement assignments for me under the central government. Indeed, Dr Manmohan Singh did ask me whether I would go as Governor of a small state. I spoke to Chidambaram, then the Home Minister, who told me in his usual unequivocal manner, 'If you go there as Governor, you will be a vegetable in six months.' Sane advice, but I was still open to an assignment with the central government, having tasted the joy of working at very high levels with the most important people in the country and engaging in discussions and debates in the highest body in the country, the Union Cabinet. It was also a wrench to give up my right—and my pass—to walk in and out of the PMO and the Prime Minister's residence to sit with the highest authority in the land and discuss national issues.

Throughout my tenure as Cabinet Secretary, all my dealings were only with the Prime Minister. There has been much talk of two centres of authority during the UPA regime but I must candidly say that, as far as I was concerned, there was never any dealing except with the PM. I did not meet even Sonia Gandhi officially. Of course, we used to come across each other at some functions and I used to call on her early in January to extend New Year greetings as I did with the two leaders of the Opposition in the Rajya Sabha and Lok Sabha, and my neighbour, L.K. Advani. There was never any attempt by Sonia Gandhi or anyone working closely with her to influence my decisions in any way. I met Rahul Gandhi only once, and that too, quite by accident in the lobby of the main pavilion of the Jawaharlal Nehru Stadium on the occasion of the inauguration of the Commonwealth Games. Of course, several important decisions of Mrs Gandhi's National Advisory Committee, such as the Right to Information Act, the Right to Education Act and food security legislation, used to pass through me for implementation. Certain concerns such as the continuing scourge of manual scavenging and the rights of forest dwellers were conveyed to me by the PMO for review and implementation.

I wonder, too, whether it is good for this large and diverse country to have a single centre of authority. In my view, there should be multiple centres in a federal structure of governance such as ours. Any attempt to centralize power will ultimately lead to bad decision-making. In a country like India, used as it is to colonial ways, it is very easy for a single authority to be misled into a wrong decision. The governance of India has necessarily to be collective. We cannot allow our hard-fought freedom to regress into autocracy.

The movement from mainstream Indian administration to an advisory position in a state government was not easy, particularly for a civil servant who has retained his integrity through his career. Chidambaram told me once that he had seen officers who were models of integrity until a couple of years before their retirement. Then, suddenly, they would see before them their bleak future in which they have to live on a niggardly pension without the system of support that had kept them afloat throughout their careers. They would then be induced to make a somersault in their approach to integrity and try to make up for lost time. Officers, after retirement, reacted to the new life in different ways until they were able to gather themselves again. I was lucky because the descent was broken by my new assignment in Kerala.

It was not easy adjusting once more to a job that drew much less out of me. It was difficult to look at issues on an entirely different scale. I had lost touch with state politics and the state's preferred way of doing things. Economic decisions were seen through the prism of politics. My advantage was that I knew the Chief Minister well and all his senior ministers. I had worked with them and developed a certain degree of familiarity. In 2007, Oommen Chandy, as Chief Minister, had made a determined bid to get me back to the state as Chief Secretary. I was then Revenue Secretary. I did not want to go back to Trivandrum at that time because I knew I had a fair chance of becoming Cabinet Secretary in another few months. Oommen Chandy and his Finance Minister, Vakkom Purushothaman, with whom I had worked earlier in my career as Deputy Secretary in the Secretariat, would not let go and piled on enormous pressure. Finally, Prime Minister Manmohan Singh had to tell them explicitly that my services were required in Delhi and that I could not be spared. I felt a little guilty about this episode and thought I could make up a bit for it by working again for a few more years in Trivandrum.

The readjustment proved painful in the beginning. Strangely, I missed the strains and stresses of my job in Delhi, the late hours at my desk, the backlog of files I had to clear after working hours and on holidays at home, the incessant flow of telephone calls, the pressures on me for appointments and the fulsome cut and thrust of administration at the highest level. Having been in the thick of things for so long, it was difficult for me to adjust to a new job that was clearly not in the mainstream of administration. The state in which I saw the Planning Board office made me even more depressed. It was filthy, unkempt and disorderly. Fortunately, I had two good members, Vijayaraghavan, who had worked with me years ago in Technopark and made a remarkable success of it, and C.P. John, who himself led a political party and narrowly missed becoming a minister as he lost in the Legislative Assembly elections. John's strength was his familiarity with the political world of Kerala, his incessant curiosity that drove him to listen and learn, his capacity to deal with ministers and political leaders of all hues and his ability to dispassionately assess where money was most needed or to make system changes as necessary. I roped in two external members also; E. Sreedharan, the celebrated 'Metro Man' of India and Tarun Das, the man responsible for the phenomenal growth of the Confederation of Indian Industries. The appointment of Tarun Das immediately raked up the old and dead controversy of the Radia tapes in which he was found talking loosely about potential Cabinet Ministers and Cabinet formation after the 2009 elections. The Left rose in protest but this was easily quelled by the Chief Minister pointing out that Tarun Das was Member, Planning Board, West Bengal, when the Left was in power in that state. He said that the Left wanted Das to help West Bengal, but was denying the same to Kerala.

The Planning Board was the first job I held where I had no control over the outcome, no responsibility for the results. The Planning Board merely allocates funds to the extent available after meeting the current expenditures of the government. Board officers take part in the approval process but the spending is left entirely to the line departments and their ministers. The result has been traditionally a huge mismatch between planned expenditure and the actual spending. The plan estimates for each department are finalized after discussions, by no means easy, as Heads of Departments have the fixed notion that the whole process is one of bargaining. They demand allocations far in excess of their spending capacity and it becomes a difficult exercise to prepare realistic estimates. As government spending also generally goes askew during the year, the correlation between plan and non-plan spending gets further distorted.

Generally, planning becomes an incremental process but a good planner can always identify areas in which higher spending would yield more results. I was lucky when, with the help of Arbind Modi, we were able to ascertain that, in the Budget for 2011–12 presented by the previous government, the estimates of central revenue accruing during the year had been underestimated by Rs 10 billion. We did not distribute this amount on a pro rata basis to all the departments. Instead, we selected key ones like agriculture, tourism, health and education, and reset the figures. This had a multiplier effect as the incremental system of estimating plan outlays meant that increased allocations in subsequent years would start from higher bases. Thus, in one stroke, the entire structure of planning had been reset not only for 2011–12, but for all succeeding years.

The Decline and Fall of Planning and Federalism

'Give me six hours to chop down a tree and I will spend the first four sharpening the axe.'

—Abraham Lincoln

Planning became a bad word after Narendra Modi assumed office in 2014. His antipathy towards the Planning Commission, not entirely undeserved, and also shared by some other Chief Ministers and central ministers, translated into a sudden and impulsive decision to discard the entire planning apparatus, announced from the ramparts of the Red Fort in his very first Independence Day address. From then onwards, there was no Plan allocation in the Central Budget and the Finance Ministry reigned supreme.

Planning was not Jawaharlal Nehru's invention, although he strongly believed in it. As early as 1876, Dadabhai Naoroji conceived of a systematic way of alleviating poverty in India. In 1933, M. Visvesvaraya produced a ten-year plan for doubling India's national income. In 1938, the Indian National Congress set up a National Planning Committee. In 1941, the Government of India set up a Committee for Planning, converted into a Reconstruction Committee directly under the Governor General in 1943. In 1946, an Advisory Planning Board was set up by the Government of India. There was obviously clear realization that the massive economic problems that plagued the country required a structured and planned approach. We are in a similar situation today. The economic slowdown since 2018–19 has been further immeasurably aggravated by the blow struck by the virus. Our situation today is no better than after the Second World War, when India endeavoured to pull itself up by its bootstraps, even as the world was recovering from a devastating war. Nonetheless, the resilience of the Indian people and the adaptability of Indian industry is such that a rosy future is still within reach.

Was the erstwhile Planning Commission an anachronistic and decrepit entity which served no purpose? The first two Five Year Plans, with their accent on agriculture and heavy industry, clearly laid the foundations for future growth. Perhaps, over the decades, it had lost the bite and purpose that Nehru and the early votaries of planning had envisioned. But, in my view, it continued to serve a very useful purpose by ensuring allocation of sizeable resources to development. I recall the intense conflict that used to take place between the Planning Commission and the Finance Ministry over the size of the Gross Budgetary Support (GBS) to the Plan during my years as Revenue Secretary, conflicts that were settled only through a peremptory decision by the then PM, himself a renowned economist.

The concept of the GBS and the Plan/non-Plan distinction in the budgets of ministries and states ensured that they thought deeply about expenditure on development while preparing their budgets. The same purpose was served by the annual debate between State Planning Boards or Commissions and State Finance Departments. This, too, was settled usually with the intervention of the Central Planning Commission and Chief Ministers. This system also served to curb the tendency of the Finance Ministry at the centre and Finance Departments in states to sacrifice development expenditure to meet the more pressing needs of revenue expenditure or to put unnecessary curbs on development spending.

Today, this system has been brought down like a house of cards by the centre. No longer do ministries and states have to reflect deeply on development schemes and projects while preparing their annual Plans. The Ministry of Finance and State Finance Departments hold sway. After providing for revenue expenditure and schemes promoted by the PMO, only the residue goes into development.

The Fourteenth Finance Commission endeavoured to redress the fiscal imbalance between states and the centre by raising vertical devolution of central revenues to states from 32 to 42 per cent. This, they said, was only a 'compositional shift'. The centre clawed back its share of resources by reducing central shares in central schemes and centrally sponsored schemes. The resultant surpluses and the savings out of the dip in oil prices in the early years of the present government went into spawning a new generation of centrally sponsored schemes. Participative scheme formulation was replaced by a top-down approach, which has indeed characterized government policy generally in all areas.

The NITI Aayog did play some role in formulation of schemes in the early days, but now seems to engage itself primarily in the preparation of indices to compare states. I have doubts about such indices, even those prepared by international agencies, because the results depend on parameters chosen and the areas and samples selected. The World Bank's Ease of Doing Business Index, which showed improvement for India in 2018–19, is compiled on the basis of identified regulatory areas including speed of starting businesses and issuing construction permits, registration of property, getting credit, tax rates and tax paying mechanisms, enforcement and resolution of contracts, training, trading across borders and dissemination. Scores are calculated based on improvements in the selected areas. Results for 2018–19 were weighted in India's favour by better practices adopted in Delhi and Mumbai to grant construction permits.

The fact that Pakistan and Togo were ahead of India in the list of countries showing most improvement must make us sit up and think. If the Ease of Doing Business Index of the World Bank ranked India higher in 2018–19, the Global Competitiveness Index brought out by the World Economic Forum shows that India had slipped down from the fifty-eighth to the sixty-eighth position out of 141 countries based on 103 indicators organized into twelve pillars. These twelve pillars are assigned scores and cover data on institutions, infrastructure, adoption of information and communication technology, macroeconomic stability, health, skills, product market, labour market, financial system, market size, business dynamism and innovation capacity.

India and Brazil are the lowest ranked among BRICS countries at sixty-eight and seventy-one, respectively. The divergence between the two indices in essentially the same sphere of business competitiveness underscores the unreliability of short-term indices in determining performance in a limited area. The same applies to interstate comparisons too. Kerala may be below Gujarat in terms of infrastructure and ease of doing business, but the way in which it handled the Nipah virus in 2018 and its performance in the early days of the Covid pandemic showed its strength in promoting public welfare. We cannot compare apples with oranges.

This is not to say that the erstwhile Planning Commission smelt of roses all the time. Over the years, it had deteriorated badly. It had become a giant bottom-heavy bureaucracy. As is the problem with bureaucracies, it allowed control freaks to proliferate. Its procedures, in line with bureaucratic mindsets, became long-winded and stalled development instead of speeding it up. It became a dumping ground for civil servants who could not find room in mainstream ministries. Chief Ministers resented being lectured in annual Plan meetings. Some central ministers also felt that the Planning Commission was a drag on their people-friendly schemes and projects. In his farewell address to the Commission, Dr Manmohan Singh had asked, 'Are we still using tools and approaches which were designed for a different era? Have we added on new functions and layers without any restructuring of the more traditional activities in the Commission?'[75]

There was obviously much that needed to be done. Prime Minister Modi's abrupt decision to abolish the Planning Commission, announced in his first-ever Independence Day address, even before any thinking of substitute arrangements, was treated as part of his election promise of 'minimum government, maximum governance'. Yet, now, as we struggle to survive in economic turbulence and come across manifest management failures as in the ongoing power crisis, we must ask ourselves the question: was it necessary to throw the baby out with the bathwater? Is instinctual, impulsive decision-making better than structured forward planning based on participative consultation?

These are questions that we need to ask as we move forward to repair our economy. We need to chart out the way ahead, not leave it to chance and react to crises blindly and without direction as and when they arise. Planning and forward thinking are not antithetical to a market economy. We can perhaps take a leaf out of China's book. As Dr Santosh Mehrotra wrote in *Economic & Political Weekly*:

The government must recognize that one source of China's strategic economic growth is an institution with strategic planning capacities, the National Development and Reform Commission. The success of China with the NDRC tells us that fiscal decentralisation, accountability mechanisms, experimentation, learning, and openness to expertise, form the core of any institution that seeks to provide vision and strategic

---

75   *Financial Express*, 'In farewell speech, PM Manmohan Singh says "India story is work in progress"', 1 May 2014, https://www.financialexpress. com/archive/in-farewell-speech-pm-manmohan-singh-says-india-story-is-work-in-progress/1245663/

economic planning. Further, strategic planning institutions in Asian economies, like India's Planning Commission, have helped deal with various regional and global economic crises; a lesson we must keep in mind.[76]

Whether in the form of a revived and restructured Planning Commission or the NITI Aayog in a new garb or an institution by any other name, planned development has once more to capture centre stage in the days ahead. Budgets, whether of the centre or the states, must reflect once again the primacy of development. The Gross Budgetary Support mechanism, in whatever form, must come back as a countervailing force to rein in the Finance Ministry. Narendra Modi's cherished dream was, 'Through the NITI Aayog, India will move away from the one-size-fits-all approach and forge a better match between schemes and needs of states.'[77] The NITI Aayog, composed of all chief ministers and some central ministers, rarely met and never became an instrument for promoting federalism and creating Team India. With no resources at its command, the links that existed between the Planning Commission and the states were progressively severed.

On 24 March 2020, the Prime Minister announced a total lockdown of the country to arrest the spread of Covid-19 after a dress rehearsal in the form of a Janta Curfew on Sunday, the twenty-second. In a way, his hand was forced because, like the WHO and other countries, India has been behind the curve in dealing with this virus. In hindsight, we can say that we should have introduced international travel curbs earlier, reduced social interaction months ago by cancelling international conferences and prevented people from participating in events abroad. I believe the fault here lies with the WHO, which should have gone into global control mode much

---

76	Santosh Mehrotra, 'The Reformed "Planning Commission"', *Economic & Political Weekly*, Vol. 49, No. 37, 13 September 2014.

77	V. Srinivas, *Towards a New India: Governance Transformed 2014–2019* (New Delhi: Konark Publishers Pvt. Ltd, 2019).

earlier, even as the epidemic raged in China. The WHO had burnt its fingers and diminished its capacity to get countries to swing into action when they exaggerated the impact of swine flu or H1N1. This time, they erred too much on the side of caution, with the result that the world was totally unprepared when the epidemic, now a pandemic, had established its footprint in many countries, growing in intensity by leaps and bounds and taking an immense toll on lives.

The Prime Minister had no choice. He had to play for time to flatten the curve of expansion of the epidemic as best as India could to enable quick enhancement and strengthening of healthcare facilities, to pray that a drug already in use and approved by drug control authorities would miraculously save the situation and give the country time to build up stocks of necessary drugs, to hope that rapid testing facilities would be set up in sufficient volumes to take care of our massive population and that medical research would find solutions where none existed at present.

The country recognized the gravity of the situation and largely responded positively. Yet, was it right on his part to put in place so draconian a measure with just four hours' notice? Perhaps it would have been more appropriate to consult with chief ministers and his own ministers and give the country some time to prepare. Must everything be done centrally by the Government of India? As with other measures, there was a burst of enthusiasm and hectic activity at the centre, followed by a realization that the task was beyond them, and then quickly dumping the whole problem on the states without supporting economic measures or transfer of funds to the states, which would have mitigated the crisis that followed.

The resilience of the economy, the monetary measures taken by the RBI and the enterprising nature of the Indian people have kept our economy afloat, even though the government failed on the fiscal front to add a further impetus by stimulating demand. Instead, we saw the extraordinary spectacle of such measures as farm reforms being pushed through under the garb of stimulus, triggering a prolonged stand-off with farmers in areas that had built their prosperity on the Minimum Support Price system which had been in vogue for many decades. This, too, signals the collapse of federalism and the rise of incipient autocracy.

What holds India together, what enabled it to survive foreign marauders, colonial rule, periods of oppression and misrule and ruthless regimentation from time to time, is its infinite capacity to absorb shocks and to reinvent itself, sustaining its deep belief in a syncretic culture, which treats all mankind as part of one great human family. Even while the country grows, as its values undergo transformations, the roots of Indian culture remained firmly embedded in the concept of 'Vasudhaiva Kutumbakam'. This is a concept that pervades India from Kashmir to Kerala, from Gujarat to the eastern extremes of our country. Like a tree bowing before a storm, India has resisted and gently overcome any forcible attempt to impose a single ideology or religious dogma. India exults in its diversity.

Planning for Kerala

I was new to planning and, for the first time in many years, I was separated from real administrative action. Having been away from the state for many years, I had gotten used to much higher outlays, schemes of much greater magnitude. When Mizoram wanted Rs 40 billion for changing their agricultural practices, the decision was taken in my conference room and later went through the Cabinet. I was used to dealing with many thousands of crores and dealing with much smaller amounts posed its own problems. I was also unused to the freewheeling manner in which people barged into my room even when I was busy with something else. I had become unfamiliar, too, with seeing developmental issues through the prism of regional politics.

My advantages were my familiarity with senior politicians and having to deal with the courteous, unfailingly polite and positive Chief Minister

Oommen Chandy, who was also the Chairman of the State Planning Board. While Oommen Chandy is known to have been closer to A.K. Antony than to Karunakaran, he has inherited the latter's capacity to mingle easily with the people. As in my days with him when he was Finance Minister, his office was invariably crowded with petitioners of all kinds and it was difficult even to gain access to his room through the milling crowds outside on the corridor. Nor were the crowds confined to his office. Even at six in the morning and late in the night, there would be petitioners waiting to see him at the Chief Minister's official bungalow, Cliff House. He would be constantly on the move, too, by road and by train, and, each month, he would have traversed almost every part of his small state. He has become, in fact, the stuff of legends.

An ambassador wanted to meet him one evening. He was in his constituency in Alappuzha district. The flight got delayed and the ambassador landed at the nearest airport, Kochi, only around midnight. He rang up the Chief Minister on his mobile to seek an appointment for the next day. The Chief Minister, directly picking up the phone to speak to him, said, 'I am waiting for you. You can come now.' The meeting took place in the early hours of the morning. He needed little sleep in the night, refreshing himself from time to time with short snatches of sleep as he travelled.

Accessibility to the people is a two-edged weapon. While easy accessibility makes a leader popular, it can also work against him when people later found to have not-so-honest intentions are seen in his vicinity. This happened to Chandy, just as it has happened to many others. Yet, he believed that by being accessible, he did more good for the people and was willing to take the risk of things occasionally going astray. He was always open, friendly and willing to believe in the innate honesty of those that met him. His office was so open that one morning, while he was away in the Cabinet room, a mentally unstable person came and sat in his chair and started making telephone calls from the Chief Minister's room. This, too, did not ruffle him; he was only highly amused.

As Chairman of the Planning Board, he was generally supportive. During the five years I was Vice Chairman, we reset some priorities within the limits of political acceptability. I believed always that the board had to function within the contours of policy as laid down by the elected government. I have referred already to the resetting of base allocations to some major departments. The board genuinely wanted elected local bodies to play a growing role in the development of the state. The procedures stipulated for them were greatly simplified. Ideally, we would have liked to substantially enhance plan allocations to them but we did not entirely succeed in this because political disputes within the Panchayati Raj institutions slowed down spending, with the result that most of them could not even spend what was allotted. My colleague C.P. John, as Member, did a great deal of work for cooperative societies and in the education sector, introducing a BA (Honours) course for the first time in select colleges. Vijayaraghavan, the other full-time Member, worked on strengthening the social justice sector, particularly on schemes for the differently abled. He has now set up, on his own, an institution for autistic children in Trivandrum, funded entirely through private donations.

On the direction of the Chief Minister, we drew up also a Perspective Plan for Kerala until 2030, working jointly with the National Council of Applied Economic Research (NCAER). This Perspective Plan laid down a framework for the growth of Kerala as a knowledge-based welfare state, replicating systems followed in Nordic countries. The preparation of the Perspective Plan involved multiple meetings at various levels with a cross section of society, including one meeting with MLAs. As the NCAER puts it on its portal:

The Kerala Perspective Plan 2030 (KPP) prepared by NCAER for the Kerala State Board of Planning is a strategic path forward for Kerala to achieve economic and living standards equivalent to Nordic countries. KPP 2030 targets leapfrogging the high middle income threshold in the next 15 years and the high income threshold in the next 15 years. It seeks to position Kerala among the Nordic countries in terms of human capital and social and environmental indices. The mission is to achieve sustainable prosperity which includes economic, human well-being, social and green prosperity. To achieve that, Kerala needs to build a sustainable development framework, which involves building a 'knowledge economy' and incorporate principles of 'sustainable development'. The approach of KPP 2030 is to build on Kerala's achievements, discuss the challenges faced by the state in a globalizing economy and propose strategies to achieve the goals. That is the why the KPP is organized in four volumes, which elaborate on four interconnected themes that together constitute its central tenet of balancing economic prosperity, social inclusion and environmental stewardship. Volume 1 begins with the an analysis of the growth of the economy, identifies growth drivers and dynamism of enterprises in different sectors. Volume 2 discusses the key bases to develop a knowledge economy. Volume 3 is the environmental sustainability volume. Infrastructure which is linked to both growth and environmental sustainability is included in this volume. The last volume is the social sustainability volume. Health, which is both foundational and a key engine of economic growth is included in this volume.[78]

The aim, in terms of GDP per capita, was to raise it from the then prevailing level of about $4,700 to $19,000 by 2030 and to $36,000 by 2040 and, that too, in a sustainable manner based on existing and future growth drivers. It is good to see that the present Left-led Kerala government also continues to lay emphasis on building Kerala into a knowledge economy with a strong infrastructure.

---

78   A. Aggarwal, B. Bhandari, S. Paul and P.C. Parida, 'Kerala Pespective Plan 2030', NCAER (July 2015), https://www.ncaer.org/publication_details.php?pID=255

Another innovation that we made was related to the infrastructure sector. I was rather proud of this change. The allocations for big projects were hitherto made within the plan budgets of respective departments. Generally, considering the importance of these projects, we would allot whatever the departments asked for, but they would not be able to spend the bulk of the amounts and they would then divert the unspent amounts to unproductive or less productive areas. We decided to aggregate all such outlays under a single head of account for identified big projects from which allocations would be made according to need by a committee headed by the Finance Secretary. We also worked with SBI and with the Finance Secretary to make the Kerala Infrastructure Investment Fund Board an active player in infrastructure financing. All the necessary sanctions were obtained but, before they could be implemented, the government changed. The new government took up this scheme, but they made one fundamental change, which, I believe, was not in the interests of the state.

The original idea was that this institution would only borrow funds for self-sustaining schemes, which would generate returns to pay back borrowed funds. The new government tweaked the scheme, making return of funds part of future budgeted outlays, thus creating a new burden on future governments and also diverting part of the state's inflows into the institution. The weakening of the State Finance Department and of the Planning Board, and the creation of multiple points from which funds flowed out during the years after 2016, are not salutary developments and future governments will struggle to meet the repayment commitments that have been incurred. Fortunately, the Fifteenth Finance Commission appears to have put a stop to this practice by bringing all borrowing within allowed borrowing limits, including funds borrowed through institutions but repaid through budgetary sources. On the plus side, there were direct and visible changes on the developmental side, which may have never taken place in a time bound manner through cumbrous and rule-bound departmental systems.

Oommen Chandy's UDF government was responsible for some significant developments in infrastructure. The Kochi Metro was completed. The bulk of the work on the Kannur airport was finished. The most significant achievement was probably the commencement of work on the Vizhinjam container terminal in the Public Private Partnership (PPP) mode. Vizhinjam was a sleepy fishing village near Trivandrum, which woke up in the wake of the burst of tourist activity that followed the explosive growth of Kovalam as a destination for tourists. It had some natural advantages which could make it into an important seaport. The depth of the water close to the shore was high, enabling the port to receive large vessels without continuous dredging. Siltation and the requirement for regular dredging was the bane of the Kochi port, strangulating its growth. It was also located closer to the international sea route, now serviced largely by Colombo. Many attempts had been made to develop this new project but all of them had failed.

Knowing the importance of this project, I persuaded Gajendra Haldea, who had been Adviser to Montek Singh Ahluwalia in the Planning Commission and an acknowledged authority on PPP projects, to help us. He spent countless hours redoing and redesigning the project. Since this was the first state port to be set up in the PPP mode, an entirely new Model Concession Agreement was drawn up and approved by the State Cabinet. Union Finance Minister Arun Jaitley also helped and the Government of India agreed to give a Viability Gap Fund amounting to 20 per cent of the cost of the project, the State meeting another 20 per cent.

There were several rounds of bidding, several pre-bid meetings, but eventually, we got only one bid from Adani Ports & SEZ Ltd and, that too after much persuasion of the bidders left in the fray after technical evaluation. It is not easy for a political government to accept a single bid in a project of these dimensions but Oommen Chandy showed his courage and the Cabinet approved the project. The CAG came out with an uninformed report after a brief 'performance audit', based on a Model Concession Agreement drawn up by the Planning Commission for port terminals in brown field ports. After the UDF government fell, the new Left government constituted an inquiry commission under a former judge of the High Court. The commission found no irregularities in the process that had been followed. The work is now well under way and despite the pandemic and the shortage of building materials, will hopefully soon see completion. For myself, I am happy that I had a role to play in both the great ventures that changed the landscape of Trivandrum. The first was Technopark and, very soon, the second will be a new trans-shipment port at Vizhinjam.

If Oommen Chandy showed immense political courage in accepting a single bid for Vizhinjam, I cannot understand the position taken by both the fronts to oppose the establishment of a full-fledged new airport in Trivandrum by Adani in a PPP mode through a transparent process of bidding followed by the Ministry of Civil Aviation. Kochi and Kannur have good airports, set up with equity participation by the state government. When the Government of India is willing to develop Trivandrum airport without any financial participation by the state, why should we protest? The people who will use the airport, the passengers as well as the trading circles, want the new airport in the PPP mode. The state company formed for the purpose had also bid for the project, but they were outbid by Adani. A new and modern airport will give a further fillip to tourism, develop new trade and lead to more business. Ever since the first industrial policy was announced by the state in the early nineties, Kerala has been proclaiming that it welcomes private business with open arms. Why, then, should we send a signal, loud and clear, that we are reversing our direction and going back to the old days when private business were bad words? Fortunately, this too is behind us now as the Government of India did not budge from its stand. With a spanking new airport, a new trans-shipment port and an expanding Technopark, the capital city is poised for phenomenal growth.

Reflections on Banking and the Economy

'The economy is the start and end of everything. You can't have successful education reform or any other reform if you don't have a strong economy.'

—David Cameron

After retirement, I have also been exploring new vistas and gaining new experience. I became the Independent Director, and later, Chairman, of a publicly owned private bank, the Federal Bank, headquartered at Aluva in Kerala. I had dealt with government economic policy in the past, but it was interesting to see how a banking system works from the inside. Its Chief Executive, Shyam Srinivasan, is a committed man with the sole ambition of pulling up the bank from the category of also-rans to a position of some eminence in the banking stratosphere. My colleagues on the board were hardcore bankers of repute in the financial sector and their way of looking at issues was a new experience for me. The bank has no access to taxpayers' money, unlike public sector banks, and, therefore, has to be careful with use of money and selection of creditors.

Arun Jaitley, as Finance Minister, once came to Trivandrum towards the end of 2018 and invited me for dinner at the Southern Air Command guest house. Jaitley, at that time, was also the Defence Minister. He was visibly amazed when I told him, in answer to his question, that net non-productive assets in the bank's loan portfolio were just over one per cent. 'How did you do it?' he asked. I told him that when a bank has to fend for itself and has no access to government support, it has no choice but to be cautious. I was on the board for five years, retiring when I turned seventy, as was then stipulated by the RBI.

For years on end, commercial banks, particularly public sector banks, were able to maintain a facade of normalcy, even of profit and prosperity, by the simple device of restructuring and evergreening of loans. Many of the large borrowers also assumed that loans once taken can continue forever and banks would assist in ensuring and adding to their wealth. This situation suddenly changed when the RBI came down heavily on loans given by banks over time and stopped effectively the process of evergreening. The result was a dramatic increase in gross and net non-performing assets which stressed assets in the economy and led to a decline in the profitability of banks. As the Governor, RBI, said in one of his speeches, the situation was further exacerbated by external shocks, induced by such events as the cancellation of coal licenses, the scrapping of 2G licenses, dumping of Chinese iron and steel in the Indian market and delays in government permissions affecting the construction industry.

The crusade against bad loans revealed the startling fact that most of it was attributable to large borrowers. The share of large borrowers in the total loan portfolio of Scheduled Commercial Banks was 51 per cent and their share in total gross non productive assets was as high as

79 per cent. The public sector banks were primarily responsible for the ballooning of bad loans. It was clear that bank officials in general found it easier to give bulk loans to large borrowers rather than diversify their portfolio. The rating agencies also played a role in facilitating such loans by giving high ratings to large borrowers and corporate groups without detailed analyses of their financial positions. Risk management systems in individual banks were found wanting and there was insufficient control at all levels.

Once the magnitude of the problem became manifest, the government, the RBI and the regulatory and investigative agencies swung into action to limit the damage—in the process, creating collateral damage to the economy as a whole. It was found that the existing debt recovery mechanisms, consisting of Lok Adalats, the Securitisation and Reconstruction of Financial Assets and Enforcement of Securities Interest (SARFAESI) Act (enabling non-recovered bank loans to be treated as arrears of land revenue) and Debt Recovery Tribunals were ineffective and measures were initiated to strengthen them. The management of public sector banks was sought to be improved through the 'Indradhanush' scheme, involving breaking up the post of Chairman cum Managing Director, strengthening the boards and management of banks through a Bank Boards Bureau, recapitalization of public sector banks and, above all, the introduction of the Insolvency and Bankruptcy Code.

The RBI came out with its own set of measures, compelling scheduled banks to make provisions for non-performing assets and stressed assets, creating a database of large loans accessible to all banks to trace incipient sickness, replacing promoters under the Strategic Debt Restructuring (SDR) scheme, converting loans into part equity through the scheme for sustainable restructuring of stressed assets (S4A), and insisting on time-bound resolution of defaults. Investigative agencies wielded the big stick, creating panic all around and bringing credit flows to a virtual standstill.

While it would appear that stability indicators of the banking sector look healthier than some years ago, the fact is that the slowdown in the economy, followed by the pandemic, could cause further damage. In response to the pandemic, the RBI and governments and central banks all over the world have had to perforce loosen their purse strings and infuse liquidity into the system. While this was inevitable, the way back to financial normalcy has to be charted out very carefully. Otherwise, there could be further jolts to the economy in the form of inflation, economic instability and rising bad debts, together with wild gyrations and uncertainty in stock markets.

The economic situation is rapidly changing with surging inflation and growth rates moderating as an unexpected war between Russia and Ukraine broke out, leading to a spate of sanctions against Russia, which, considering the size and economic might of that country and its dominant position in the energy sector, will have unpleasant ripple effects on the global economy for many years. There is threat also to the value of the dollar as Russia and other countries scramble to find other currencies with which to manage trade. The WTO now expects merchandise trade volume growth of 3 per cent in 2022 as against its previous forecasts of 4.7 per cent. The Reserve Bank, in its April 2022 policy review, displays more caution both on the inflation front and in terms of growth. Nevertheless, in its State of the Economy report of 10 April 2022, it expresses optimism in the following words:

Notwithstanding this unsettled global environment, the domestic economic situation continues to improve. The Union Budget 2022-23 and the monetary policy announcement of February 10, 2022 have set the tone for a durable and broad-based revival. The renewed emphasis on public investment through infrastructure development is expected to crowd in private investment and strengthen job creation and demand in 2022-23.[79]

---

79   Reserve Bank of India, 'State of the Economy,' RBI Bulletin, Vol. LXXVI, No. 2, February 2022, https://rbidocs.rbi.org.in/rdocs/Bulletin/PDFs/ BULLETINFEB20220AA3C61D698B4A76995677735F2AE71D. PDF

Yet, present indicators do not presage smooth recovery. The Reserve Bank itself displayed its concern on rising inflation by raising bank rates by 40 basis points in a surprise move. Private consumption as share of GDP continues to decline, having dipped from 60.5 per cent in 2019–20 to 58.6 per cent in 2020–21 and, now, to 57.5 per cent in 2021–22. Capacity utilization in the last quarter of 2021 was around 68 per cent, a far cry from the peak level of 83 per cent in early 2011. The international economic situation remains uncertain and gloomy. Stock markets display high volatility.

If the government and the RBI wield the big stick prematurely, the economy could go into a tailspin from which it may be difficult to pull out. Banking is a profession, now a major industry, that is based on trust. We keep money in banks on trust. Bank lending to creditors is also based on trust, although that trust is now hedged in part by collaterals, guarantees, letters of credit and the like. A bank cannot make money unless it lends the money that is kept with it with a margin. The creditor also borrows money believing that he will be able to invest it in productive enterprises that will give a return which will enable him to repay the principal and interest. Occasionally, this assumption goes awry because of adverse economic conditions or because the product manufactured or service offered does not find acceptance in the market. On such occasions, the bank has two choices. It can assess once again whether the creditor has genuinely faced a problem beyond his control, whether his intentions were honourable, whether, with some more time, the loan will be repaid and then give him flexibility in some form or the other. Or else, he can come down hard, call in the collateral and throw the law book at him. Small borrowers and farmers will benefit from a more flexible approach. Inability to repay loans and relentless pressure from lenders has often resulted in suicides, particularly in our farming community.

There are, of course, those who deliberately cheat the lending banks with or without the connivance of bank officials. Sometimes, bank officials are coerced into giving loans by those in authority in government or higher up in the bank hierarchy, who can call in their favours later for their own benefit. This is corruption and has to be dealt with as such. However, building up an entire system of regulation on the belief that all are corrupt can be as harmful to society as the belief that all human beings are thieves. Fortunately, the RBI is under mature leadership today and the monetary response has been more measured and better calibrated.

I am glad to see that focus is now visibly shifting from ease of doing business for investors, particularly foreign investors, to ease of living for the Indian people, a far more wholesome concept. Ultimately, we cannot shed our welfare orientation in a mad race to improve our position in global indices. Sometimes I wonder if we are obsessed with indices and inter-country comparisons made by international bodies. Intra-country comparisons, pitting state against state, create what is thought to be 'competitive federalism'.

The conditions are different, the base is different, yardsticks used are different. Indices can, at best, provide some policy pointers; they cannot form the basis of development administration. Good administration is beyond indices. Good administration means understanding the nature, needs and internal diversity of the entity that is administered, and finding ways to address challenges and to fulfil needs. It means planning, not for sectoral growth but for holistic, inclusive growth, maintained over a sustained period of time. It means being alive to changes, never falling into traps like the middle income trap, which interrupt the momentum of growth. It means, too, dealing with crises as and when they arise, without engaging in intellectual debates on whether they are structural or cyclical.

India is a large country with its own strengths and we must rely on ourselves to grow. We must not evaluate ourselves or the Indian states by indices reflecting only parts of the whole. If we do, it will be like the story of the four blind men and the elephant. We must also never lose focus. Our battle is not per se to bring in investment but to eradicate poverty and raise standards of living. The goal of governance in a poor country such as ours cannot be expressed more clearly than in the words of Mahatma Gandhi:

> I will give you a talisman. Whenever you are in doubt, or when the self becomes too much with you, try the following expedient: Recall the face of the poorest and the most helpless man whom you may have seen and ask yourself, if the step you contemplate is going to be of any use to him.[80]

Gandhiji's talisman will need to continue to guide our policies and our administration for many decades until we lift ourselves from the depths of poverty.

---

80   M.K. Gandhi as quoted in Salil Tripathi, 'Mahatma Gandhi's Talisman is More Relevant than Ever Today', *Mint* (2 April 2020), https://www.livemint.com/opinion/columns/mahatma-gandhi-s-talisman-is-more-relevant-than-ever-today-11585772154724.html.

On Power, R&D and Defence

'You and I come by road or rail, but economists travel on infrastructure.'

—*Margaret Thatcher*

I became an Independent Director also for Tata Power, my first exposure to the power sector as it is today. It is easier to deal with a Tata Group company because its manner of working and its ethical principles are like the government at its best. This, too, was a learning experience. More than three decades ago, I had been Collector of the district that had the biggest hydroelectric project in Kerala. Hydel dams were then the cheapest form of electricity and Kerala was lucky in meeting all its needs through such power. In the first decade of this millennium, there was a great surge in thermal power as the economy boomed and the hunger for power was great. In its wake came several stranded projects strewn across the country after the abrupt withdrawal of coal linkage. They also became non-productive assets in banks.

Some years ago, the Manmohan Singh government wanted India to look increasingly at environment-friendly renewable power. There were several forms of renewable energy on which scientific research was in progress, including solar, wind and even tidal energy. Windmills gained traction initially, thanks to a very liberal tax break in the form of high depreciation rates allowed in the very first year. Windmills were not only for energy, they sprouted also in the gardens of the very rich as ornamental showpieces. Solar energy showed the greatest potential and India decided to go ahead with solar farms. The question arose, who will buy this power? This was left to the Committee of Secretaries under me as the Cabinet Secretary to resolve. No easy task, as the cost per unit was then as high as Rs 17. Ajay Shankar, then Secretary of the National Competitiveness Council, came up with the idea that the giant state-owned NTPC may buy the power initially proposed to be produced, add it to the huge amount of thermal power they were producing and fix an average price accordingly. This was accepted and soon became a government decision. Thus started the saga of solar energy in India.

When I joined Tata Power, I was startled to find that solar energy prices had come down to around Rs 3 per unit. There were even fly-by-night operators who would quote impossibly low prices in bids called by various state governments. Even the NTPC, under investor pressure to diversify into renewable power, quoted below Rs 2, some time ago. The expansion of solar energy worldwide was fed by low cost solar panels from China, which accounts today for 90 per cent of world production. Today, Kochi airport is powered entirely by solar energy; so is the Brabourne Stadium in Mumbai where all the big cricket matches used to be held. Both these were set up by Tata Power. Solar power now energizes the country in solar farms, on rooftops, even in the form of floating panels on water. Newer and newer ways of providing energy through solar power are developing. Solar power will hold sway for the next few decades until cheaper forms of energy are found. Hydrogen cell-based energy is snapping at its heels and may supplant it sooner than later.

The power sector in India is a developing success story. Like the IT and the telecom sectors, wise policies and timely correction have taken the sector into a significant growth path under successive governments. The UPA government gave it a sharp impetus on the generation side through thermal power plants. Thermal plants, which had to face deadly blows from the CAG's action on coal and the subsequent judicial overreach, are now on the way out, thanks to the phenomenal growth of renewable energy and the rising global concern on climate change. The Ministry of Power, under present Minister R.K. Singh, has correctly identified the severe problems on the distribution and consumption side which need to be corrected if the industry is to remain healthy.

Reforms by state governments in the pricing of power and in uncontrolled leakage of power were sought to be rectified by linking part of the capacity of states to borrow from the market to concrete reforms. Finance Minister Nirmala Sitharaman, in her 2021 Budget speech, announced the arrival of 'open sourcing', whereby consumers will have the choice of service provider, thus putting an end to cross-subsidization for political reasons and giving a new global competitive edge to Indian industry. The Electricity (Amendment) Act and the new Tariff Policy, now on the anvil, will be harbingers of great change, not only for the power sector but for all of India.

New experience came also through the Sree Chitra Tirunal Institute of Medical Sciences and Technology, an institution set up by the redoubtable Dr M.S. Valiathan, Padma Vibhushan, who started it virtually from scratch as an institution for research and development (R&D) in the field of medical devices, combined with a hospital specializing in cardiology, neurology and radiology. I was lucky to work with an outstanding Director, Dr Asha Kishore, an eminent neurologist and, even more, a strong administrator. The institute also taught me all over again the problems involved in running a governmental institution in Kerala, the political forces one has to confront and the fact that a small group of mischief-makers can destroy the growth potential of an organization. This association also made me understand that India's R&D activity is in dire need of massive improvement.

The Prime Minister's Economic Advisory Council, in a report titled 'R&D Expenditure Ecosystem' released in 2019, pointed out that India's expenditure on R&D remained constant over the years, hovering around 0.6 per cent to 0.7 per cent, well below major countries such as the US (2.8 per cent), China (2.1 per cent), Israel (4.3 per cent) and South Korea (4.2 per cent). The council made several suggestions to stimulate private sector R&D, such as mandating that a certain proportion of the turnover of large and medium enterprises be invested for such activity, joint action be taken by states and the centre to fund R&D and reconsidering the government's decision to withdraw weighted deduction for tax purposes.

Indeed, it is China that shows the way. R&D expenditure in China zoomed up from 0.7 per cent in the 1990s to 2.1 per cent of the GDP currently. China is fast catching up with the current world leader, the US. Huawei Technologies is presently at the forefront of telecom technology, preparing to roll out 5G. In every new sphere of modern science and technology, China is striving to develop its strength. New breakthroughs in defence technologies have made the Chinese more self-sufficient in weapons and systems. President Xi Jinping highlighted the importance of continuously upgrading defence technology at the National People's Congress in 2016 by saying that, 'The capacity to innovate will determine the future of the Chinese armed forces.'[81] China employs 7,38,000 people in R&D as compared to 1,58,000 in India. Their vision is clear. In the words of their Science and Technology Minister Wan Gang, 'China needs to enter the ranks of innovative countries and become a big technological innovation power by 2050.'[82]

---

81   Claude Arpi, 'R&D Key to India's Status', *The Pioneer*, 25 April 2019.

82   *South China Morning Post*, 'China's spending on research and development up 14pc in 2017 to US$279 billion, science minister says', 27 February 2018, https://www.scmp.com/news/china/policies-politics/article/2134895/chinas-spending-research-and-development-14pc-2017

We have not only to pump in more resources, we have to make procedural and systemic changes to ensure flexibility and cost-effectiveness in the R&D structure in India. The Space Commission and the Atomic Energy Commission are outliers. The autonomy that was given to them from their very inception and their strong leadership, reporting only to the highest level in the political executive, gave them muscle power far in excess of that available to other institutions and departments engaged in science and technology. The success of these two organizations itself provides a model that can be replicated in all other areas by creating one or more strong organizations on similar lines with funding and with autonomy. R&D institutions must have the space to grow by themselves, adopting their own systems, untroubled by the shackles of routine-bound bureaucracy.

Defence is another area that can provide a springboard for sharp economic acceleration. The US and Israel, France, Sweden and Germany, and lately, China, have shown how investment in defence can pay off. India starts with an advantage as our armed forces are huge and hungry for modernization and technological innovation. Development of defence production, backed by strong R&D, will not only make our country impregnable, it will also spawn a whole range of upstream and downstream industries which would create business and employment opportunities everywhere. The Defence Research and Development Organisation (DRDO) and the public sector alone cannot meet this need. The private sector, with its resources, skills, flexibility and innovative capacity, needs to be fully harnessed. In several other countries, the private sector has been at the forefront of defence production and R&D. As part of the stimulus package announced by the Finance Minister, Foreign Direct Investment limits have been raised to 74 per cent. This, by itself, may not produce a spurt in foreign investment in defence as foreign investors would have concerns relating to intellectual property rights. For the same reason, foreign investment may not benefit us unless we have access to intellectual property. Some items for procurement have been earmarked for domestic industry but, so far, the list is not sufficiently broad-based to attract much domestic investment. The slowness of procedure and the quirky changes that are made in policy and specifications make investment in defence risky for private investors.

The centre, the states, centres of higher learning and the private sector can together create a new environment conducive to rapid growth of R&D. Together, we need to lay out time-bound roadmaps for the future. We have been repeating the mantra of achieving the goal of spending 2 per cent of the GDP for too long—in speeches, in plans, even in party manifestos. We still remain at levels considerably short of 1 per cent. We need to put our heads together and devise a game plan. We have the brains, the skills, the spirit of innovation and the entrepreneurial abilities. If we add to these organization, imagination and drive, we have all the ingredients for a quick and efficient take-off.

My continuing assignment as honorary advisor to the Arya Vaidya Sala, Kottakkal, is one that gives me a great deal of pleasure and satisfaction. This is a hundred-year-old Ayurvedic institution that combines in itself medical care of the highest quality and production of Ayurvedic medicines and their marketing in all parts of the country and abroad. This is a distinct institution, maintaining high ethical and quality standards with focus on patients and their health rather than on profits. Indeed, its income is used entirely for charitable purposes, a fact that has been recognized by the income tax department. Old family traditions govern its mode of functioning but it remains open to new methods of diagnosis and treatment. Many new formulations have originated here and lines of treatment developed for several different disorders. It remains a simple, transparent organization with a temple on its premises, patronizing the ancient Kerala dance form of Kathakali. Overall, it maintains a profile that is very different from the profit-oriented products and services that we observe in the markets for alternative medicine today. The long waiting list of patients desiring treatment at the hospitals of the Arya Vaidya Sala and the fact that these patients come from many different countries stand testimony to the faith that it has been able to generate among the people at large.

The Constitutional Balance and Reflections on the Present

'Our ability to reach unity in diversity will be the beauty and the test of our civilization.'

—*Mahatma Gandhi*

It is not easy to build that fine balance that is needed in a democratic system between the political executive, the administration, the judiciary, regulatory authorities, investigative agencies and the military. We still recall with embarrassment the days of the Emergency, when the political executive went berserk and pushed into the background all the other arms of governance. We recall with horror the events of 1984 in Delhi, 1992 in Ayodhya and 2002 in Gujarat, when communal forces were given free rein to do whatever they wanted for some days, causing unimaginable havoc to the fabric of our society. In our neighbouring countries, democratic structures have often been attacked and overcome

251

by military forces. We saw repeated episodes of military rule in Pakistan and Bangladesh.

Administration has generally been the weakest element in this interplay of forces. It has generally followed the lead of their political masters, be they elected representatives of the people or the military. It is generally comfortable in a state of political anonymity. Constitutional and statutory authorities wax and wane, depending largely on the personality of the persons who man these high offices. Very often, we come across the phenomenon of civil servants occupying positions of Constitutional power finding it difficult to handle their new roles with equanimity. They often strike out in a maniacal fashion and the victims are generally other civil servants.

Among the Constitutional authorities, the CAG has always been a source of much terror among civil servants. When I first came to Kerala for training in the districts, full of energy and zeal and the desire to do good, I quickly learnt that my colleagues in the lower rungs of the bureaucracy lived in abject fear of the CAG. I was intrigued by the fact that even young persons who had barely served for a few years in administration saw, as their primary goal, retirement many years hence with their pensions secure. I was mildly contemptuous of them, but realized, towards the end of my career, with the 2G case and the coal case, that officers who did nothing more than follow set procedures as their predecessors had done, and who had generally been uncontroversial, could spend the evenings of their lives traversing the corridors of courts and eventually languishing in jail for months on end. Civil servants, by and large, are not fearless enough to face such misery in their last days nor do they have the resources to fight cases entirely on their own. The same kind of fear is generated by a vigilance establishment and by whimsical regulatory authorities.

It requires maturity and wisdom to navigate the seas of governance. The instruments of the government are powerful. They need to be used with care and foresight to build a balanced structure as envisaged in our Constitution. A nation with such diversity as ours can disintegrate unless the spirit of the Constitution is fully imbibed by all those who administer the powers given by it. The tragedy today is the belief that grew for some time that even the judiciary is not above pressure, strong or fiercely independent. The bases of judgments of the Supreme Court itself were doubted. Questioning the logic of judgments was itself being characterized as contempt of court. After Independence, the Indian Civil Service disappeared and the IAS was never a 'steel frame'. Indeed, the IAS or the civil services collectively were not expected to be the steel frame. Colonial governance required a steel frame to sustain itself. The steel frame of independent India is its Constitution and, if this backbone of our democratic system of governance begins to come apart, the future could get increasingly dismal.

During the past seven decades, India and the world have changed dramatically. This period of change in our country will be seen in the distant future as an era of transformational change, much like the Meiji restoration in Japan or the Industrial Revolution in Britain and Europe. Successive governments have left their own imprint on Indian society and have built on the foundations laid by past administrations. Make in India, Direct Benefits Transfer, Jan Dhan Yojana, infrastructure development schemes and the Aadhar mechanism are logical offshoots of paradigm shifts accomplished by past governments. The introduction of GST, a massive alteration in the taxation and federal structure of India, itself evolved from the modified VAT and VAT regimes created in the past.

The reforms effected in the last three decades signify a change of direction and of momentum. However, this may not have been possible had we not, during the early years, laid strong foundations of democracy and made public investments in basic capital-intensive industry and revolutionary changes in agriculture. The role of the giants of Indian industry of the time, the J.R.D. Tatas and the G.D. Birlas, reinforced and strengthened the growth momentum.

The concept of India as a united country was treated with derision by our colonial masters until well into the twentieth century. Ramachandra Guha, in his book *India After Gandhi*,[83] talks of an event in 1891, when Rudyard Kipling visited Australia and a journalist asked him about the possibilities of self-governance in India. 'Oh, no,' said Kipling, 'They are 4,000 years old out there, much too old to learn that business. Law and order is what they want and we are there to give it to them and we give it to them straight.' Guha also mentions a cricketer and tea planter who predicted:

Chaos would prevail in India if we were ever so foolish to leave the natives to run their own show. Ye gods! What a salad of confusion, of bungle, of mismanagement and far worse would be the instant result. Themselves, they are still infants as regards governing or statesmanship. And their so-called leaders are the worst of the lot.

And yet India triumphed, the Constitution stayed firm and secure, the institutions of governance evolved, albeit at varying paces and, within the broad embrace of democracy, the concept of Indian nationhood blossomed, despite divergences in society, despite the divisions of religion, caste, language and even ethnic variations and, but for a short period in the mid-'70s when authoritarian rule was thrust upon the people in the form of the Emergency, the instruments of democracy have prevailed. While India changed and grew, we had to contend with massive global changes, the decline of socialism as a development doctrine, the end of the Cold War and the consequent political changes, the emergence of Europe as an economic entity, the geopolitical changes wrought by the competitive battle for energy, the growth of

---

83   Ramachandra Guha, *India After Gandhi* (New Delhi: Pan Macmillan, 2007).

terrorism and the phenomenal rise of information technology, to name only a few.

India has been at the forefront of global transformation in all directions. Unlike many other formerly colonial countries, we have been able to transcend our weaknesses and scale great heights of success in many areas. Why did we succeed while others are still struggling?

The answer probably lies in the manner in which our Constitution-makers accepted our diversity and endeavoured to build a polity that would accommodate our multicultural society. The problems that Kipling mentioned, that the British visualized as factors that would divide India forever, were all thought through and built into the fabric of the State. Not that explosive situations never arose which could have torn the country apart, as they did with its erstwhile twin, which culminated in the split into two nations in the west and the east of India.

The communal divide and subnational ambitions often flared up later in history, too. For many years in the '60s and '70s, Sikh nationalistic feelings surfaced in the form of the Khalistan movement. The Sikhs have always been strong patriots and great soldiers, willing to give up their lives for the national cause. For some years, however, Punjab was in the grip of a militancy that seemed to have virtually spun out of control. It was the return of democracy, the willpower of a Prime Minister, a Chief Minister and a Police Chief acting in tandem, that brought order back to that troubled land. The communal flare-up in Delhi in 1984, directed this time against the Sikhs, was an unimaginable event. Fortunately, this did not leave a lasting impact on the communal equation and the Sikhs again became the nationalists they had always been. The Hindu–Muslim divide, never satisfactorily resolved, flared up again in Gujarat in 2002 and remained always uneasy. Even if the incidence of communal conflict has declined, it remains under the surface and breaks out sporadically in various forms—in these days in an accentuated form, as basic trust is lacking.

The diversity of India is reflected also in ethnic and tribal divides. The Mizo movement of the past, the Bodo agitation, the demand for

Gorkhaland and the continuing demand for Nagalim are assertions of cultural diversity assuming militant forms. The left-wing extremist movements in forested areas in the heartland of India is again rooted in tribal identity and the perception that tribals and forest dwellers have been treated unfairly. Even in the relatively urbanized northern states of the country, the Jat and the Gujjar communities occasionally assert their rights and firmly adhere to cultural practices like khap panchayats.

The Constitution of India was designed in a flexible manner to accommodate cultural differences. Recognizing the diversity of India and creating a single structure that provided both for unity and for differences in thought, practice and cultural mores was an unparalleled exercise in statecraft for which we have to be grateful to the stalwarts who created the document. As the Jawaharlal Nehru University professor Dr Gurpreet Mahajan put it in her book, *Accommodating Diversity: Ideas and International Practices*:

> If we look at the functioning of the Indian State since Independence, it is evident that it has been remarkably successful in accommodating diversity in this kind of way. In fact, the ease with which it has been done can only be appreciated and understood fully when we look at the challenges that are currently being faced in this regard by many liberal democracies in the west.[84]

What is of deep concern today is the danger that lies ahead in democracy itself thriving on division of society rather than in bringing our peoples together. The conflict generated by the Citizenship Amendment Act, the National Register of Citizens and the perceived attempt to discriminate on the basis of community signals a strong deviation from the path of reconciliation and unification that we have hitherto followed. One of

---

84   Gurpreet Mahajan, *Accommodating Diversity: Ideas and Institutional Practices* (New Delhi: Oxford University Press, 2011).

the tasks Dr Manmohan Singh had specifically asked me to look at when I became Cabinet Secretary in 2011 was the creation of identity cards for the people of India. My predecessor, B.K. Chaturvedi, had struggled with it for a couple of years. I, too, tried my hand at it with the help of the Home Ministry and the Registrar General of Census Operations. Frankly, I had little technical knowledge and made no headway. Also, a task as big as this required a dedicated organization. It could not be another part-time occupation of the Cabinet Secretary, loaded as he was with a great many assignments across many different sectors.

It was then that the Prime Minister thought of appointing Nandan Nilekani to take up the humongous task of providing a mark of identity to every person living in the country. That was when the project took wings. With his technical background and his capacity to go into minute details, the contours of a solution gradually took shape. I helped by holding meetings of Secretaries to iron out differences. Nilekani is a determined man and he generally managed to get what he wanted, including an organization consisting of handpicked officers, mostly from the IAS. There were several issues that had to be resolved. One such was whether biometric identification was to be confined to fingerprints alone, which would have been a great deal cheaper, or if it should include irises, too. Nandan was insistent on the inclusion of irises and finally this was agreed to, despite the high costs. Thus was born the concept of the Aadhaar.

There was immediately a conflict with the Home Ministry. In 2004, the Citizenship Act of 1955 had been amended to provide for the issue of national identity cards. Through this amendment, the central government had acquired the power to 'compulsorily register every citizen of India and issue national identity card to him'.[85] For this purpose, a National Register of Citizens had to be maintained. This

---

85 Government of India, Amendment Act of the Citizenship Act 1955, 2004, https://egazette.nic.in/WriteReadData/2004/E_7_2011_119.pdf

fell within the domain of the Home Ministry. With the intervention of the then Home Minister, Chidambaram, this dispute was resolved. Nilekani said that Aadhaar numbers would not be tantamount to establishment of citizenship. At that time, there was no intention even to issue Aadhaar cards. It was only after Prime Minister Modi recognized the advantages of the Aadhaar and decided to link it to a wide range of governmental activities that the Aadhaar card came to occupy the position of pre-eminence that it presently does.

The National Register of Citizens has again gained prominence. The work on preparing the register was taken up in a desultory manner and never made much progress. It could not, therefore, address the issue of millions of migrants, primarily from erstwhile East Pakistan, who had illegally entered Assam and the other Northeast states and West Bengal. This huge influx had resulted in mass agitation in Assam, headed by the All Assam Students Union, which ended only with the Assam Accord of 1985 upon the initiative of then Prime Minister Rajiv Gandhi. The accord sought to legitimize migrants who had entered Assam illegally until 1971. Migrants who came into Assam thereafter would be detected and expelled in accordance with law. Neither this accord nor subsequent actions of the central or state governments made any distinction between illegal migrants in the name of religion.

The Supreme Court, in 2013, directed the central and state governments to update the register in Assam, and this task was to take place under direct monitoring by the Court. Accordingly, the updating process commenced and the final list was published in August 2019. As against 33 million people who applied for registry, 31.1 million were found eligible to be registered, leaving 1.9 million out in the woods, facing threat of expulsion. This led to another storm of protests, as many people, including a sitting MLA representing the Abhyapuri South constituency in lower Assam, were left out in the cold. It was alleged that many genuine citizens, including Bengali Hindus, were not included in the final list.

It was in this context that the central government decided to push through amendments to the Indian Citizenship Act, whereby Hindus, Sikhs, Buddhists, Jains, Parsis and Christians from Afghanistan, Bangladesh and Pakistan, who entered the country on or before 31 December 2014, became eligible for citizenship. The original act provided for citizenship only to applicants who had stayed in India in the last twelve months continuously and for eleven out of the previous fourteen years. This, too, was relaxed and they needed to have stayed only for five years to qualify for citizenship. With their dominance in the Lok Sabha and their new-found majority in the Rajya Sabha, the government was able to ram through these amendments. To be fair, they had been trying to get amendments to the Citizenship Act passed in Parliament since 2014, in line with their election manifesto, but they had not succeeded since they did not have the requisite majority in the Upper House.

The newly passed bill was seen as a change in the direction of Indian polity. Never before had religion formed the basis of any legislative action, except where such discrimination was deemed necessary to redress perceived economic or social inequality. This was seen purely as a measure to exclude Muslims from the definition of legal migrants and to fast-track the legitimization of migrants belonging to the six identified religions. Since the bulk of the migrants were Hindus, this was clearly seen as a highly discriminatory move, striking at the very heart of the Indian Constitution and the spirit of equality that it embodies.

Article 14 of the Constitution states that, 'The State shall not deny to any person equality before the law or the equal protection of the laws within the territory of India.' Article 15 provides explicitly that the citizen shall not be discriminated against on grounds of religion, race, caste, sex or place of birth. Article 16 assures equality of opportunity in matters of employment and exemption from any kind of discrimination on grounds of religion, race, caste, sex, descent, place of birth or residence. While it can be argued that these provisions relate to citizens and not to those who are yet to become citizens, there is no gainsaying the fact that people who have been living for years in India suddenly face the threat of dispossession of their rights. Besides, the thought that majority governments, representing only a part of the electorate, can tinker with the very concept of citizenship, should set alarm bells ringing. What safeguard is there against future governments introducing new clauses to further change the definition of citizenship? This battle will be fought in court and its result will be vital to the very concept of our nation.

The deliberate, well-considered exclusion of Muslims holds dangerous portends for the future. India has prided itself on its inclusiveness, its policy of complete non-discrimination. This is a thought process that defined the Independence movement, which became the cornerstone of the Constitution. 'In nature,' Mahatma Gandhi had said, 'there is a fundamental unity running through all the diversity that we see about us. Religions are given to mankind so as to accelerate the process of realization of fundamental unity.'[86] This is the concept of Advaita, or non-duality, that lies at the core of the *Bhagwad Gita*, the Upanishads and the Prakarana Granthas composed by Shankaracharya. Advaita is uniformly acknowledged to define the essence of Hindu religious philosophy. To this concept of oneness, Gandhiji returned again and again in his messages to the people of India.

In Kevadia Colony in Gujarat stands the world's tallest statue, 597 feet high, commemorating the immense contributions made by Sardar Vallabhbhai Patel to the making of India. This was the man who, as Home Minister, spent sleepless nights trying to contain the horrors of the holocaust that followed the Partition. After Independence, when Gandhiji went on a fast, protesting the Cabinet's decision to withdraw the amount of Rs 550 million given to Pakistan, Patel had said, 'If, in spite of having achieved Independence, Gandhiji has to fast today to

---

86   T.N. Khoshoo, *Mahatma Gandhi: An Apostle of Applied Human Ecology*, (New Delhi: Tata Energy Research Institute, 1995).

achieve real Hindu–Muslim unity, it is a standing shame for us. We have just heard people shouting that Muslims should be removed from India. Those who do so have gone mad with anger.'[87]

Many a time in the history of independent India, there has been conflict, finally resolved through mature political decisions. In mid-'60s, there was mayhem in Tamil Nadu on a perceived attempt by the then Congress government of Lal Bahadur Shastri to force Hindi down the throats of unwilling Tamilians. This issue had been resolved earlier by the Constitution-makers by deciding that English will continue as official language for another fifteen years alongside Hindi. It came up again in the early '60s as the fifteen-year period drew to a close. Nehru endeavoured to put a lid on it in 1963, continuing use of English as official language beyond that year through the Official Languages Act. C.N. Annadurai, DMK leader in the Rajya Sabha, raised his voice against this legislation on the grounds that it stated only that English 'may' continue as the official language, not that it 'shall' continue.

Nehru died in 1964. The attempt made by the Congress government in Tamil Nadu to introduce legislation for adopting a three-language formula led to widespread unrest, including agitation, resulting in 70 deaths as officially estimated, 500 otherwise. This, too, was resolved by the Prime Minister Lal Bahadur Shastri, who announced over All India Radio that Nehru's assurances would be honoured. The net result of the agitation was the extinction of the Congress Party as an entity that could form and run a government in Tamil Nadu. Since then, Tamil Nadu has been ruled by either the DMK or the All India Anna Dravida Munnetra Kazhagam (AIADMK).

Social differences again came to the fore during the V.P. Singh government in the late '80s. The Mandal Commission had recommended in 1980 that 27 per cent reservation in government jobs and public universities may be given to Other Backward Communities.

---

87   The Sardar Patel Portal, 'Painful Partition', http://sardarpatel.nvli.in/
     thematic-collections/painful-partition

V.P. Singh endeavoured to implement the recommendation. Again, there was uproar, led by the students of Delhi, soon spreading to other locations in the north. In September 1990, a Delhi student, Rajiv Goswami, attempted self-immolation. This was followed by self-immolation attempts in many other places like Hissar, Sirsa, Ambala, Lucknow, Gwalior, Kota and Ghaziabad. There was rioting and destruction of public property. This was a spontaneous uprising and the students largely prevented political leaders from taking advantage of the situation. L.K. Advani and Madan Lal Khurana of the BJP were not allowed to meet the parents of Rajiv Goswami.

V.P. Singh took a rigid stand on the matter. He said, 'I wish to make it clear that, should a situation arise in which I have to choose between a cause that I believe in so intensely and my chair, I will not hesitate for an instant to choose the former.' He was alone even in his Cabinet. *India Today* observed on 15 October 1990 that a 'severe dysfunction had afflicted the government' as was evident from the fact that 'while Singh was absorbing the flak, Home Minister Mufti Mohammed Sayeed, who is responsible for law and order, is virtually in hiding.'[88]

The result was the same, the fall of the V.P. Singh government and the early disappearance of V.P. Singh from Indian politics. Reservation, however, was accepted and is now part of policy. With the slew of reforms that started in 1991, the economy expanded and dependence on government jobs and government educational institutions declined. Moreover, it came to be recognized that reservation was a correction of an inequality rather than an attempt to give an advantage to one section at the expense of another.

The Assam agitation of the late '70s and '80s can be considered to be a direct result of the perception that the culture of Assam was

---

88   *India Today*, 'Storm created by Mandal Commission poses serious threat to V.P. Singh's political survival,' 15 October 1990, https://www. indiatoday.in/magazine/cover-story/story/19901015-storm-created-by-mandal-commission-poses-serious-threat-to-v.p.-singh-political-survival-813100-1990-10-15

threatened by the influx of foreigners. The agitation started in March 1979 and was led by the All Assam Students Union. There was widespread agitation and much bloodshed, including the murder of a high-ranking civil servant, E.S. Parthasarathy, in a bomb attack. This, too, was resolved through the Assam Accord of 1985.

The Citizenship Amendment Act and the veiled threat of distinguishing between communities that together constitute the Indian ethos boomeranged unexpectedly, particularly in urban areas. Riots, agitations, hartals and violence rocked the country. This was not an agitation spearheaded by the Muslims. It was a spontaneous outburst in which all communities were together expressing their ire. It was not masterminded or led by any political party. Political leaders of parties other than the ruling party appeared to be following the agitators rather than the other way round. The young, in particular, were outraged.

The government's defence that this is intended only to target foreigners and only to help those who face religious persecution in neighbouring Muslim countries has thus far carried no conviction. Many questions arise. The migrants targeted by the act have been living in India for years; many for decades. Some were born in India. They are largely impoverished and thus will have no documents to show. There may be a concentration of migrants in the Northeast, but they are to be found in other parts of India, too. Does the government want to follow two different procedures to identify citizens, one for Muslims, another for others? Will Muslims be subjected to stricter procedures for registration than the others? How will the government distinguish between 'Indian Muslims' and 'foreigner Muslims' in, say, Malappuram in Kerala or Moradabad in UP? How do they propose to deal with the demand of many in Assam, where the Assamese now find that a large number of non-Muslim migrants will be given legitimacy in violation of the Assam Accord of 1985, which had specified 1971 as the cut-off year? Too many questions remain unanswered. The advent of the pandemic has quietened the agitation for the time being. There are still rumblings under the surface and the feeling of marginalization is acutely felt within sections of Indian society. Prudence lies in healing wounds and bringing estranged people together again.

The pandemic did not, however, prevent the government from opening another area of controversy, an unnecessary provocation at a time when the country was in the throes of fear and despair: the farm laws. These were intended to provide more opportunities to farmers to sell their produce at more remunerative prices by allowing the private sector to open new aggregation centres for agricultural products and removing powers entrusted with the government to regulate wholesale and retail trade in times of scarcity. Farmers, particularly in Punjab and Haryana, who had built their fortunes by selling their crops in regulated markets at the minimum support price fixed by governments, rose in revolt against the new measures. The states saw it as in invasion of their federal rights guaranteed by the Constitution. The fact that these deep reforms were sought to be smuggled in under the cover of a stimulus package to deal with the pandemic made farmers even more suspicious. They saw it understandably as the thin end of the wedge that would, in time, undermine the support system now in place, in the same manner as privatization of public enterprises was initially introduced through baby steps to deal with loss-making enterprises and has now extended to profit-making ones and, in its latest avatar, as monetization of public assets. Fortunately, better sense prevailed and the laws were withdrawn.

The Constitution was carefully crafted by wise lawmakers under the leadership of the incomparable B.R. Ambedkar, keeping in mind the diversity of India and the multiplicity of cultures within the fledgling nation and realizing full well the importance of finding common denominators that will keep it together. In an article titled 'India's Enduring Document of Governance' in *The Hindu* published on 26 November 2019, N.L. Rajah, Senior Advocate in the Madras High Court wrote:

What is noteworthy is the fact that inclusiveness during the formative years of the Constitution-making debates; specificity of the provisions that produced an excellent balance between redundant verbosity and confounding ambiguity; fundamental rights and judicial review being made sheet anchors of the instrument; a workable scheme of amending the Constitutional provisions ... to ensure longevity of Constitution, were all applied even in the 1940's by our Constitution makers.[89]

'There is simplicity in every Indian and there is unity in every corner of India,' Prime Minister Narendra Modi said on 15 August 2015. He called it 'the strength of India'. 'If the unity of India is destroyed, then the dreams of the people are also destroyed,' he said.[90] The challenge is to ensure that we keep our strength intact through strict adherence to the Constitution. It requires statesmanship of the highest quality to bring the country together, giving prominence to centrifugal rather than centripetal forces. It calls for the resurgence of federalism, of problem-solving through discussion and debate amongst peoples, and the restoration of the true spirit of democracy everywhere. The larger share of the responsibility obviously lies with the government and ruling party as the Opposition is at present distracted and in disarray, and cannot provide a cohesive platform. Dissent in society can ultimately tear the fabric that binds the country together.

There is no logical reason to believe that hatred and division should be considered a winning formula for electoral gain. The lessons that we learn from the electoral history of the past few decades are quite different. They tell us that the electorate is chafing at the bit to move

---

89   N.L. Rajah, 'India's Enduring Document of Governance', *The Hindu*, 26 November 2019.

90   *Business Standard*, 'There is unity in every corner of India: Modi', 15 August 2015, https://www.business-standard.com/article/news-ians/there-is-unity-in-every-corner-of-india-modi-115081500096_1.html

beyond the shibboleths of the past. Many distinctive features are clearly discernible. First, while the voters largely ignore painfully prepared and elaborate party manifestos, they are looking for clarity in policy. They cannot accept a leadership unclear about the direction in which they move or a leadership that is not able to state its position unequivocally. Old cliches and hackneyed expressions no longer impress them. They also welcome changes in political and economic stances in the interests of the nation, as happened in 1991, when the time-honoured economic approach of the nation was turned on its head; later, when the civil nuclear bill was adopted despite opposition; and in more recent times, when Atmanirbhar was adopted as a creed, harking back to the self-reliance ideology of yore and an independent, non-aligned position was assumed in the Russia–Ukraine war. Rigid adherence to positions will not win votes as the Left has found to its cost at the all-India level over the years. Secondly, they want their chosen representatives to have the courage to take firm decisions and move forward fearlessly. They are willing even to forgive mistakes, provided they believe in the good faith behind them, as demonstrated by the demonitization fiasco and the more recent decisions to backtrack from the farm laws. Thirdly, strong governmental actions to subdue oppression by a few influential blackguards in rural society yield rich electoral dividends in states where such persecution has prevailed in the past, as in Bihar and UP. Fourthly, the people are impressed by visible development, as shown by the Aam Aadmi Party with its public schools, hospital care, mohalla clinics and reasonably priced utility services in Delhi or by the central government's free rations, housing schemes, women centric programmes and social welfare measures. Fifthly, whether or not there is actually integrity in the system as a whole, the electorate likes to see an image of austerity and integrity at the very top and the ability to defend actions convincingly without being pushed into a corner. Finally, whatever is done at the top, it cannot be driven home unless there is a powerful party apparatus which can reach down to the lowest level, which has its nose close to the ground and is politically savvy.

Electoral success no longer requires the division of society on communal, caste or linguistic lines. Performance, trust and ability to communicate carry more weight than engendering hatred through division. Our democracy is maturing and the aspirations of our people have grown far beyond the narrow confines of caste and community. Why, then, must we resurrect old notions of division, using the media, social media and films? Why must we revive memories of old conflicts and reopen past wounds and allow them to fester until sepsis sets in and begins to gnaw at the vitals of our nation? Statesmanship demands encouraging and nurturing harmony in society, based on concord, not alienation. The Constitution must remain the steel frame that binds the nation together. In the words of Martin Luther King Jr., 'We must live together as brothers or perish together as fools.'

Epilogue

'At the end of the day, you can't control the results: you can only control your effort level and your focus.'

—Ben Zobrist

I was lucky to be elected Chairman of the Centre for Development Studies, Trivandrum, a think tank affiliated to Jawaharlal Nehru University and founded by the illustrious Dr K.N. Raj, the famed development economist. I succeeded an equally celebrated economist, Dr Bimal Jalan, whose contributions to Indian economic policy over the years have been immense. I confined myself primarily to improvements in administration, leaving the academic environment free as it should be. From time to time, I could make use of their huge library. I have been writing, too, contributing articles to various newspapers, web papers and periodicals on a range of subjects.

Retirement has given me the time to indulge my natural inclination towards the spiritual side of life. The 'Direct Path', propounded by such mystics as Ramana Maharshi, Nisargadatta and Atmananda, based on Advaita, Zen and Tao, attracted me in particular. The Direct Path is now popularized all over the world by the likes of Mooji Baba, Greg Goode, Eckhart Tolle, Rupert Spiro, Gary Zukav and others, and finds uncanny resonance in Albert Einstein's relativity theories and quantum mechanics as it evolves. It is reflected in literature in the writings of such luminaries as Paulo Coelho and Richard Bach.

This philosophy is not new; it was first enunciated in the Upanishads. The universe is seen as one—indivisible, indestructible, eternal. The Buddha, after many years of arduous penance, came to the same conclusion, but he called it 'Shunyata' (nothingness). Moses, too, seemed to convey a similar thought in Exodus 3.14 in which God told him '*Ehyeh 'ǎšer 'ehyeh*' (I am that I am), which is very similar to the Mahavakyas in the Upanishads, '*Aham Brahmasmi*' (I am Brahman), '*Tattvam Asi*' (You are that), '*Ayam Atma Brahma*' (This Self is Brahman). These concepts are agnostic of religion. They could apply as much to Islam (as the Sufi saints revealed) or Christianity and Buddhism, as to Hinduism. In the words of Rumi, 'I am in you and I am you. No one can understand this until he has lost his mind.'

As physics progresses, as cosmology evolves, similar thoughts are developing in the scientific world, too. The connectedness of the universe; the existence of a single force in the form of energy; the free convertibility of matter into energy and energy into matter; the fact that space and time are interrelated, and together they form the fabric of the universe; that time and space began only at the point of origin, the Big Bang; that the limits of scientific knowledge stops as of now at the Big Bang; and that consciousness could have preceded time and space—these are all concepts that evolved through the late nineteenth and the twentieth centuries.

The advent of quantum mechanics opened a whole new world of physics. The double slit experiment, Schrödinger's cat and the Copenhagen equation created new mysteries—the particle may no longer be a particle, but shows the characteristics of waves when not observed and the position of a particle cannot be defined except in the form of a probability wave. The search for a unified force that brings together gravity, the electromagnetic force, the strong and the weak nuclear force, continues. Given our three-dimensional perspective and the limitations of language that can often mislead, it is difficult for us to comprehend a single force from which all is derived and in which all manifests. We are like waves searching for water, having forgotten that we are water.

In the words of Paulo Coelho in *The Witch of Portobello*: 'This has been a growing trend over the last few years. We may be witnessing a very important moment in the history of the world, when the Spirit finally merges with the Material, and the two are united and transformed.'

At the end of the day, what are my learnings? Do I have a message to give? Each person has to live his own life, learn his own lessons. The circumstances may be different, the environment is subject to change, technology advances, priorities vary as time passes. What I learnt is not necessarily what others will learn. I can only talk of a few things that seemed important to me:

- Change is a constant in an administrative career. The India that I saw in the 1970s is not the India of today. Our conditions of living have changed, requirements have changed, expectations have changed. Adapt to change without batting an eyelid.

- Life is flow. Ultimately, it will take its own course. Attempts to bend it in a particular direction will cause frustration. If life is allowed to flow smoothly like a river, there will be less tension, more peace of mind and, strangely, greater achievement.

- Remain professional. It is easy to give up professionalism and succumb to the lures of office. There will always be greater respect for the true professional.

- One of the things we were told in Mussoorie was never to run after publicity. Let the media approach you for what information they want. You lose respect if you keep projecting yourself endlessly. The media are fickle. They may praise you today, bring you down tomorrow. They are themselves human beings and have all the strengths and weaknesses of human beings. Do not judge yourself or others by what the media writes. Learn to form your own judgement.

- Your job requirements change dramatically from time to time. Learn to work fast and learn fast. Keep your meetings, appointments, and telephone calls short. There are some people who will tell you they have worked fourteen or sixteen hours, day after day, seven days a week. Believe me, they have been wasting time. No job requires so many hours of sustained work, even though there may be occasions when you have to work longer, even for days at a time.

- In my life, integrity has been a given. As I have mentioned before, integrity is either present in your DNA or it is not. Integrity has made me feel good. I have always been respected even though I have had to live a life of frugality, which continues even now. But do not wear your integrity on your sleeve. Sometimes, I have found this to deteriorate into an offensive and irritating holier-than-thou attitude.

- There are phases in life when things do not go your way. Every life has its lows and its highs. There are some jobs in which you excel, others where you are unable to contribute. They will pass.

- Rewards do not await you as a matter of course. You will be respected for a job well done but this is not going to lead necessarily to recognition or material compensation.

- Keep your expectations moderate. If expectations are too high, frustration follows.

- Build your team. It should consist of people who complement your strengths and supplement your weaknesses.

- You can make a mistake, others can make mistakes. Every life is replete with mistakes. Forgive yourself, forgive others.

- Allow the team to function freely and cohesively. Riding roughshod over your team is the worst way of managing it and is guaranteed to produce negative results.

- You do not have all the answers. Be open to ideas, listen carefully. Let your team feel they are one unit thinking alike, not a ragged bunch of disparate individuals pulling in different directions under a tyrant.
- More work gets done when the atmosphere is calm and peaceful. Strive to create that atmosphere. Above all, do not regard your own team member as your rival and do not, for God's sake, indulge in games with your superiors to pull others down. You will be appreciated for your own merit, not for your skill in undermining others.
- Ten people working together will obviously achieve more than one person trying to do everything. You can achieve a great deal more by delegating work and authority and trusting your team.
- Look beyond the immediate requirements of your job. Visualize your organization as it will be ten years hence, and plan accordingly.
- Give free rein to imagination and to new ideas. Some good ideas are generated in this process. Sometimes, ideas are clearly beyond the realm of practicability. In such cases, I have found it easier to defuse them by asking the person who generated the idea to implement it. You will not hear of it again.
- Do not allow criticism to weigh you down. Sometimes, your critic may be right and you may find it of advantage to change course. Sometimes, criticism is intended only to put you down and you will only serve your critic's cause by feeling low.
- Put your heart and soul into the job. Do not fritter away your energies in several different directions. If you have given your life to a profession, let your focus be unwavering.
- It is good to learn how to centre yourself. Prayer and meditation are useful tools to center yourself. For others differently inclined, golf and bridge might serve the purpose.
- You can have good bosses and bad bosses. This, too, will pass.
- Interaction with politicians and political leaders is an integral part of a civil servant's life. They represent the people and have deep connections with them. Many have excellent ideas, distilled from

long years of public contact. Do not consider them to be enemies who are to be kept at the distance. At the same time, maintain your professional integrity.

- Once you have left a job, shed the practice of looking over your successors' shoulders to find fault with them. Likewise, do not waste your energies finding fault with your predecessor. The predecessor–successor syndrome is rampant in the civil services. Stay out of it. There are all kinds of people that make up the world. Let them be, leave them alone.

- There will be occasions in your life when you are vested with great authority. Let not your powers overwhelm you. Authority is to be exercised with discretion, wisdom, humility and maturity. Do not ever have the feeling that it is necessary to wave your baton hither and thither to exhibit your power.

- At the point of retirement, you are at the height of your power and authority. Suddenly, on the day you retire, you become a common citizen. That sinking feeling is inevitable. Your skill lies in the manner in which you adjust to it and how you keep your body and your brain alive and kicking.

- The world has been around for ages. People have come and gone, yet the world proceeds at its own pace. Be under no illusion that after you, there is the apocalypse. The world will go on as smoothly as ever.

- Do not labour under the mistaken belief that your successors cannot manage without your expert advice. Do not badmouth your successors because they think differently or have committed the cardinal sin of sitting on the chair you once occupied.

I am in a happy place now. There is nothing to achieve, no goals to set, no pressures, no expectations, no ambitions, no fears. I am in a place where I can enjoy the flow of life and, along with it, accept the occasional storm, the ripple, the barrier, the twists and the turns that comes in its way. What lies ahead?

'Still, in the end, we die. With us our universe: every concept, every name, everything we know dies as well. The personal meaning it had is very perishable as it is its own creation. Some might say "after we die, things around us continue". And this is true. But they are our things, perceived through our eyes, understood through our minds, and are thus our creations. So, in a way, the universe ends with each of our deaths.'

—Harvey Daiho Hilbert Roshi,
Living Zen: The Diary of an American Priest

Index

About the Author

K.M. Chandrasekhar is a former IAS officer of the 1970 batch, who served as the Cabinet Secretary of India from 2007 to 2011. In a career spanning five decades, he has traversed many sectors—district administration, public finance, taxation, national security and international diplomacy, among others. He was the Founder Chairman of the Spices Board, India's Ambassador to the WTO and the Union Revenue Secretary. He was Vice Chairman, Kerala State Planning Board, and has also held the position of Secretary for Industries and Finance departments in the Kerala government.

30 Years *of*

HarperCollins *Publishers* India

At HarperCollins, we believe in telling the best stories and finding the widest possible readership for our books in every format possible. We started publishing 30 years ago; a great deal has changed since then, but what has remained constant is the passion with which our authors write their books, the love with which readers receive them, and the sheer joy and excitement that we as publishers feel in being a part of the publishing process.

Over the years, we've had the pleasure of publishing some of the finest writing from the subcontinent and around the world, and some of the biggest bestsellers in India's publishing history. Our books and authors have won a phenomenal range of awards, and we ourselves have been named Publisher of the Year the greatest number of times. But nothing has meant more to us than the fact that millions of people have read the books we published, and somewhere, a book of ours might have made a difference.

As we step into our fourth decade, we go back to that one word – a word which has been a driving force for us all these years.

Read.